LIVING MUSICIANS

First Supplement

LIVING MUSICIANS

MUSICIANS

First Supplement

Compiled and Edited

by

DAVID EWEN

THE H. W. WILSON COMPANY

NEW YORK   1957

Introduction

This volume is the first supplement to LIVING MUSICIANS, published in 1940. In the almost two decades that have elapsed since the publication of LIVING MUSICIANS, many musicians have come to prominence, and some of them are now artists of the first magnitude. Their absence from LIVING MUSICIANS was a gap that had to be filled. This supplement includes approximately 150 such biographies. The plan originally pursued has been adhered to: to place particular emphasis on American musicians, or those foreign musicians whose art is most familiar to American audiences. Several musicians who have come to prominence in the 1940's and 1950's, but who have since passed from the concert stage either through death or retirement, have been included; in this category belong Guido Cantelli, Kathleen Ferrier, William Kapell, and Aksel Schiøtz.

Besides including these new biographies, the present supplement brings up to date the biographical information on those musicians in the original volume concerning whom there is important new material. Supplementary material has been supplied for about half of the five hundred original biographies.

The marks used to indicate the pronunciation of names follow the system of Webster's *New International Dictionary*.

I want to express my indebtedness to Angel Records, the Boston Symphony Orchestra, the Cleveland Orchestra, Columbia Artists Management, Columbia Records, Hurok Attractions, London Records, the Metropolitan Opera Association, *Musical Courier*, National Artists Corporation, the Philharmonic-Symphony Society of New York, and the San Francisco Opera Association, among others, for their cooperation in providing photographs and essential biographical data.

DAVID EWEN

Little Neck, New York

Contents

Living Musicians: First Supplement

ABENDROTH, HERMANN, conductor. For his earlier career, see *Living Musicians,* 1940.

* * *

After World War II, Abendroth was appointed director general of music in East Germany, and musical director of the Weimar State Orchestra. During this period he became the first German conductor since World War II to be invited to the Soviet Union. He died of a stroke in Weimar on May 29, 1956, and was given a state funeral.

ABRAVANEL, MAURICE DE, conductor. For his earlier career, see *Living Musicians,* 1940.

* * *

Between 1941 and 1949, Abravanel conducted several notable musical productions on Broadway, including *Lady in the Dark, One Touch of Venus, Street Scene,* and *Regina.* He was appointed principal conductor of the Utah Symphony Orchestra in 1947, and has since then been elevated to the post of musical director. He is also professor of music at the University of Utah.

ADLER, CLARENCE, pianist. For his earlier career, see *Living Musicians,* 1940.

* * *

During the 1942-1943 season Adler performed a cycle of fourteen piano concertos, five of them American premières, at Town Hall, New York.

AITKEN, WEBSTER, pianist. See *Living Musicians,* 1940.

ALBANESE, LICIA, lyric soprano, was born in Bari, Italy, on July 22, 1913. The daughter of an agent for a large grocery-store chain, she was one of six children. Her first lessons were in dancing. One day, however, her sister's piano teacher noticed that Licia had a beautiful voice and prevailed upon her to sing an aria from *Tosca* at a party honoring her father's birthday. Her father became so deeply impressed that he encouraged Licia to abandon dancing for music study. This happened when Licia was twelve. For three years after that, she studied voice with a local

LICIA ALBANESE

tenor. Professional training followed in Milan with Giuseppina Baldassare-Tedeschi.

She had been studying only a brief period in Milan when, in 1934, she made an unscheduled debut at the Teatro Lirico in *Madama Butterfly.* The principal soprano having become suddenly indisposed, the opera-house director was induced by Mme. Baldassare-Tedeschi to allow Albanese to serve as a last-minute replacement in the role of Cio-Cio San. Albanese gave such a good account of herself that she was invited to audition for La Scala. But, feeling she was not yet ready, she preferred returning to her studies. One year later, in 1935, she won first prize in a national contest for singers sponsored by the Italian government. Since this award carried with it an appearance in a leading Italian theatre, Albanese made a more official debut at the Teatro Reale in Parma—once again in *Madama Butterfly*—on December 10, 1935. She was now hailed as a new star. (The role of Cio-Cio San, in which she has since made over 150 appearances, has become one of her greatest. Shortly after the end of World War II, the Metropolitan Opera revived *Madama Butterfly* expressly for her.)

After this Parma debut, she appeared at La Scala, where she attracted the interest and

Albanese: äl-bä-nä′sä

received the support of its leading tenor, Beniamino Gigli. Success at La Scala was followed by triumphs in other major Italian opera houses. Within a few years she became such a favorite throughout Italy that she was invited to sing for King Victor Emanuel at the royal palace, and for Pope Pius XI at the Vatican. She was one of the few women ever to perform for His Holiness, and the only woman both to broadcast over the Vatican Radio and to be decorated by the Pope.

Her artistic stature in Europe grew after appearances at the Paris Opéra, and at Covent Garden where she was heard in 1936 during the Coronation festivities. Finally she came to the United States, making her American debut at the Metropolitan Opera on February 9, 1940, in *Madama Butterfly*. "The most important thing about her," said Edward Johnson, then general manager of the company, "is her unlimited promise for the future. The more the public comes to know her and demand her—and it will—the more scope we can give her in new roles and more appearances." During that first season at the Metropolitan, Albanese was also seen and acclaimed in the roles of Mimi in *La Bohème* and Micaela in *Carmen*.

Albanese has been a principal soprano of the Metropolitan since 1940, appearing in a variety of roles. The most successful, besides those already mentioned, have been Violetta in *La Traviata*, Marguerite in *Faust*, Manon in the operas by Massenet and Puccini, Nedda in *Pagliacci*, and Desdemona in *Otello*. She appeared as Desdemona when opera was televised for the first time from the stage of the Metropolitan Opera — on October 29, 1948. She also appeared in the leading opera houses of South America and Europe, and was selected by Toscanini for his broadcasts of *La Bohème* and *La Traviata* over the NBC network, which were recorded by Victor. Other important radio appearances included those on her own program, "The Treasure Hour of Song."

Albanese became an American citizen in 1945. In the same year she married Joseph Gimma, a New York stockbroker who is also a native of Bari. They have two homes—a spacious apartment on Park Avenue in New York City decorated with Chinese art, and a waterside cottage in Huntington, Long Island. Her favorite diversions are fishing, clam digging, gardening, designing her own shoes and clothes, and cooking regional dishes.

ALCOCK, MERLE, contralto. See *Living Musicians*, 1940.

ALDA, FRANCES, soprano. For her earlier career, see *Living Musicians*, 1940.

* * *

Alda was active in war relief work during World War II. She died in Venice, Italy, on September 18, 1952.

ALESSANDRO, VICTOR, conductor, was born in Waco, Texas, on November 27, 1915. His father was director of music and school bands for the Houston public school system. His first recollection of hearing music goes back to his second year when he attended one of his father's band concerts. When he was three, Victor was taken by his parents to an opera performance. "I think I knew from that day on I would be a conductor." (Curiously, he later made his debut as opera conductor of the very same opera he heard that day—*Tosca*.) He also began attending symphony concerts. Often, upon returning home from one of these performances, he played at being a conductor by waving a pencil as a baton and singing parts of the orchestral work at the top of his voice. He was not yet four when he conducted a child's rhythm band. "I was a lot harder on that baby orchestra than I am on my own orchestra today. Somehow, somewhere, I got the impression that a conductor had to throw tantrums, and so I threw tantrums all over the place."

After studying music with private teachers, he attended the Eastman School of Music from 1933 to 1937. (When, in 1948, the University of Rochester conferred on him the

Gittings

VICTOR ALESSANDRO

honorary degree of Doctor of Music he became the first graduate of the Eastman School to be thus honored.) A fellowship in conducting brought him to the Mozarteum in Salzburg, after which, on still another fellowship, he studied composition with Ildebrando Pizzetti at the Santa Cecilia Academy in Rome.

Returning to the United States in 1938, he was appointed musical director of the Oklahoma Symphony Orchestra. He held this post until 1951. During his last two years in Oklahoma, he attracted international attention when he and his orchestra started a weekly hour-long broadcast on a national hookup which was relayed by transcription throughout the world over the Armed Services network and the Voice of America.

While serving with the Oklahoma Symphony, Alessandro also made guest appearances with other American orchestras. Three performances with the San Antonio Symphony, in January 1951, were so successful, that he was then engaged as its musical director. Alessandro took over the orchestra on November 3, 1951, and in 1952 he also became head of the San Antonio Grand Opera Festival, even though up to then he had had virtually no experience in opera. He has retained both positions, and has proved equally successful in both. "His adroitness, sensitivity and obvious flair for the medium have had everything to do with the success and permanency of the venture," reported Alfred Frankenstein from San Antonio in the San Francisco *Chronicle*.

In 1956 Alessandro received the Alice M. Ditson Award for distinguished service to American music.

ALSEN, ELSA, soprano. See *Living Musicians*, 1940.

ALSEN, HERBERT, bass-baritone. For his earlier career, see *Living Musicians*, 1940.

* * *

Alsen's principal appearances since World War II have been with Covent Garden and the Vienna State Opera. In Vienna he received the honorary appointment of Kammersänger in 1947. On August 6 of the same year he appeared at the Salzburg Festival in the world première of Gottfried von Einem's *Dantons Tod*.

ALTHOUSE, PAUL, tenor. For his earlier career, see *Living Musicians*, 1940.

* * *

Althouse left the Metropolitan Opera after the 1939-1940 season, thereafter devoting himself to teaching and coaching young singers. His pupils included Richard Tucker and Eleanor Steber. Althouse died in New York City on February 6, 1954.

ALVARY, LORENZO, bass-baritone, was born in Debrecen, Hungary on February 20, 1909. His family was musical, and he was given musical training from his seventh year on—first in piano, then cello. In his boyhood he often participated in chamber-music performances with various Budapest ensembles. Since his father wanted him to be a lawyer, he attended first the University of Budapest, then, from his seventeenth year on, the University of Geneva. An additional period of study of languages and philosophy took place at the Sorbonne.

He returned to music study in his twentieth year, having by then become determined to enter music professionally. After intensive voice training with Fernando Tanara in Milan, and Oscar Daniel in Berlin, he made his opera debut at the Budapest Royal Opera in 1933 as Ramfis in *Aida*. Guest appearances in other European opera houses followed. In Florence, Bruno Walter heard him and engaged him for the Vienna State Opera where, in 1936, Alvary made his debut as Sparafucile in *Rigoletto*.

It was Bruno Walter who encouraged him to come to the United States. He arrived in 1939 to fill an engagement with the San Francisco Opera, but his American debut took place in St. Louis, where he appeared as Leporello in a performance of *Don Giovanni* that starred Ezio Pinza. One year later he finally appeared at the San Francisco Opera; the general manager, Gaetano Merola, became his mentor, and since that time, Alvary has been a permanent member of the company. Alvary's debut at the Metropolitan Opera took place on November 26, 1942, as Zuniga in *Carmen*, Sir Thomas Beecham conducting. Alvary has since appeared successfully at the Metropolitan in many roles, including Baron Ochs in *Der Rosenkavalier*, Rocco in *Fidelio*, Arkel in *Pelléas et Mélisande*, Varlaam in *Boris Godunov*, Leporello in *Don Giovanni*, and Mephistopheles in *Faust*.

"From every point of view, visually, vocally, and histrionically," said the New York *Herald Tribune* on January 13, 1954, after Alvary's appearance as Arkel, "Mr. Alvary's evocation of the ancient, brooding monarch was a joy to behold. When he was singing, the strength and resonance of his basso and the unusual intensity of his musical

Alvary: äl-vä're

LORENZO ALVARY

conception commanded from the listener a level of attention that was no less intense. When he was not singing, his presence on the stage was itself sufficient to underline the dreamy, other-worldly character of the Maeterlinck drama, adding a quality of withdrawn pensiveness to serve as backdrop for the more overt demeanor of other characters."

While pursuing his career in America, in the 1940's, Alvary continued studying voice with Giuseppe Danise and Alexander Kipnis.

Alvary has been heard frequently in recitals and as soloist with major symphony orchestras. For several successive seasons he appeared with the New York Philharmonic-Symphony Orchestra under Bruno Walter in performances of such choral masterworks as Bach's *Passion According to St. Matthew* and Beethoven's *Missa Solemnis*. He was also heard with the NBC Symphony Orchestra under Toscanini in Beethoven's Ninth Symphony. In 1948 he appeared at the Central City (Colorado) Festival, and in 1949 toured Rio de Janeiro, Mexico City, and Cuba.

He has also appeared extensively in the major opera houses of Europe. When he appeared in *Der Rosenkavalier* at the Carlo Felice Theatre in Genoa in 1955, he became the first non-Italian to sing the role of Baron Ochs in the Italian language.

One of his major hobbies is to scout Europe for forgotten comic operas. He made a "find" in Cherubini's *The Portuguese Inn*, which received its American première in 1954 at the San Francisco Opera. Five of his discovered comic operas were revised, orchestrated, and rearranged by Guilio Confalonieri, in whose version they were introduced at the Florence May Music Festival, La Scala, and other major European music centers.

AMANS, JOHN, flutist. For his earlier career, see *Living Musicians,* 1940.

* * *

Amans resigned as first flutist of the New York Philharmonic-Symphony Orchestra at the termination of the 1942-1943 season. After World War II, he went into retirement in the city of his birth—Amsterdam, Holland.

AMATO, PASQUALE, baritone. For his earlier career, see *Living Musicians,* 1940.

* * *

Amato died in Jackson Heights, New York, on August 12, 1942.

The AMERICAN SOCIETY OF ANCIENT INSTRUMENTS. For its earlier history, see *Living Musicians,* 1940.

* * *

The founder and director of the American Society of Ancient Instruments—Ben Stad—died in Gloucester, Massachusetts, on August 19, 1946. The organization has since passed out of existence.

AMFITEATROFF, DANIELE, conductor. For his earlier career, see *Living Musicians,* 1940.

* * *

From 1938 to 1941, Amfiteatroff was the assistant conductor of the Minneapolis Symphony Orchestra. Since 1941, he has appeared as guest conductor of major American orchestras, and has worked in Hollywood writing music for the screen.

ANDA, GEZA, pianist, was born in Budapest, Hungary on November 19, 1921. His father, a schoolmaster, was a competent amateur violinist, and his mother played the piano well. Anda was eight years old when he attended his first concert, a recital by Ernst von Dohnányi which fired him with the ambition to become a concert pianist. His parents, however, wanted him to be a schoolteacher and saw to it that his academic training kept pace with his music study.

In his thirteenth year, Anda entered the Royal Academy of Music in Budapest. During his six years there—the last two as Dohnányi's pupil—he supported himself by playing the harmonium in salon and radio orchestras, and by teaching the piano to

GEZA ANDA

successful performances at the Edinburgh and Lucerne festivals.

Anda's name first became known to American music lovers through his recordings for Angel Records, which led a critic of the *Saturday Review* to describe him as "a star of the first magnitude." He made his American debut in the fall of 1955, when he appeared as soloist with the Philadelphia Orchestra under Ormandy in Brahms' B-flat major concerto. "He is a solidly accomplished pianist," wrote Howard Taubman in the New York *Times*, when both orchestra and pianist visited Carnegie Hall, New York, on November 1, "not overpowering but satisfying in his sane and sensitive musicianship. . . . His tone is big and firm. . . . One was never diverted from the grand design of Brahms' work." The excellent impression made at these initial appearances with the Philadelphia Orchestra was strengthened in the tour that followed which included appearances in recitals and as soloist with major orchestras.

beginners. In his last year at the Academy, he won the Franz Liszt Prize, a national competition among Hungarian pianists held once every three years. As a result of this award, Anda was able to make his debut. This took place in Budapest when he appeared as soloist with the Budapest Philharmonic under Willem Mengelberg in Brahms' B-flat major Concerto.

In the winter of 1941, a state scholarship sent him to Berlin. There, one year later, he appeared with the Berlin Philharmonic under Furtwängler in Franck's *Symphonic Variations*. In that same year he left war-torn Europe through the influence of the American consul and settled in Zurich. Now a Swiss citizen, Anda regards Zurich as his permanent home.

After the war, Anda spent nine months in Paris studying French music and culture. He resumed his concert work with performances in France, Holland, Belgium, Spain, Denmark, and Sweden. He appeared with most of the principal European orchestras and under such eminent conductors as van Beinum, Klemperer, Paray, Scherchen, and Schuricht. The *Images Musicales* of Paris said of him: "Mr. Anda touches mastery. . . . His manner of playing, of precision and clarity without default, is virile and strong. . . . His soul is artistic in every conception." *De Telegraaf* of Amsterdam called him a "poet of music." In 1951 he appeared for the first time at the Salzburg Festival, which he revisited for several years after that; and in 1955 he gave

ANDERSEN, STELL, pianist. See *Living Musicians,* 1940.

ANDERSON, MARIAN, contralto. For her earlier career, see *Living Musicians,* 1940.

* * *

Marian Anderson made her debut in opera and became the first Negro to sing a major role at the Metropolitan Opera, on January 7, 1955, when she appeared as Ulrica in *Un Ballo in Maschera.* In 1957 she sang the national anthem at the ceremonies attending President Eisenhower's second inauguration.

ANDRESEN, IVAR, basso. See *Living Musicians,* 1940.

ANGELES, VICTORIA DE LOS, soprano, was born Victoria Gamez Cima, in Barcelona, Spain, on November 1, 1923. Her father was a caretaker of the University of Barcelona campus. While still a child, she was presented with a guitar by her uncle. Once she had acquired the rudiments of guitar-playing, she often spent hours singing songs to her own accompaniment. Revealing an unusual gift for musical expression at the Instituto Balmes, she was sent to the Conservatorio del Liceo, where she studied voice with Dolores Frau and where she completed a six-year course in three years. After that she continued studying singing by herself.

Her concert and opera debuts took place in her twentieth year with a recital in Barcelona

VICTORIA DE LOS ANGELES

and an appearance at the Barcelona Liceo as the Countess in *The Marriage of Figaro*.

In 1947 she won first prize among 120 contestants at the International Singing Contest in Geneva, Switzerland. Opera appearances in Barcelona followed immediately, in such roles as Elsa in *Lohengrin*, Eva in *Die Meistersinger*, Elisabeth in *Tannhäuser*, Manon in Massenet's opera of the same name, Marguerite in *Faust*, and Agathe in *Der Freischütz*. During the same year she made her first appearances at La Scala (in *Ariadne auf Naxos*) and was acclaimed at Covent Garden, the Stockholm Royal Opera, the Copenhagen Royal Opera, the Teatro Colón in Buenos Aires, and at major music festivals in Edinburgh, Florence, and Holland.

Her American concert debut took place in Carnegie Hall, New York, on October 24, 1950. "Here is a vocal delight unique in our time," said Virgil Thomson in the New York *Herald Tribune*. Louis Biancolli wrote in the New York *World Telegam and Sun* that she was "one of the greatest vocal talents since Claudia Muzio."

She returned to the United States in 1951, and on March 17 made her debut at the Metropolitan Opera in *Faust*. When she was heard as Cio-Cio San in *Madama Butterfly* a few weeks later, Irving Kolodin wrote: "Her Butterfly is certainly the most interesting new one we have heard since Licia Albanese first sang the part here." In later appearances at the Metropolitan Opera she extended her reputation with excellent performances as Mélisande in *Pelléas et Mélisande*, Mimi in

La Bohème, Rosina in *The Barber of Seville*, Eva in *Die Meistersinger,* and Donna Anna in *Don Giovanni*. Besides her performances in New York, she has been heard in recitals and operas in every part of the musical world, and at most of the leading European music festivals.

On November 28, 1948, she married Enrique Magrina Mir, an impresario whom she had met in Barcelona seven years earlier. They make their home in Barcelona. Away from her singing, she enjoys knitting, reading, cooking, and playing the guitar. Frequently, at her concerts, she accompanies herself on the guitar in renditions of Spanish Flamencan folk songs.

ANSERMET, ERNEST, conductor. For his earlier career, see *Living Musicians,* 1940.

* * *

After an absence of eleven years, Ansermet returned to the United States in 1948 for guest appearances with the major symphony orchestras.

ANTOINE, JOSEPHINE, soprano. See *Living Musicians,* 1940.

ARÁNYI, YELLY D', violinist. See *Living Musicians,* 1940.

ARRAU, CLAUDIO, pianist. For his earlier career, see *Living Musicians,* 1940.

* * *

Arrau made his first tour of Australia in 1947, and his first tour of South Africa in 1949. In 1953 he presented in Carnegie Hall a cycle of all the piano sonatas of Beethoven.

AUSTRAL, FLORENCE, soprano. For her earlier career, see *Living Musicians,* 1940.

* * *

Austral appeared at the Berlin State Opera until the outbreak of World War II. After the war she went into retirement in London.

BACCALONI, SALVATORE, basso buffo, was born in Rome, Italy, on April 14, 1900, the son of a building contractor. He received his first musical instruction at the San Salvatore in Lauro school, which he entered when he was five. In 1907 he was enrolled in the school of choristers attached to the Sistine Chapel. When his voice broke five years later, he decided to abandon music for architecture. He attended the Academy of

Baccaloni: bä-kä-lō'nē

Fine Arts in Rome, from which—after a period of service in the signal corps during World War I—he was graduated with a degree in architecture in 1920.

One day in 1921 he sang at a musicale where he was heard by Giuseppe Kaschmann, a famous baritone. Kaschmann persuaded Baccaloni to become a singer and for two years was his teacher. In 1922 Baccaloni made his debut in a small opera house in Rome as Bartolo in *The Barber of Seville*. For the next four years he gained valuable experience in several of Italy's minor opera houses.

In 1925, appearing in Bologna in a minor role in *Louise*, he was heard by Toscanini, who arranged to have him appear at La Scala, where, for the next thirteen years, Baccaloni was to be principal basso. About a year after his first La Scala appearance, Baccaloni was induced by Toscanini to specialize in comic roles. "Comic roles in opera are always played by old men who have lost their voices," Toscanini told him. "I should like to have a young man in full voice play them. You have a fine voice and an aptitude for comedy. You should become a specialist in comic roles."

Baccaloni's subsequent performances in buffo parts helped restore to them an eminence they had once enjoyed. In such roles as Don Pasquale, Falstaff, Dulcamara in *L'Elisir d'Amore*, and Leporello in *Don Giovanni*, Baccaloni combined distinguished singing and brilliant acting with a personal gift for projecting broad comedy and burlesque. He was acclaimed not only at La Scala but throughout Italy, and in 1934 was decorated Knight of the Crown of Italy. He also appeared in other leading European opera houses.

His American debut took place at the Chicago Opera during the 1930-1931 season. But not until nine years later, on December 3, 1940, did he join the company of the Metropolitan Opera, making his debut there as Bartolo. He dominated the performance so completely that one New York music critic remarked the opera should have been renamed *The Bartolo of Seville*. Three weeks later he scored another personal triumph as Don Pasquale, Donizetti's opera being revived expressly for him. Virgil Thomson described his performance in the New York *Herald Tribune* as "the finest piece of lyric acting in the comic vein I have ever seen, not excepting Chaliapin." From then on, Baccaloni appeared at the Metropolitan Opera in most of his successful buffo parts, becoming a favorite of American opera audiences. As Oscar Thompson wrote at the time, in Baccaloni "the Metropolitan has made . . . its happiest dis-

SALVATORE BACCALONI

covery . . . since Kirsten Flagstad joined the company. If Italian and French opera at the Metropolitan could possess in each significant role a singing actor or actress of the gifts and skill of Mr. Baccaloni, then indeed we could boast of having the finest opera in the world." Besides appearing at the Metropolitan, Baccaloni toured the United States with his own company in performances of major scenes from the most celebrated Italian comic operas.

Baccaloni, who weighs over three hundred pounds, is one opera star who enjoys his rotund figure, since it is an essential part of his stock in trade. "I owe it to my public to be fat," he explained to an interviewer. His partiality toward rich Bulgarian recipes, spaghetti with rich sauces, and other succulent dishes prepared by his wife, is the insurance that he will retain his ample circumference.

Since his boyhood studies at the Rome Academy of Fine Arts, he has retained an interest in painting, sketching, and etching. He is particularly fascinated by the problems of designing scenery and costumes. Other interests include reading history and philosophy, and hiking.

After leaving the Metropolitan Opera in the early 1950's, Baccaloni devoted himself to the concert stage. He made his motion-picture debut in 1957 in a non-singing comedy role in *Full of Life*, starring Judy Holliday.

BACHAUER, GINA, pianist, was born in a suburb of Athens, Greece, on May 21, 1913. Her father was a dealer in foreign cars. Piano study began when she was five, and three

GINA BACHAUER

years after that she gave a public recital in Athens. Subsequent music study took place with Ariadne Casasis at the Athens Conservatory, from which she was graduated with honors; with Alfred Cortot at the École Normale in Paris; and from 1932 to 1935 privately with Serge Rachmaninoff.

In 1933 she won first prize, the Gold Medal of Honor, in a state competition for pianists held in Vienna; and in the same year she gave her first public recital as a mature artist, in Paris. Two years later she played the Tchaikovsky Concerto in B-flat minor in Athens with the Athens Symphony under Dimitri Mitropoulos. On this occasion, King Paul and Queen Frederika of Greece presented her with a platinum vanity box inlaid with sapphires and diamonds. She then went on a tour of Italy, Yugoslavia, Austria, and Egypt.

En route to Italy for her third tour of that country, she heard the news that her native land had plunged into World War II. She forthwith canceled her Italian appearances and returned home. When the Nazis invaded Greece she fled to Egypt. During the next few years she made so many appearances for the armed forces (over six hundred) that she was dubbed the "Myra Hess of the Middle East." Her programs included not only the classics and semi-classics but even popular songs and boogie-woogie.

After the war, she returned to the professional concert stage. On January 21, 1946, she made her debut in England, appearing with the New London Symphony under Alec

Sherman in the Grieg Concerto in A minor. (Four years later, on November 21, 1951, Alec Sherman became her husband.) Appearances throughout Europe and the Near East now brought her to a front rank among women pianists. Her virtuosity led some of the critics to describe her as a second Teresa Carreño.

Her American debut took place at Town Hall, New York, in 1950. Jerome D. Bohm wrote in the New York *Herald Tribune* that she performed "miracles of virtuosity," while Harold C. Schonberg described her playing in the New York *Times* as "liquid" and "authoritative." She scored an even greater success a few months later when she appeared as soloist with the New York Philharmonic-Symphony under Mitropoulos in the Tchaikovsky Concerto. In 1951-1952 she returned to the United States to fill fifty-two engagements, and since then her tours of this country have been even more extensive.

During the summer of 1955 she returned to her native land to appear with the National Symphony of Athens under Alec Sherman in a command performance before King Paul and Queen Frederika. She also became the first pianist to play before the royal pair in the ancient open-air theatre constructed in the hollow of the hill on which the Parthenon stands. In addition to these honors she was twice decorated by King Paul for her services to Greek Relief.

BACHAUS, WILHELM, pianist. For his earlier career, see *Living Musicians,* 1940.

* * *

After an absence of twenty-eight years, Bachaus returned to the American concert stage in 1954, to begin a nation-wide tour with a triumphant appearance at Carnegie Hall on March 30.

BACON, KATHERINE, pianist. See *Living Musicians,* 1940.

BADURA-SKODA, PAUL, pianist, was born Paul Badura in Vienna, Austria, on October 6, 1927. His father died when Paul was only four months old. His mother later married a Viennese furniture dealer named Skoda. He has retained the names of both his father and stepfather.

Paul began taking lessons in piano when he was six. However, he showed such a gift for drawing, mathematics, and science that up through his boyhood he thought of becoming an engineer. The turning point came in his sixteenth year with a piano recital by Edwin Fischer. This performance inspired him to

Badura-Skoda: bȧ-dōō′rȧ skō′dȧ

become a concert pianist. Encouraged by his stepfather, he pursued piano study intensively with Otto Schulhof, Viola Thern, and for three years with Edwin Fischer.

In 1945 he entered the Vienna Conservatory, where he stayed two years. Winning the first prize in the Austrian Music Competition entitled him to a debut performance, which took place in June 1947 with the Vienna Symphony under Rudolf Moralt in Liszt's Concerto in E-flat. One year later, Badura-Skoda won the Bartók Competition in Budapest, and in 1949 the International Music Competition in Paris.

His concert career began officially with a successful recital in Vienna in 1948. One year later he appeared twice as soloist with the world-renowned Vienna Philharmonic, once under Wilhelm Furtwängler and the other time under Herbert von Karajan. These two appearances did much to establish his reputation in Vienna, but it was not long before his fame spread throughout the rest of the music world. In 1950-1951 he toured Italy and Scandinavia as soloist with the Vienna Chamber Orchestra under Franz Litschauer. In November 1951 he made his first appearance in London; in 1952, he toured Australia; and in 1953 he played in South America. He also scored major successes at the Bach Festival in Vienna, the International Festival in Cannes, and the Salzburg Festival.

He first became known to this country through his recordings for Westminster. Consequently, when he made his first tour of the United States, during the season of 1952-1953, he found a large and appreciative audience awaiting him. His North American debut took place in Toronto, Canada, on November 1, 1952. A few days later, on November 7, he was heard in the United States for the first time, when he played Mozart's Concerto in B-flat major with the Cincinnati Symphony Orchestra under Thor Johnson in Cincinnati. On January 10, 1953, he gave his first New York recital. "Not in a long time has a new pianist appeared among us so thoroughly prepared, it would seem, for a great career," reported Virgil Thomson in the New York *Herald Tribune*. "His technique is impeccable; his musicianship utterly mature and first-class. He has brains, too, as can be read from the completeness, the clean simplicity with which he exposes any musical passage. And the loving care with which he details a passage without any sacrifice of the whole work's architectural proportions is proof of the finest musical sensibilities."

Since then, besides appearing in Europe, Badura-Skoda has toured this country several

PAUL BADURA-SKODA

times. With each reappearance he has demonstrated ever-growing interpretative powers. After a New York recital in 1954, the New York *Times* wrote: "It must be said that Mr. Badura-Skoda improves each time he has appeared in this city. . . . His music making is now that of a real artist."

BAILLY, LOUIS, violist. For his earlier career, see *Living Musicians,* 1940.

* * *

After World War II, Bailly established his home in Canada where he joined the faculty of the Pelletier School of Music in Montreal.

BALDWIN, SAMUEL ATKINSON, organist. For his earlier career, see *Living Musicians,* 1940.

* * *

Baldwin died in New York City on September 15, 1949.

BALOGH, ERNO, pianist. See *Living Musicians,* 1940.

BALOKOVIČ, ZLATKO, violinist. See *Living Musicians,* 1940.

BAMBOSCHEK, GIUSEPPE, conductor. For his earlier career, *see Living Musicians,* 1940.

* * *

In 1957 Bamboschek was elected general manager of the Philadelphia Grand Opera Company.

BAMPTON, ROSE, soprano. For her earlier career, see *Living Musicians,* 1940.

* * *

In 1943 Bampton was heard for the first time in Wagnerian roles: Elsa in *Lohengrin,* Elisabeth in *Tannhäuser,* and Kundry in *Parsifal.* She left the Metropolitan Opera in 1951 and for a while appeared with the New York City Opera. She was subsequently heard in numerous concert and television performances in this country, and in opera in South America.

BARBIERI, FEDORA, mezzo-soprano, was born on June 4, 1920, in Trieste, then part of Italy. She did not receive music instruction until her eighteenth year. Meanwhile she attended local schools, after which she worked as a clerk in a little shop owned by her parents. While working in the store, she would sing "to make the days pass faster." One day a customer heard her and urged her to begin cultivating her voice. Heeding this advice, Barbieri became a pupil of Federico Bugamelli, with whom she studied in Trieste for two years. An additional nine-month period of training followed with Luigi Toffolo. She then made her debut at the San Giusto Church in Trieste, where she had been baptized.

She went to Florence, there to study for a year with Giulia Tess. On November 4, 1940, her opera debut took place in Florence, where she appeared as Fidalma in *Il Matrimonio Segreto.* Her physical stamina attracted as much attention as her singing, for one day after her debut she was heard in the taxing role of Azucena in *Il Trovatore,* while on the third day she reappeared as Fidalma.

During the next two and a half years, Barbieri appeared at La Scala. In 1943 she went into temporary retirement, after marrying Luigi Barlozzetti, administrative director of the Florence May Music Festival. They have two sons.

Her "second debut," as she describes it, took place at the Teatro Verdi in Florence in 1945 when she was acclaimed for her performance of Amneris in *Aida.* It is from this point on that she began to assume a position of first importance among Italian sopranos, particularly through her performances at La Scala and her remarkable recordings, which carried her fame throughout the world of music. The wide range of her voice (from low E to high C) enabled her to appear in many works long neglected because suitable mezzo-sopranos were not available, including many lesser known works of Monteverdi and Rossini, and Donizetti's infrequently heard *La Favorita.* In 1949 she was acclaimed at the May Music Festival in Florence for her performance in the title role of Monteverdi's *Orfeo.*

She made her London debut in 1950 when the company of La Scala toured England. Her American debut took place at the Metropolitan Opera on November 14, 1950 (not only the opening night of the season but also the first performance under the new directorial regime of Rudolf Bing), when she appeared as Princess Eboli in *Don Carlos.* Since she was already known to American audiences through her recordings, she was given a warm welcome. Her magnetic stage presence and her remarkable voice, however, brought her many new admirers.

In the summer of 1956, Barbieri scored a personal triumph at both the Verona Arena and the Caracalla Baths in Rome. On the opening night of the 1956-1957 season, she returned to the Metropolitan Opera after a two-year absence to appear as Adalgisa in *Norma*—opposite Maria Callas, then making her Metropolitan Opera debut in the title role.

BARBIROLLI, SIR JOHN, conductor. For his earlier career, see *Living Musicians,* 1940.

* * *

Barbirolli left the New York Philharmonic-Symphony after the 1940-1941 season. In 1943 he was appointed permanent conductor

FEDORA BARBIERI

Barbieri: bär-byâ′rē

of the Hallé Orchestra in Manchester, which he reorganized and raised to a position of first importance among European orchestras. For his services to English music he was knighted in June 1949, and in 1950 was awarded a gold medal by the Royal Philharmonic Society of London.

BARER, SIMON, pianist. For his earlier career, see *Living Musicians,* 1940.

* * *

Barer died while performing the Grieg Concerto in A minor in Carnegie Hall on April 2, 1951.

BARLOW, HOWARD, conductor. For his earlier career, see *Living Musicians,* 1940.

* * *

Barlow resigned as conductor of the Baltimore Symphony Orchestra in 1943, and from 1943 to 1945 was one of the conductors of the New York Philharmonic-Symphony. In 1943 he also resigned as music director of CBS to assume the post of musical director of "The Voice of Firestone" program, broadcast first on radio, then simultaneously on television and radio.

BAROMEO, CHASE, basso. See *Living Musicians,* 1940.

BARRÈRE, GEORGES, flutist. For his earlier career, see *Living Musicians,* 1940.

* * *

Barrère died in Kingston, New York, on June 14, 1944.

BARTLETT, MICHAEL, tenor. See *Living Musicians,* 1940.

BARTLETT and ROBERTSON, duo-pianists. For their earlier careers, see *Living Musicians,* 1940.

* * *

Rae Robertson died in Los Angeles on November 4, 1956.

BARZIN, LEON, conductor. For his earlier career, see *Living Musicians,* 1940.

* * *

When the New York City Ballet was organized in 1948, Barzin was appointed musical director. He was also appointed artistic director of the Symphony of the Air in 1956, and was one of its conductors when that orchestra toured the Near East that fall.

While holding these posts, Barzin continued to serve as music director of the National Orchestral Association, celebrating his twenty-fifth anniversary with this organization in 1955.

BAUER, HAROLD, pianist. For his earlier career, see *Living Musicians,* 1940.

* * *

Bauer died in Miami, Florida, on March 12, 1951.

BAUM, KURT, tenor, was born in Prague, Czechoslovakia, on March 15, 1908. His father, a merchant, wanted him to become a doctor. After completing his high school and college education in Cologne, Baum enrolled in the medical school of the University of Prague in 1927. During this period he was an exceptional all-around athlete, the amateur boxing champion of Czechoslovakia. He also attracted attention with his singing, which—as one story has it—improved in tone quality and resonance after he had his nose broken in a boxing bout with Max Schmeling. Several friends urged him to consider music seriously as a career. Since this was in line with his own wishes, he left medical school after his third year and entered the Music Academy of Berlin.

In 1933 he won first prize among seven hundred contestants in the Vienna International Competition. Among those who heard him was the director of the Zurich Opera who engaged Baum for his company. Baum's debut, then, was made at the Zurich Opera in November 1933 in *Il Trovatore.* After singing lyric roles in Zurich for a year, Baum was engaged by the Deutsches Theater in Prague, where he appeared in the leading dramatic tenor roles in *Aida, Cavalleria Rusticana,* and *La Gioconda.*

Further intensive training in Italian opera took place with Edoardo Garbin in Milan and at the Santa Cecilia Academy in Rome, following which Baum appeared in opera houses in Vienna, Budapest, Paris, Salzburg, and Monte Carlo, distinguishing himself in the leading tenor parts in the French and Italian repertory. Paul Longone, director of the Chicago Opera, heard him in Monte Carlo and signed him for his company. Baum's American debut took place in Chicago on November 2, 1939, as Radames in *Aida.*

An engagement at the Metropolitan Opera followed. Baum's first appearance there took place on November 27, 1941, in *Der Rosenkavalier.* Though he was cast in the minor

Baum: boum

KURT BAUM

role of Italian Singer, he impressed Robert Lawrence of the New York *Herald Tribune* with "the excellent quality" of his singing, "topped by ringing climactic tones." Baum soon began assuming major tenor roles not only in Italian and French but also in German operas, and became recognized as one of the most valuable members of the entire company. Of his Manrico in *Il Trovatore*, the New York *Times* said it was "perhaps the best sung since the days of Lauri-Volpi. His high C's packed a wallop, and he sang throughout with rousing sonority." When Baum appeared in *La Gioconda* at the San Francisco Opera, Alfred Frankenstein compared him favorably to Caruso.

Shortly after World War II, Baum returned to Europe to make his debut at La Scala as Manrico. He later appeared in other major European opera houses, at the Florence May Music Festival, and during the Coronation festivities in London in a command performance of *Aida* for Queen Elizabeth II.

Baum married Renata Schall, a Powers model, on June 6, 1944. They make their home in New York City. Baum loves the sea, and his favorite pastimes include swimming and deep-sea fishing. Indoors his main diversion is photography.

BAUME, ÉMILE, pianist. See *Living Musicians,* 1940.

BEATTIE, DOUGLAS, basso. See *Living Musicians,* 1940.

BEECHAM, SIR THOMAS, conductor. For his earlier career, see *Living Musicians,* 1940.

* * *

Beecham made his debut at the Metropolitan Opera on January 2, 1942, in a dual bill comprising *Le Coq d'Or,* and Bach's cantata, *Phoebus and Pan,* staged as an opera. He remained at the Metropolitan through the 1943-1944 season. Since World War II, he has directed notable opera performances at Covent Garden and Glyndebourne. In 1949 he toured the United States with the Royal Philharmonic Orchestra in London. In 1944 he married the concert pianist Betty Humby.

BEHREND, JEANNE, pianist. See *Living Musicians,* 1940.

BEINUM, EDUARD VAN, conductor, was born in Arnhem, Holland, on September 3, 1901. He came from a family which for several generations had produced professional musicians. His father was a bass player and assistant conductor of the Arnhem Philharmonic Orchestra; his older brother, Co van Beinum, was a violinist and choral conductor. Eduard received instruction on the violin from his brother; later on he also received piano lessons from F. Hiller. At sixteen, he joined the violin section of the Arnhem Philharmonic. One year later, he entered the Amsterdam Conservatory where his teachers included Sem Dresden, Bernard Zweers, and J. B. C. De Pauw.

He completed his studies in 1921, when he was appointed conductor of the Toonkunst Choir in Schiedam. He held this post until 1930. During this period he also conducted an orchestra and choir in Zutphen, and from 1927 on, the Haarlem Philharmonic.

In 1931 he succeeded Cornelis Dopper as second conductor of the renowned Concertgebouw Orchestra of Amsterdam led by Willem Mengelberg. When, in 1938, ill health compelled Mengelberg to cut down his schedule, van Beinum was selected to share the post of conductor with Bruno Walter. He also made guest appearances with major orchestras of Europe and the Soviet Union.

Van Beinum abandoned all his musical activity after the Nazis invaded Holland in 1940. Following the liberation—with Mengelberg completely discredited as a collaborationist—van Beinum was made music director of the Concertgebouw. Only three men have held this post since the founding of the orchestra in 1888; van Beinum is the third.

As the conductor of the Concertgebouw (with which he toured Europe in 1945), as

Beinum: bĭ′nŭm

EDUARD VAN BEINUM

the sole conductor of the London Philharmonic during the 1948-1949 season, and as a guest conductor of other major European orchestras, van Beinum achieved international recognition as one of Europe's leading conductors, the foremost to arise in Holland since Mengelberg. A musician of impeccable taste, a penetrating interpreter of an extensive repertory, and a master of orchestral technique, van Beinum commanded the respect and admiration of the music world.

He made his American debut as guest conductor of the Philadelphia Orchestra in January 1954. When he was heard with that orchestra in New York, Olin Downes wrote in the New York *Times* that he was "clearly a past master of his craft, being indeed one of the most skillful and polished conductors we have heard in seasons."

In the fall of the same year, van Beinum returned to the United States to tour the country with the Concertgebouw Orchestra—the first time this organization was being heard in America. The tour opened in New York on October 13, 1954. Mr. Downes wrote: "It was the glory of the orchestra itself, the sincerity and passion of the players to give of their best, and the high musicianship and evident idealism of Mr. van Beinum, that made the occasion a triumph of art."

On January 12, 1956, van Beinum made a guest appearance with the Los Angeles Philharmonic which proved so successful that he was engaged as its music director on a two-year contract. He held this post while fulfilling his commitment with the Concertgebouw Orchestra in Holland.

Van Beinum is the recipient of numerous honors, including the Chevalier of the Legion of Honor, Officer of the Order of Orange Nassau, Order of the North Star from Sweden, and Order of the Dannebrog from Denmark. He is married to a former concert violinist and they have two sons.

BELLISON, SIMEON, clarinetist. For his earlier career, see *Living Musicians,* 1940.

* * *

Bellison retired from the New York Philharmonic-Symphony in 1948, and died in New York City on May 4, 1953.

BENTONELLI, JOSEPH, tenor. For his earlier career, see *Living Musicians,* 1940.

* * *

In 1944 Bentonelli joined the voice department of the University of Oklahoma. He was elected to the Oklahoma Hall of Fame in 1951, and became honorary Colonel on the staff of the Governor of the State.

BENZELL, MIMI, soprano, was born on April 6, 1924, in Bridgeport, Connecticut, where she received her earliest musical training. After her family moved to New York City, she appeared in a minor role in a high school performance. Soon after that she entered Hunter College but was compelled by her family's critical financial situation to leave school and find a job as a department store sales clerk. But while working, she continued to sing. A successful audition brought her a scholarship for the David Mannes School where she studied with Olga Eisner. Her first solo appearance took place in a church for a $5.00 fee which she used at once to buy an opera score; up to this time she had never seen an opera performance.

After completing her studies with Mme. Eisner, Benzell made several appearances over radio, in summer operetta performances, and finally in a season of opera conducted by Sir Thomas Beecham in New Mexico. Sir Thomas became interested in her and arranged for her to audition for the Metropolitan Opera. Singing the taxing recitative and aria of Zerbinetta from *Ariadne auf Naxos,* she made such an impression that the day after the audition she was given a contract.

She made her debut at the Metropolitan Opera on January 5, 1945, as the Queen of the Night in *The Magic Flute.* "Her coloratura is neat and finished," wrote Olin Downes

Benzell: běn-zěl'

MIMI BENZELL

in the *New York Times.* "She has style in acting and singing. . . . [Her] performance . . . was highly intelligent and artistic." During the next five years she appeared sixty-five times in eight starring roles, including Gilda in *Rigoletto,* Philine in *Mignon,* Zerlina in *Don Giovanni,* and Musetta in *La Bohème.* "A figurine of grace and delicate femininity," wrote the New York *World Telegram* critic, "she brought down the house time after time."

Benzell has also appeared with other opera companies in America, including the festival in Central City, Colorado, where, in 1952, she was seen in *Ariadne auf Naxos,* and heard in several recitals. The critic of the Detroit *News* said at this time: "Her voice with its power, flexibility and warmth, together with her personality, make her a favorite with her audiences." She has also been a great favorite over radio and television, and in films.

On July 29, 1949, she married Walter Gould, a concert manager and music publisher, and brother of the famous composer, Morton Gould. They have a son.

BERGER, ERNA, soprano, was born in Dresden, Germany, on October 19, 1900. She was still a child when her family moved to Paraguay, where she was raised on a farm in a jungle clearing. In her late teens she worked as a governess for a French family. She saved enough money to return to Dresden to pursue in earnest the study of singing. While studying with a local teacher, and mastering five opera arias, she applied for a scholarship at

the Dresden Opera School. Fritz Busch, musical director of the Dresden Opera, happened to hear her audition and engaged her at once for his company. She scored her first successes in Dresden, principally in the French and Italian repertory. Later on, as the principal soprano of the Berlin State Opera, her interpretations of the Mozart operas attracted world attention—combining as they did coloratura singing of a high order with a keen understanding of the classic style. She was now invited to the foremost European opera houses, and to such world-famous music festivals as those in Salzburg and Bayreuth. Sir Thomas Beecham considered her so indispensable for the role of Constanza in *The Abduction from the Seraglio* that he postponed his recording of this Mozart opera for a year so that Berger might appear in it.

In 1948-1949 she made the first of several successful tours of Australia, where one critic called her "the greatest singer since Melba." Her American debut took place on the opening night of the Metropolitan Opera season of 1949-1950, when she appeared as Sophie in *Der Rosenkavalier.* Since this performance was televised, her debut was witnessed by millions. Irving Kolodin described her performance as "a wonderfully pure, well-phrased Sophie." Somewhat later, when she was heard as Gilda in *Rigoletto,* one New York critic said she was "a singing actress of the great tradition." Subsequent appearances at the Metropolitan Opera, mostly in coloratura parts, succeeded in making her as much a

James Abresch

ERNA BERGER

favorite in this country as she was in Europe. "She is," wrote Virgil Thomson in the New York *Herald Tribune,* "one of the great sources of musical satisfaction in our time." She also became an idol of the concert world, described by Louis Biancolli of the New York *World Telegram* as "the first lady of *Lieder,*" after a highly successful American concert debut in Carnegie Hall in February 1950.

BERNSTEIN, LEONARD, conductor, was born in Lawrence, Massachusetts, on August 25, 1918. In childhood he was attracted to the piano and after a single lesson "I knew with finality I would become a musician." Later study of the piano took place with Helen Coates and Heinrich Gebhard, while he pursued his academic education in public schools and at Harvard College. At Harvard, where with the regular curriculum he took music courses with Walter Piston and Edward Burlingame Hill, he continually amazed teachers and fellow students with his remarkably retentive musical memory and his sure musical instincts. He was graduated in 1939.

Soon after his graduation, several celebrated musicians, including Dimitri Mitropoulos, persuaded him to consider conducting as a career. To prepare for this calling Bernstein attended the Curtis Institute of Music, studying conducting with Fritz Reiner, piano with Isabella Vengerova, and orchestration with Randall Thompson. In 1940 and 1941 he attended the Berkshire Music center at Tanglewood, in Lenox, Massachusetts, as a pupil of Serge Koussevitzky. Koussevitzky became so interested in him that from then on he regarded Bernstein as his protégé. In 1942 Koussevitzky appointed Bernstein his assistant at the Berkshire Music Festival. One year later, Koussevitzky recommended him to Artur Rodzinski, then recently appointed music director of the New York Philharmonic-Symphony. So completely was Rodzinski won over to Bernstein that though he knew the young man had never conducted a major orchestra, he appointed him his assistant with the Philharmonic.

Bernstein soon had an opportunity to reveal his talent to the entire country. About a month after the opening of the 1943-1944 season, Bruno Walter—scheduled to conduct a Sunday afternoon performance, on November 13—suddenly fell ill, and Bernstein was called as a substitute. Since he was given notice only a day before the concert he had no opportunity to rehearse the orchestra, and only several hours to become acquainted with a rigorous program that included a world première.

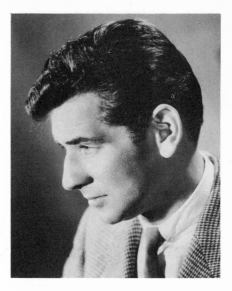

LEONARD BERNSTEIN

His performance—relayed throughout the country over the CBS radio network—was a sensation. The following morning, Olin Downes wrote in the New York *Times,* and on the front page: "It was clear at once . . . that he was conducting the orchestra in his own right and not the orchestra conducting him; that he had every one of the scores both in his hands and in his head and though he logically and inevitably conformed in broad outline, he was not following slavishly in the footsteps of his distinguished senior." The New York *Times* also discussed Bernstein's achievement in an editorial. Rodzinski, who had motored in from Massachusetts to hear the performance, pronounced Bernstein "a prodigious talent." Koussevitzky, who heard him over the air, sent effusive congratulations by wire. That single performance made Bernstein famous—literally overnight.

After that he was often called upon to conduct guest performances with the New York Philharmonic-Symphony and with other major American orchestras. He proved himself to be no flash in the pan, but a born conductor with a penetrating musical intelligence, a keen insight into musical interpretation, and a commanding personality. In 1945 he was appointed musical director of the New York City Symphony with which, for several seasons, he led many distinguished concerts, including provocative premières and novelties. In May 1946 he scored a sensation at the International Music Festival in Prague, and in 1948 he repeated his triumphs in Palestine as principal conductor of the Palestine Symphony Orchestra. He has since then led most of the great orchestras of the world, acclaimed everywhere. In 1953 he became the first American-born conductor to lead a performance at La Scala, in Milan—a distinguished revival of Cherubini's *Medea.* In the fall of 1956 the New York Philharmonic-Symphony announced that Bernstein had been engaged to share the direction of that orchestra with Mitropoulos beginning with the 1957-1958 season; and in 1957 Bernstein was engaged to direct the New York Philharmonic-Symphony Young People's Concerts during the same 1957-1958 season.

Bernstein has also achieved prominence as a composer: in serious music with two symphonies, a ballet, a one-act opera, and various other works; in popular music with the scores for two resounding musical-comedy successes —*On the Town* in 1944 and *Wonderful Town* in 1952—and for *Candide* in 1956. His remarkable musical versatility is also demonstrated by his appearances as pianist (often in concertos in which he himself leads the orchestra in the accompaniment), and by his success as a teacher at Brandeis University and the Berkshire Music Center, and as a lecturer on various musical subjects on the "Omnibus" television program.

His expansive and trenchant intellect has made him unusually well informed in art, literature, politics, psychology, philosophy, and poetry. On September 9, 1951, he married Felicea Montealegre, who subsequently made several successful appearances as an actress on television. They make their home in a spacious New York apartment on Fifty-seventh street, near Carnegie Hall. They have two children.

BETTI, ADOLFO, violinist. For his earlier career, see *Living Musicians,* 1940.

* * *

Betti was in Paris during World War II when, because he was Italian, he was classified an enemy alien and denied the right to return to the United States. He subsequently resettled in the town of his birth, Bagni di Lucca, where for a brief period he served as mayor. Ill health compelled him to withdraw from politics. He died there on December 2, 1950.

BIGGS, E. POWER, organist, was born in Westcliff, Essex, England, on March 29, 1906, and was baptized George Edward Power-Biggs. After attending Hurstpierpoint College in Sussex he decided to study engineering, even though music was already a

E. POWER BIGGS

major interest and he had for some time now been studying the organ. After two years of courses in engineering, he won the Thomas Threlfall Organ Scholarship, which enabled him to attend the Royal College of Music in London. This award led him to exchange engineering for music. After studying at the College with Sir Henry J. Wood and George D. Cunningham, he was graduated in 1929 with highest honors in organ, piano, harmony, and counterpoint, and with the Hubert Kiver Organ Prize.

His debut, which took place in the same year of 1929, was unscheduled. Sir Henry J. Wood was conducting an orchestral concert at Queen's Hall in London which called for the services of an organist. The regular organist became indisposed two days before the concert, and Wood called on Biggs to substitute. After this event, Biggs played in several concert halls and cathedrals in England.

His first visit to the United States also took place in 1929. Though he had come as an accompanist for a Welsh singer, he also managed to tour the country for six months and make almost two hundred solo appearances. He came to the United States again in 1932. This time he settled here permanently, and became an American citizen in 1938. On March 31, 1932, he gave an organ recital at the Wanamaker Auditorium in New York. Soon after this he received an appointment as choirmaster and organist of the Christ Church in Cambridge, Massachusetts. He started giving impressive concerts of organ music at the Harvard Memorial Church and in various auditoriums and churches throughout the United States. He was subsequently appointed to his present positions of organist and music director of the Harvard Church in Brookline and official organist of the Boston Symphony Orchestra.

In 1937 he first started playing on the instrument with which he has since become identified—a baroque organ in the German Museum of Harvard which (except for electrification) is virtually identical with the one Johann Sebastian Bach used to play in Weimar. Biggs' concerts at the German Museum, especially in programs of Bach's music, in which he was now a recognized authority, attracted the admiration of musicians everywhere. Biggs' fame spread from the specialist to the ordinary music lover on September 20, 1942, when he gave the first of a series of half-hour Sunday morning broadcasts over the Columbia Broadcasting System. This first series, on a national hookup, proved so popular that since that time Biggs has continued to broadcast. In 1945-1946 he became the first organist to perform over the air all of Bach's organ works. Since 1947 he has been recording this music for Columbia Records. He has also on several occasions given cycles of Bach's complete organ works in public recitals.

Biggs has frequently appeared as soloist with the major orchestras of America and England. In 1949 he was called upon to dedicate the new organ erected in Symphony Hall, Boston. In 1952 he received a citation from the National Association of Composers and Conductors for his service to American music.

BJÖRLING, JUSSI, tenor. See *Living Musicians*, 1940.

BLACK, FRANK, conductor. See *Living Musicians*, 1940.

BLECH, LEO, conductor. For his earlier career, see *Living Musicians*, 1940.

* * *

During World War II, Blech was deposed by the Nazis as musical director of the Berlin State Opera. After the war he conducted extensively in Stockholm, and in 1949 he returned to Berlin to assume the post of principal conductor of the Municipal Theatre.

BLOCH, SUZANNE, lutist. See *Living Musicians*, 1940.

BLOOMFIELD, THEODORE, conductor, was born in Cleveland, Ohio, in 1923. He started to study piano when he was seven. He was still in his boyhood when, fired with the ambition of becoming a conductor, he undertook the study of the French horn to gain experience in orchestral performances. After graduation from the Oberlin Conservatory of Music in 1944, he attended the Juilliard Graduate School for two years on a fellowship, specializing in conducting; at the same time he played the horn in the National Orchestral Association. For two summers he also studied conducting with Pierre Monteux in Maine. In 1946 Monteux conducted the première of Bloomfield's transcription of Bach's Toccata and Fugue in C major with the San Francisco Symphony Orchestra.

Bloomfield's first appearances as conductor took place in 1945 when he led the New York Little Symphony at the Carnegie Chamber Music Hall in New York. When George Szell was appointed music director of the Cleveland Orchestra, he arranged a nationwide competition among young musicians for an apprentice and assistant. Bloomfield was chosen in 1946 from among one hundred applicants. Bloomfield now gained valuable experience for one season by studying Szell's methods, assisting him at rehearsals, and playing the piano in the orchestra when one was required.

In 1947 Bloomfield organized the Cleveland Little Symphony Orchestra, made up of thirty-three members of the Cleveland

THEODORE BLOOMFIELD

Orchestra. Until 1952 he directed it in numerous programs requiring a smaller symphonic ensemble. In 1949 he also organized and led the Civic Opera Workshop. Despite these activities in Cleveland, he managed to give performances over radio networks, to serve as accompanist for Licia Albanese, and to be on the opera staff of the Berkshire Music Center at Tanglewood, in Lenox, Massachusetts.

His European debut took place in February 1952 when he led a performance of *Salome* in Como, Italy. He next conducted two symphony concerts in Milan, and in the summer of the same year toured Germany in nine piano recitals under the auspices of our State Department. He has since then made many appearances as conductor not only in Italy, but also in Vienna, Brussels, Monte Carlo, Switzerland, and Spain. A critic in Vienna wrote that "he left an excellent impression . . . through his precise and polished baton technique, sense of sound, majestic line, and unusually fine feeling for a live, pulsating rhythm." In 1955 he was invited to direct Gluck's *Orfeo* at the season's opening performance in Turin.

In November 1954 he gave two great performances with the Portland Symphony Orchestra. Hilmar Grondahl of the *Oregonian* spoke of his "remarkable skill, musical insight, depth and variety." The following spring Bloomfield was engaged as the permanent conductor of the Portland Symphony.

BODANYA, NATALIE, soprano. For her earlier career, see *Living Musicians,* 1940.

* * *

Bodanya left the Metropolitan Opera after the 1941-1942 season and for the next few years devoted herself to the concert stage.

BOEHM, KARL, conductor, was born in Graz, Austria, on August 28, 1894. His father, a lawyer, insisted that his son follow in his footsteps. Karl Boehm received his Doctor of Law degree in Graz in 1919. Even while he was attending law school, he studied music intensively, principally at the Vienna Conservatory, where he was a pupil of Eusebius Mandyczewski. In 1917, he found a job as prompter at the Graz Opera. By 1920 he had completely abandoned law for music, and in that year he received an appointment as one of the principal conductors of the Graz Opera. During one of his performances, the distinguished conductor Karl Muck heard him and recommended him for the post of

KARL BOEHM

conductor at the Munich Opera. Boehm made his debut there in 1920, and four years later was elevated to the post of principal conductor. In 1927 he went on to Darmstadt as first conductor of the Opera; in 1931, he was appointed musical director of the Hamburg State Opera; and in 1933 he became musical director of the Dresden State Opera. While in Dresden he led the world premières of Richard Strauss' *Daphne* and Heinrich Sutermeister's *The Magic Isle,* both dedicated to him.

Since World War II, Boehm has risen to a position of first importance among Europe's conductors, particularly through his appearances at the Salzburg Festival, and guest performances at the Vienna State Opera. Since 1951 he has conducted the German season of opera in Buenos Aires.

In 1954 Boehm was appointed artistic and musical director of the Vienna State Opera on a five-year contract. He inaugurated his regime on November 5, 1955, with a performance of *Fidelio* which opened the rebuilt Opera House on the Ringstrasse, an event that attracted world attention and which a year later was recreated by television for American audiences.

Boehm's tenure of his office with the Vienna State Opera was short-lived. He resigned as artistic and musical director in March 1956 following criticism by the State Opera management that he was filling too many engagements with other opera companies and orchestras. Nevertheless he continued to serve as one of its conductors. In

Boehm: bûm

the fall of 1956 he signed a two-year contract with the company calling for twenty-five performances the first year, and thirty-six the second.

Boehm made his first appearances in America in February 1956 as a guest conductor of the Chicago Symphony Orchestra. In 1957 he was engaged by the Metropolitan Opera to conduct performances of *Don Giovanni* and *Der Rosenkavalier.*

In 1956 he received from the International Mozarteum Foundation in Salzburg the Golden Mozart Memorial Medal in recognition of his outstanding performances of Mozart's music.

BOEPPLE, PAUL, conductor. See *Living Musicians,* 1940.

BOLET, JORGE, pianist, was born in Havana, Cuba, on November 15, 1914. Both parents were of Catalonian descent, and neither was a musician. Jorge began studying the piano when he was seven. Five years later he gave a recital in Havana. In 1927 a scholarship enabled him to attend the Curtis Institute of Music, the funds for this trip to Philadelphia having been raised through a benefit concert in which he appeared as soloist with the Havana Symphony. For several years Bolet attended the Curtis Institute, a pupil of David Saperton. Before the studies were concluded, he made his American debut at Carnegie Hall, in 1933, with an orchestra directed by Artur Rodzinski, in the Tchaikovsky B-flat minor Concerto. One year later, after his graduation from the Curtis Institute, the Cuban government financed an extensive tour of Europe. There, for the next two years, he made appearances in London, Paris, Amsterdam, Vienna, Berlin, Milan, and Madrid. Back in the United States he was appointed to the faculty of the Curtis Institute as an assistant to Rudolf Serkin. In 1937 he won the Naumburg Award, entitling him to a concert appearance at Town Hall, New York. One year after that he received the Josef Hofmann award, the highest honor the Curtis Institute could confer on a graduate.

When World War II began, Bolet was called back by President Batista to Cuba to serve in the army. As a commissioned officer he served as assistant military attaché to the Cuban Embassy in Washington, D.C. After Batista's fall, Bolet was permitted to leave the Cuban army, and soon afterwards he enlisted as a private in the United States army. After receiving his American citizenship he was

JORGE BOLET

commissioned a lieutenant. One of his army assignments was with the occupation forces in Japan, where he led a performance of Gilbert and Sullivan's *Mikado,* the first time the comic opera was seen in that country.

Returning to civilian status, Bolet resumed his concert work. He has since filled approximately seventy engagements a season, including appearances with major American orchestras. The New York *Herald Tribune* has described him as "an artist to whom the grand manner is neither affectation nor pose. His performance [is] polished, elastic. . . . Warm of tone, incisive of rhythm, he places a whirlwind technique at the services of music whose cyclonic temperament demands a masterful treatment."

In the spring of 1954 he became one of five American musicians invited for a four-week visit to Western Germany as guests of the Federal Republic of Germany; this was the first time a foreign government had acted as host to American artists. While in Germany, Bolet appeared as soloist with the Berlin Philharmonic. *Der Tag* described him as "a pianist of astounding technique and unfailingly impressive power."

Bolet's favorite hobby is photography. His New York apartment is equipped with a dark room where he does his own developing and printing. He is also a sports-car enthusiast.

BONCI, ALESSANDRO, tenor. See *Living Musicians,* 1940.

Bolet: bō-lĕt'

BONELLI, RICHARD, baritone. For his earlier career, see *Living Musicians,* 1940.

* * *

Bonelli left the Metropolitan Opera after the 1944-1945 season. Previously, in 1943, he had become head of the voice department of the Academy of the West at Santa Barbara, California, and from 1947 to 1949 was chairman of the board at the Academy. He was cited by the city of Santa Barbara for his services to the community. From 1950 to 1955 he taught voice at the Curtis Institute.

BONNET, JOSEPH, organist. For his earlier career, see *Living Musicians,* 1940.

* * *

Bonnet died in Sainte-Luce-sur-Mer, in Quebec, on August 2, 1944.

BORI, LUCREZIA, soprano. See *Living Musicians,* 1940.

BORKH, INGE, dramatic soprano, was born in Mannheim, Germany, into a family which had been prominent in the theatre. Her first ambition being the stage, she studied acting at the Reinhardt Seminar in Vienna. However, she soon demonstrated a strong gift for music and was induced to study seriously at the Vienna Academy, which she entered in her sixteenth year. Later music study took place in Italy.

INGE BORKH

Borkh: bôrk

Her first professional appearance took place in Lucerne, Switzerland, after which she appeared in opera performances in several other Swiss cities; in Geneva she appeared in Menotti's *The Consul.* Her successes in Switzerland led, in 1951, to engagements at the festivals in both Munich and Berlin. After that she appeared extensively in opera throughout Italy, Germany, Great Britain, and Portugal, scoring major successes in the leading soprano roles in *Fidelio, Elektra, Tosca, Salome, Turandot,* and *The Flying Dutchman,* among other operas.

Her American debut took place with the San Francisco Opera on September 25, 1953, when she appeared and was acclaimed in the title role of *Elektra.* Reporting this debut for *Musical America,* Marjory M. Fisher wrote: "Miss Borkh was quite superb. A handsome woman, she had a voice that sounded young, fresh, beautiful, and voluminous. Her singing was mature and remarkably impressive, capable of conveying a great range of emotions. She also used her entire body as an instrument of expression, and while her actions were stylized they never became merely stereotyped operatic gestures. Her facial expressions were wonderful to see." During that initial season with the San Francisco Opera she was also seen in *Die Walküre* and *Turandot,* and she was reengaged by the company for the 1954 and 1955 seasons.

Borkh made her New York debut on November 16, 1956, when she appeared in Carnegie Hall as soloist with the visiting Pittsburgh Symphony in Berg's concert aria, *Der Wein,* and Beethoven's *Ah, Perfido!* Hers was, wrote Louis Biancolli in the New York *World-Telegram* and *Sun,* a voice "of striking size and strength," while Howard Taubman remarked in the *New York Times* that she sang "with style and vocal amplitude." A few days later, on November 20, Borkh again appeared in New York, this time in a concert performance of *Fidelio* with the American Grand Opera Society. Borkh has also appeared at leading American music festivals including those at Ann Arbor, Ravinia, and Cincinnati.

In 1955 she was seen in two important world premières, Respighi's *La Fiamma* at La Scala in Milan and Werner Egk's *The Irish Fairytale* at the Salzburg Festival. In 1957 Borkh was engaged by the Metropolitan Opera for the following season.

BOULANGER, NADIA, conductor. For her earlier career, see *Living Musicians,* 1940.

* * *

Between 1940 and 1946, Boulanger lived in the United States, lecturing and teaching. She returned to France after World War II, joined the faculty of the Paris Conservatory and, in 1948, became director of the American Conservatory in Fontainebleau.

BOULT, SIR ADRIAN, conductor. For his earlier career, *see Living Musicians,* 1940.

* * *

In 1942 Boult resigned as musical director of the British Broadcasting Corporation, while retaining his post as principal conductor of the BBC Symphony. He retired from the latter post in 1950 to become principal conductor of the London Philharmonic. After leaving the London Philharmonic in 1956 he was named its honorary musical adviser.

BOVY, VINA, soprano. For her earlier career, see *Living Musicians,* 1940.

* * *

After World War II she appeared at the Paris Opéra, and in opera performances throughout France.

BRAILOWSKY, ALEXANDER, pianist. See *Living Musicians,* 1940.

BRANZELL, KARIN, contralto. For her earlier career, see *Living Musicians,* 1940.

* * *

Karin Branzell resigned from the Metropolitan Opera after the 1943-1944 season. She appeared subsequently as a guest artist with various European opera companies. She also entered upon a successful new career as concert artist and as teacher of voice at the Juilliard School of Music.

BRICE, CAROL, contralto, was born in Sedalia, North Carolina on April 16, 1918. Her father was a chaplain and her mother a teacher of history at the Palmer Memorial Institute. Carol began singing with the Sedalia Singers when she was only three and even toured with them. After receiving her academic education at the Talladega College in Alabama, she went to New York to attend the Juilliard School of Music on a fellowship. For five years she studied voice with Francis Rogers. During this period she appeared in the chorus of *The Hot Mikado,* produced at the New York World's Fair.

CAROL BRICE

In 1940 she was chosen to sing on the program for President Roosevelt's third Inauguration. Two years later she became the first Negro singer to win the Naumburg Foundation Award. She made her concert debut at Town Hall, New York, on March 13, 1945, and was generally well received. Soon after this, she sang for Fritz Reiner, who engaged her to appear as soloist with the Pittsburgh Symphony. "I predict," Reiner said at the time, "that she will become one of the outstanding singers of our generation." One of these concerts was broadcast, and was heard by Serge Koussevitzky. He was so impressed by Brice's performance in Manuel de Falla's *El Amor Brujo* that he asked her to sing for the Friends of the Boston Symphony. "Today we discover another great singer," he said upon introducing her. On August 3, 1947, Carol Brice sang the Brahms *Alto Rhapsody* under Koussevitzky at the Berkshire Music Festival in Tanglewood. Olin Downes reported in the New York *Times*: "The voice has a nearly instrumental maintenance of line —like a gorgeous colored band against the tapestry of the orchestral and choral sonorities." A year later, Brice returned to the Berkshire Music Festival to appear as Jocasta in Stravinsky's *Oedipus Rex*.

Besides her performances at Tanglewood and with the Boston Symphony in Boston, Carol Brice has been heard in recitals, over the radio, and as soloist with the principal orchestras. In 1954 she was one of five musicians invited to Germany as guests of the Federal Republic of Germany, the first time a foreign government was host to American artists. There she was acclaimed in a performance of Mahler's *Songs of a Wayfarer* with the Berlin Philharmonic Orchestra.

In May 1956 Carol Brice created the role of the Voodoo Priestess in Clarence Cameron White's opera, *Ouanga*, given a concert performance at the Metropolitan Opera House. She once again sang the role when the opera received its first stage production the following fall in Carnegie Hall.

BRICO, ANTONIA, conductor. For her earlier career, see *Living Musicians,* 1940.

* * *

Late in 1946, Brico went on a five-month tour of Europe, conducting orchestral and operatic performances in Sweden, Finland, Austria, Holland, Yugoslavia, and several other countries. After directing an all-Sibelius concert in Helsinki on December 8, 1946, she was awarded the Pro Finlandia Medal. In 1948 she became permanent conductor of the newly-founded Denver Community Orchestra, and subsequently was appointed musical director of the Denver Philharmonic.

BRISELLI, ISO, violinist. See *Living Musicians,* 1940.

BRITT, HORACE, violoncellist. See *Living Musicians,* 1940.

BROSA, ANTONIO, violinist. For his earlier career, see *Living Musicians,* 1940.

* * *

During the period of World War II, Brosa stayed in the United States, where he was heard in recitals and with symphony orchestras. During this period he also became head of the Pro-Arte String Quartet and was Artist-in-Residence at Smith College, in Northampton, Massachusetts. He resumed his concert activity in Europe in 1946.

BROWN, EDDY, violinist. For his earlier career, see *Living Musicians,* 1940.

* * *

In the years immediately after World War II, Brown lived in Italy, where, with the co-operation of the Italian government, he helped found the Accademia Internazionale di Bel Canto, in Bordighera, a school and theatre for students from all parts of the world. After returning to the United States

he was appointed, in 1956, artistic coordinator and teacher of master classes in violin at the College-Conservatory of Music in Cincinnati.

BROWNLEE, JOHN, baritone. For his earlier career, see *Living Musicians,* 1940.

* * *

In 1956 Brownlee was appointed director of the Manhattan School of Music in New York City. This post did not prevent him from fulfilling commitments with the Metropolitan Opera and other major opera companies.

The BUDAPEST STRING QUARTET. For its earlier history, see *Living Musicians,* 1940.

* * *

Jac Gorodetzky has succeeded Alexander Schneider as second violinist.

BURGIN, RICHARD, violinist and conductor. For his earlier career, see *Living Musicians,* 1940.

* * *

In 1951 Burgin was appointed principal conductor of the Portland (Maine) Symphony Orchestra. He held this post five seasons, while continuing to serve as concertmaster and assistant conductor of the Boston Symphony.

BURKE, HILDA, soprano. For her earlier career, see *Living Musicians,* 1940.

* * *

Burke left the Metropolitan Opera after the 1942-1943 season.

BUSCH, ADOLF, violinist. For his earlier career, see *Living Musicians,* 1940.

* * *

After becoming an American citizen, Adolf Busch settled permanently in Guilford, Vermont, where he helped organize the Marlboro School of Music. He died of a heart attack in Guilford on June 9, 1952.

BUSCH, FRITZ, conductor. For his earlier career, see *Living Musicians,* 1940.

* * *

From 1942 to 1945 Busch made many appearances in South America. In 1945 he was engaged as conductor of the Metropolitan Opera, where he made his debut in *Lohengrin* on November 26. He remained several seasons with that company, then conducted in Europe, particularly at Glyndebourne and the Edinburgh Festival. He died of a heart attack in the Hotel Savoy, in London, on September 14, 1951.

BUSTABO, GUILA, violinist. See *Living Musicians*, 1940.

BUXTON, EUGENIA, pianist. See *Living Musicians*, 1940.

CALLAS, MARIA MENEGHINI, soprano, was born Maria Anna Sofia Cecilia Kalogeropoulos in New York City on December 3, 1924, to Greek parents. "I was the ugly duckling of the family," she confided to an interviewer, "fat, clumsy, and unpopular." Though hers was not a musical household, she began showing an interest in opera when she was only three. In her eighth year she started taking vocal lessons, and one year later sang at assemblies at P.S. 164. When she was fourteen she was taken by her mother to Greece, where she attended the Royal Conservatory of Athens for a seven-year period on a scholarship, as a pupil of Elvira de Hidalgo. Meanwhile, when she was fifteen, she made her opera debut at the Athens Royal Opera as Santuzza in *Cavalleria Rusticana*. Her teacher said of her: "She never flirted and nobody courted her. She had a real inferiority complex about everything—except her voice. . . . She would want to sing the most difficult coloratura scales and trills. Her will power was terrific. She had a phenomenal memory and could learn the most difficult opera in eight days."

She remained in Greece during the period of World War II; there, in 1942, she sang Tosca with the National Opera Company on twenty-four hours' notice and received rave notices. Returning to the United States in 1945, she was offered a contract to appear in *Madama Butterfly* and *Fidelio* at the Metropolitan Opera, but turned it down, feeling not yet ready for such a major test. She did, however, consent to appear at the Verona Arena, in August 1947, in *La Gioconda*. This was her debut in Italy. The conductor of that performance, Tullio Serafin, was so impressed by the beauty and power of her singing that he personally coached her for several months. She then appeared at La Scala and other major Italian opera houses in such exacting and varied roles as Turandot, Isolde, Norma, Aida, and Lucia. She became so popular that many Italians re-

MARIA MENEGHINI CALLAS

ferred to her as "the queen of the prima donnas." In Trieste she was regarded as the greatest Norma of all time, and in Genoa opera lovers carried her through the streets after one of her performances.

During this period, in 1949, she married Giovanni Battista Meneghini, a prosperous builder who gave up his own business to manage her career. In that same year she made her first appearance at the Teatro Colón in Buenos Aires. One year later she opened the season of the Mexico City Opera, and in 1951 that of La Scala. In 1952 she made her debut in England at Covent Garden and was a sensation; one critic hailed her as "the greatest singer, male or female, since Nordica."

Her fame spread to the United States largely through her remarkable recordings in virtually all her famous roles. Once again she was offered a contract for the Metropolitan Opera, and once again she turned it down—this time because her husband was unable to get a visa for the United States. When she did make her American debut, on November 1, 1954, as Norma, it was with the then newly organized Lyric Theatre in Chicago. "She is the sort of artist who is likely to become legendary," wrote Irving Sabolsky in the Chicago *Daily News*. And Claudia Cassidy said in the *Tribune*: "For my money, she was not only up to specifications but she surpassed them." She appeared in six performances that season, acclaimed in all. In 1955 she returned to Chicago to open the second season of the Lyric Theatre as Elvira in *I Puritani*.

On June 12, 1956, Callas was a triumph at the Vienna State Opera in *Lucia di Lammermoor*, Herbert von Karajan conducting. Finally she made her debut at the Metropolitan Opera, on the opening night of the season, October 29, 1956, in the title role of *Norma*. "She brought to the role," wrote Howard Taubman in the New York *Times*, "the concentration of one who had studied it thoroughly. As for her singing, Miss Callas mantained a standard that one . . . rather expected. . . . When she did not force, her voice had delicacy and point. She phrased with sensitivity; she colored her tones to suit the drama; she was telling in florid passages."

Callas' permanent home is in Milan, where she and her husband occupy a $100,000 town house. "In Milan," according to *Time* magazine (October 29, 1956), "she began to live the life of the prima donna and to look the part. . . . Her life took on a sybaritic pattern. In the morning she usually sang at the piano on a glassed-in terrace outside her bedroom, polishing current roles. Afternoons, she visited her dressmaker or her beautician, taking treatments worthy of a courtesan. . . . When shopping, she added to a wardrobe that already included twenty-five fur coats, forty suits, 150 pairs of shoes, 200 dresses, at least 300 hats. . . . At night, Callas' favorite rite is to soak leisurely in the bath, steep herself in buckets of cologne, and then (after a careful weigh-in on the bathroom scale) to go to bed 'feeling absolutely luscious.' Perfumed, glowing and gowned in slinky silk, she lies awake late into the night—studying scores while husband Meneghini sleeps."

In 1957 Callas was appointed Knight Commander of the Italian Republic by President Giovanni Gronchi.

CALLIMAHOS, LAMBROS, flutist. See *Living Musicians*, 1940.

CALVÉ, EMMA, soprano. For her earlier career, see *Living Musicians*, 1940.

* * *

Calvé died in Milliau, France, on January 6, 1942.

CAMERON, BASIL, conductor. See *Living Musicians*, 1940.

CAMPOLI, ALFREDO, violinist, was born in Rome on October 20, 1906. His father was professor of the violin at the Santa Cecilia Academy, while his mother had been a concert singer before her marriage. When

Campoli: käm'pō-lē

Alfredo was five years old, he began to study the violin with his father. Four years later, when the family settled in London, the boy gave little concerts for the English troops at various branches of the YMCA.

In his thirteenth year, Campoli took part in several English competitions among violinists, carrying off seven first prizes, together with two gold medals and a silver cup. One of these prizes came from Princess Mary in 1919, after his performance of the Mendelssohn Concerto at the London Music Festival. His professional debut took place at Wigmore Hall when he was fifteen. He was so well received both by the public and critics that he was invited to appear throughout England, sometimes as soloist with major orchestras. He subsequently founded and directed an orchestra of his own which was disbanded at the outbreak of World War II.

During the war, Campoli gave innumerable concerts for British troops in army camps, hospitals, and factories. After the war he resumed his professional career. Besides making many tours of Europe, he appeared in Australia, New Zealand, India, Hong Kong, and Singapore. He also began appearing regularly over the BBC radio, and in time achieved something of a record by broadcasting over a thousand times. His many recordings for His Master's Voice (British Victor) and Columbia first made his name known to American music lovers.

Campoli made his American debut by appearing as soloist with the New York Phil-

ALFREDO CAMPOLI

harmonic-Symphony on December 5, 1949. From then on, he toured the United States several times and made appearances in many other countries, justifying the opinion of M. Montagu Nathan, who wrote in *Musical Opinion* of London that Campoli belongs with "the greatest violinists of our time."

Campoli resides with his wife, Joy, in London, where he pursues the hobbies of photography, bridge, tennis, and billiards.

CANTELLI, GUIDO, conductor, was born in Novara, Italy, on April 27, 1920. His first experience in conducting was leading his father's military band when he was only five years old. "In reality," he recalls, "the band conducted me." As a child he also sang in a church choir and performed children's parts in opera performances. All this while he studied organ with Felice Fasola and piano with his father. He was only eleven when he began to play keyboard instruments for public performances of opera, and fourteen when he gave his first piano recital.

A piano diploma for the Verdi Conservatory brought him to Milan when he was fourteen. A year later he studied composition privately with Paolo Delachi. When he reached his eighteenth year he began attending the Milan Conservatory where he studied composition with Arrigo Pebrolo and Giorgio Ghedini. In his last year at the Conservatory he directed three orchestral concerts there, one of which included his own *Theme and Variations*.

His professional debut as conductor came in 1941 when he conducted *La Traviata* at the Teatro Carlo Coccia in Novara (a theatre which Toscanini had helped open in 1889). Cantelli led many of the celebrated works of the Italian opera repertory, besides conducting several symphony concerts. In 1943 he had to abandon music to enter the Italian army. Because he refused to support the Nazi-Fascist Axis he was shipped off to labor and concentration camps in Germany and Italy. With the help of a priest he managed to escape to Novara from a camp in Bolzano. He was almost a skeleton at the time, weighing only eighty pounds. Involved in fighting between Fascists and Partisans, Cantelli was captured by the Fascists and sentenced to be shot. The liberation of Italy saved his life.

In July 1945, two months after his marriage to a childhood sweetheart, Iris Bilucaglia, Cantelli conducted a symphony concert with the orchestra of La Scala in Milan. He was immediately invited to conduct both orchestral concerts and opera performances in several Italian cities. In 1946 he made successful

GUIDO CANTELLI

appearances at the ninth International Festival in Venice, and with the Santa Cecilia Orchestra in Rome. Between 1946 and 1948 he directed performances not only throughout Italy, but also in Belgium and Austria.

The turning point in his career came in Milan on May 18, 1948, while he was rehearsing his orchestra at La Scala. Toscanini was in the auditorium and was so impressed by Cantelli that he not only attended Cantelli's concerts but was also present at all rehearsals. Toscanini invited Cantelli to come to America as a guest conductor of the NBC Symphony Orchestra. Cantelli arrived in the winter of 1948 for four performances with the NBC Symphony, making an impressive debut on January 1, 1949. "He is an unusually gifted musician," wrote Francis D. Perkins in the New York *Herald Tribune*. "In technique of conducting he seemed remarkably well versed: his gestures were clear and indicative and . . . told of a definite interpretative idea, an assurance based on a thorough knowledge of his scores."

Cantelli returned the following season to conduct four more concerts with the NBC Symphony, and a season later eight concerts. After that, he appeared as guest conductor of most of the major American orchestras. He led a part of each season of the New York Philharmonic-Symphony for six years, beginning with 1951. He also directed both operas and orchestral music in Europe, scoring major successes at La Scala, at the Salzburg and Lucerne festivals, and with the Vienna Phil-

Cantelli: kän-tĕl'lē

harmonic. At the Venice Festival, in September 1949, he conducted the first Italian performance of Menotti's *The Telephone*.

"Cantelli's capacity to assimilate and transmit music with the most exceptional clarity and intensity is paralleled at his best by the depth of his thinking and his powerful sense of form," wrote Olin Downes in the New York *Times*. "These are the things which set him apart from any colleague of equal years and experience."

Cantelli was en route from Italy to New York to conduct the New York Philharmonic-Symphony for four weeks when—on November 24, 1956—he was killed in an Italian airliner crash, just as the plane was taking off from Orly airfield outside Paris.

CARRERAS, MARIA, pianist. See *Living Musicians*, 1940.

CARRON, ARTHUR, tenor. For his earlier career, see *Living Musicians*, 1940.

* * *

Carron left the Metropolitan Opera in 1946 and became a member of the Covent Garden company in London, where he had made his debut in 1939.

CARVALHO, ELEAZAR DE, conductor, was born in Iguatu, State of Ceara, Brazil, on June 28, 1912. His childhood was spent on his parents' farm. When he was thirteen he was sent for schooling to the town of For-

taleza, where he began preparing himself for a career as seaman. He then joined the National Navy Corps in Rio de Janeiro, where he served until 1936. While devoting himself to his naval studies, he also attended music school, played the double bass in school orchestras, and undertook a six-year course in composition with Paulo Silva. In the Navy he played in naval and marine bands.

After being discharged from service, he earned his living first by playing in orchestras in casinos, cabarets, and circuses; then by playing in the orchestra of the Teatro Municipal, an opera house in Rio de Janeiro; finally by serving as assistant to Eugen Szenkar with the Orquestra Sinfonica Brasileira. At the same time he attended the University of Brazil, from which he was graduated with honors in 1940.

In 1941 he received an unscheduled opportunity to conduct the Orquestra Sinfonica. From that moment on he knew he wanted above everything else to be a conductor. He soon began conducting concerts of the Orquestra Sinfonica as well as opera performances at the Teatro Municipal, where he opened the seasons in 1942, 1943, and 1944.

In the summer of 1946 Carvalho came to the United States to study conducting with Serge Koussevitzky at the Berkshire Music Center at Tanglewood. Koussevitzky thought so highly of him that a year later he made him his assistant in the conducting class and appointed him conductor of the school orchestra. His North American debut as conductor followed on December 19, 1947, when he appeared in Boston as guest of the Boston Symphony Orchestra. Alexander Williams wrote in the Boston *Herald:* "As a conductor this young Brazilian is not one of your acrobats and shadow-boxers. He tends to his job with a minimum of gestures with his hands. As is the modern fashion, in actual performance he uses no score. The superb recreation he achieved with Berlioz' romantic, lovable, and sometimes long-winded symphony, entitled him to respect as a new figure in the field."

Carvalho has frequently appeared as guest conductor of the Boston Symphony, both in Boston and during the summers at the Berkshire Music Festival at Tanglewood, and with other major American orchestras. Besides filling such commitments, he is the principal conductor of the Orquestra Sinfonica Brasileira.

CASADESUS, ROBERT, pianist. See *Living Musicians*, 1940.

ELEAZAR DE CARVALHO

Carvalho: kĕr-vȧ'lyōō

CASALS, PABLO, cellist. For his earlier career, see *Living Musicians,* 1940.

* * *

Casals emerged from his retirement in June 1950 to appear both as conductor and solo cellist in a Bach festival held in Prades, France, a town which had been his home since 1938. The Prades Festival, with Casals as its dominating personality, has continued annually since then. Early in 1955 Casals broke his self-imposed exile from Spain by attending in the town of Vendrell the funeral of his housekeeper and friend, Francisca Capdevila; the Spanish authorities placed no obstacles in the way of his return. On January 28, 1956, Casals made his first concert appearance outside Prades since 1945, with a performance in Veracruz, Mexico. A three-month visit to Puerto Rico followed. During ceremonies celebrating the dedication of a bronze plaque at the house where his mother was born in San Juan, Casals performed a lullaby his mother had taught him, and accompanied Marta Montanez, a twenty-year-old cello pupil whom he married the following year. On October 10, 1956, at a concert in Paris celebrating his eightieth birthday, Casals conducted two of his own works, and as an encore played a brief cello solo.

Late in 1956 Casals announced he would henceforth make his permanent home in Puerto Rico, while spending several months in Europe each year fulfilling his commitments there. In honor of his eightieth birthday, the government of Puerto Rico sponsored a music festival devoted to works by Bach, Mozart, and Schubert with Casals as its central figure, both as conductor and as cellist. This festival took place between April 22 and May 8, 1957, but without Casals as a participant; while rehearsing for this festival, Casals suffered a heart attack.

CASSADÓ, GASPAR, cellist. For his earlier career, see *Living Musicians,* 1940.

* * *

Since the end of World War II, Cassadó has made his home in Florence, Italy, and has served as professor at the Accademia Musicale Chigiana in Siena.

CASSEL, WALTER, baritone, was born in Council Bluffs, Iowa, on May 15, 1910. In his boyhood, he received as a birthday gift from his uncle a trumpet on which he started to take lessons. He soon began playing in the high-school orchestra, and won several trumpet-playing contests. In school he also joined the glee club. The discovery that he had a

Cassel: kăs' 'l

WALTER CASSEL

stronger talent for singing than trumpet-playing—and the winning of a first prize in a singing contest conducted throughout the state of Iowa—made him decide to study voice seriously. While doing so, he earned his living at various jobs, including sign-painting and flour-milling, as well as playing the trumpet in dance bands and singing over a local radio station.

In 1933 Lawrence Tibbett, appearing in Iowa for concerts, heard Cassel, and advised him to go to New York for additional study. About a year later, Cassel went to New York, and two days after his arrival auditioned with the National Broadcasting Company. He was immediately engaged. During the next few years he made guest appearances on several important radio programs and was subsequently starred on his own radio show, "Calling America," over the CBS network.

During World War II he temporarily deserted radio to tour army camps. For his war services he was honored with an award from the United States Treasury.

After the war, Cassel combined radio work with appearances in performances of operettas and musical comedies in different parts of the country. As preparation for opera, he continued his musical training with Frank La Forge. He made his opera debut at the Metropolitan Opera on December 12, 1942, as De Brétigny in *Manon.* Since then he has appeared in important baritone roles at the Metropolitan Opera and has been acclaimed for his interpretations of Valentine in *Faust,* Silvio in *Pagliacci,* and the elder Germont in

La Traviata. He has also been heard with other important American opera companies, including the New York City Opera, where he scored a major success as Baron Scarpia in *Tosca* on April 1, 1948. "Full of color and variety as his singing was," wrote a critic of the New York *Times*, "it was matched by his acting. He appeared every inch the nobleman." "It was a stunning Scarpia," reported John Briggs in the New York *Post*. "I do not remember when I have seen it done better." Cassel also became a member of the NBC Opera Company upon its first tour of America during 1956-1957. Besides his opera appearances, Cassel has often been heard on the concert stage. After one of his New York recitals, the New York *Post* critic said: "The singer projects a song with vigor and intelligence. . . . A fine voice and its natural brilliance produces a variety of excitement."

Cassel married Gail Manners, his second wife, in 1953. A man of powerful physique (he is more than six feet tall and weighs over two hundred pounds), Cassel is an excellent athlete, his specialties being tennis, handball, shot-putting, and throwing the discus and javelin. His indoor pastimes include carpentry, photography, and tinkering with electrical appliances.

CASTAGNA, BRUNA, contralto. For her earlier career, see *Living Musicians*, 1940.

* * *

Castagna left the Metropolitan Opera after the season of 1944-1945, and since that time she has appeared in opera performances in Europe and South America.

CASTON, SAUL, conductor, was born in New York City on August 22, 1901. He is a descendant of a line of musicians which reaches back into the early eighteenth century. When he was eight, Saul began studying the trumpet with Max Schlessberg, then the trumpeter of the New York Philharmonic-Symphony Orchestra. Six years later Caston joined the Russian Symphony and the Young Men's Symphony, both in New York City. After graduation from a New York City high school, Caston was engaged by Leopold Stokowski as second trumpet of the Philadelphia Orchestra. Four years later he was elevated to the position of first trumpet, and in 1936 he became Stokowski's associate conductor. When Stokowski organized the All-American Youth Orchestra, Caston was appointed his assistant; at the same time, Caston served as guest conductor of the Philadelphia Orchestra

SAUL CASTON

during its transcontinental tour in 1936. In 1941 Caston became conductor of the Reading (Pennsylvania) Symphony. While holding this post, he made several guest appearances with major American orchestras, and served as music director and conductor of the Robin Hood Dell summer concerts in Philadelphia.

When Artur Rodzinski was engaged as conductor of the Curtis Institute Symphony Orchestra, Caston became his assistant. At the Curtis Institute, Caston established a class in brass instruments and trained the student body in the first Philadelphia performance of Eugen d'Albert's opera *Tiefland*. During this period Caston conducted several concerts of the Philadelphia Orchestra, and its children's and young people's concerts.

In 1945 Caston was appointed music director of the Denver Symphony Orchestra, which he has since that time led with distinction. Besides its regular performances in Denver, the orchestra has been heard for several seasons at the Red Rocks Theatre in Colorado; was chosen several times to appear on the national-hookup radio program "Orchestras of the Nation"; and has been heard throughout the world on the "Voice of America."

"Under the leadership of Saul Caston," wrote Virgil Thomson in the New York *Herald Tribune*, "the Denver Symphony Orchestra has become one of the major orchestras of America." Howard Taubman has written in the New York *Times*: "What is worthy of note is the responsive and enthusiastic quality of the playing of the Denver

Symphony Orchestra, which Saul Caston has been building with care, intelligence, and imagination." The world-famous composer Igor Stravinsky has said: "The precision, sensitivity and fine discipline of the Denver Symphony Orchestra reveals Saul Caston's exceptional ability to create a fine symphonic group. Caston is the perfect conductor to create a musical tradition for this region."

Besides his performances in and near Denver—and his extensive tours with the orchestra throughout the entire Rocky Mountain region—Saul Caston has appeared as a guest of other leading American orchestras.

He has established in Denver a training orchestra for young instrumentalists and is advisory head of the School of Orchestra at the Lamont School of Music, connected with the University of Denver.

CATHELAT, GEORGES, tenor. See *Living Musicians,* 1940.

CEHANOVSKY, GEORGE, baritone. See *Living Musicians,* 1940.

CHAMLEE, MARIO, tenor. See *Living Musicians,* 1940.

CHAPMAN, FRANK, baritone. See *Living Musicians,* 1940.

CHASINS, ABRAM, pianist. For his earlier career, see *Living Musicians,* 1940.

* * *

In 1943 Chasins became music consultant for the New York radio station WQXR and in 1947 its musical director.

CHAVEZ, CARLOS, conductor. For his earlier career, see *Living Musicians,* 1940.

* * *

Since 1936 Chavez has often visited the United States as guest conductor of the foremost American orchestras. In 1947 he was appointed director of the National Institute of Fine Arts in Mexico.

CHEMET, RÉNÉ, violinist. See *Living Musicians,* 1940.

CHERKASSKY, SHURA, pianist. See *Living Musicians,* 1940.

CHRISTOFF, BORIS, bass, was born in Sofia, Bulgaria, in 1919, the son of a university professor. While attending academic schools in preparation for a career in law, he followed singing as a hobby. The decision to make music a career was made at a festival in Sofia when he sang a solo part with an amateur chorus. King Boris considered his singing the high point of the festival and arranged a scholarship for him to study music seriously. After this preliminary training, Christoff went to Italy in 1942 to work under Riccardo Stracciari. Three years later he went to Salzburg to study the German repertory. When the war ended, he found himself in a displaced-persons camp in the Austrian Tyrol.

He returned to Italy early in 1946 and made his debut in a concert in Rome at the Santa Cecilia Academy. Several other recitals followed, as well as some radio appearances. La Scala in Milan then engaged him, and in less than two years he was singing leading basso roles.

Since then, Christoff has been heard not only at La Scala, but also at the San Carlo in Naples, and the Rome Opera. He did not appear in what is probably his most famous role, Boris Godunov, until 1949. This event took place not in Italy but at Covent Garden, where Christoff was then making his debut. He was hailed for the dramatic vigor of his performance. His interpretation of Boris was soon afterwards acclaimed both at the Teatro Colón in Buenos Aires and at the Paris Opéra.

It was also as Boris Godunov that he made his American debut—at the San Francisco Opera on September 30, 1956. (For six years,

BORIS CHRISTOFF

efforts had been made to bring Christoff to America, but the State Department had consistently denied him a visa.) Reporting the performance for the New York *Times,* Howard Taubman said: "Mr. Christoff is an outstanding singing actor and his Boris is, beyond the shadow of a doubt, the best of our generation. . . . Mr. Christoff is a volcano of emotion. When he is on the stage, opera takes on an unexpected dimension. It becomes the stuff of life, but on a larger scale, as great tragedy must be."

CICCOLINI, ALDO, pianist, was born in Naples on August 15, 1925. His family for several generations had been professional musicians and artists. Aldo started to study the piano when he was six, was enrolled in the Naples Conservatory at eight, and at thirteen gave his first public recital at the San Carlo Theatre in Naples. His promising career was interrupted by World War II. "There was a time when the south of Italy was really the front line," he told an interviewer. "Twice houses in which we lived were destroyed by bombs. But still there were concerts. We could hold them at nine o'clock in the morning because that was the safest hour from bombs, but then things got worse. From May to October 1943 in Naples it was forbidden for people to gather for any purpose, so we had no more music."

In 1943 he was taken hostage by the Nazis and condemned to die. A young Austrian soldier helped Ciccolini escape ("for what reason I do not know to this day"), enabling him to join the British Eighth Army as interpreter. When Naples was liberated, he became the first Italian artist to give a concert for American troops and to play over the American radio.

After the war Ciccolini was appointed professor of the piano at the Musical Academy in Naples. He won first prize in several national competitions for pianists, then went on to Paris in 1949 to compete with ninety-six other pianists in the celebrated Marguerite Long-Jacques Thibaud contest. He won the Grand Prix. The following month, on July 8, 1949, he gave his first recital in Paris, under the auspices of the Italian Ambassador to France. The critic of *Le Figaro* wrote: "The name of this young virtuoso will go around the world." This recital launched his successful career as virtuoso throughout the world of music. In 1950 he toured France, Italy, Portugal, Spain, North Africa, and South America. In the same year, on November 2, he made his North American debut, appearing as soloist with the New York Philharmonic-Symphony in the Tchaikovsky B-flat Concerto. Virgil Thomson in the New York *Herald Tribune* described his playing as "brilliant" and called him "a virtuoso of the first rank." When Ciccolini played the same Concerto in Boston with the Boston Symphony, Cyrus Durgin wrote in the *Globe:* "I have never heard anyone play the Tchaikovsky Concerto as he did, with no pounding, and with a style so clear, exact and bold that it put the work in a new light." His appearances in this country, as well as in Europe, have since then been extensive.

CIGNA, GINA, soprano. For her earlier career, see *Living Musicians,* 1940.

* * *

After World War II, Cigna withdrew from an active career on the opera stage to open a school for young singers in Milan.

CLIFTON, CHALMERS DANCY, conductor. For his earlier career, see *Living Musicians,* 1940.

* * *

Between 1942 and 1945 Clifton was director of the Music Workshop for veterans at Halloran Hospital, in Staten Island, New York.

CLUYTENS, ANDRÉ, conductor, was born in Antwerp, Belgium, on March 26, 1905. His father was the conductor of the Royal Theatre in Antwerp. André received an intensive musical education at the Royal Con-

Courtesy of Musical Courier

ALDO CICCOLINI

Ciccolini: chē-kō-lē'nē

Cluytens: klü-täN'

Angel Records

ANDRÉ CLUYTENS

servatory in Amsterdam, where he was trained as pianist. Upon his graduation, in his nineteenth year, he received not only the first prize in piano playing but also the highest honors in harmony, counterpoint, and fugue.

His first post was that of chorusmaster at the Royal Theatre, where his father conducted. There, in 1927, André Cluytens was elevated to the conducting staff, where he stayed five years. In 1932 he settled permanently in France and became musical director of the Grand Théâtre du Capitole in Toulouse. Three years after that he received an appointment as first conductor of the Lyons Opéra.

He first attracted attention as conductor at the Opéra-Comique, where he now serves as musical director. He also occupies two other major musical posts in Paris. In 1947 he became the principal conductor of the Paris Opéra, and in 1949 he succeeded Charles Munch as conductor of the Paris Conservatory Orchestra.

He has achieved recognition as one of the outstanding French conductors of our time outside of France through guest appearances with major orchestras and opera companies throughout Europe. He has made frequent appearances in Vienna, Berlin, and Bayreuth, where he is a particular favorite. He was directing a performance of the Vienna Philharmonic in May 1955 when, during the intermission, the chairman of the orchestra appeared on the stage to announce that the Austrian State Treaty had just been signed. Then and there, and in response to the enthusiasm in the audience, he led the orchestra in the Austrian National Anthem.

When the Paris Opéra celebrated the 150th anniversary of Berlioz' birth in 1953, Cluytens led a monumental Berlioz concert that attracted national attention. A year later, he once again scored when he led Gounod's *Mireille*, revived successfully at the Aix-en-Provence festival.

Cluytens was one of two conductors (the other being Carl Schuricht) chosen to lead the Vienna Philharmonic on its first tour of the United States. He conducted ten concerts; the first—and his American debut—took place in Washington, D.C. on November 4, 1956. One month later he appeared with the orchestra at Carnegie Hall. "Let there be no mistake about M. Cluytens' technical proficiency," wrote Howard Taubman in the New York *Times*. "He knows his job as a conductor. Granted that the Vienna Philharmonic is as responsive an ensemble as a conductor could encounter; the fact remains that M. Cluytens had everything in hand at all times. His beat and control were sure, and he knew precisely what he wanted and how to get it from his players."

The following year, Cluytens was engaged to appear as a guest conductor of the New York Philharmonic-Symphony Orchestra.

COATES, ALBERT, conductor. For his earlier career, see *Living Musicians,* 1940.

* * *

Coates died in Capetown, South Africa, on December 11, 1953.

COATES, JOHN, tenor. For his earlier career, see *Living Musicians,* 1940.

* * *

Coates died in Northwood, Middlesex, England, on August 16, 1941.

COHEN, HARRIET, pianist. For her earlier career, see *Living Musicians,* 1940.

* * *

Cohen remained in England through the years of World War II, playing for the British troops. Bombing attacks on London destroyed her home and injured her three times, one of these injuries causing the loss of vision in one eye. In February 1947 she was decorated by President Beneš of Czechoslovakia and the Prince Regent of Belgium with their highest honors: the Order of the White Lion (First Class) from Czechoslovakia; and the Order of the Commander of the Crown of Belgium. She also received the rank of Commander of the British Empire.

On February 6, 1948, she returned to the United States after an absence of eight years, making her first reappearance over the CBS network with the CBS Orchestra under Alfredo Antonini in a performance of Bach's D minor Concerto.

CONLEY, EUGENE, tenor, was born in Lynn, Massachusetts, on March 12, 1908. The son of a surveyor, he spent a normal boyhood, receiving his education in the public schools. After graduating from high school, he went to work in the plant of the local electric company. At the same time he received his first fee of $5.00 for singing as soloist in church, and was soon appearing over local radio stations and as a member of a male choir.

After a period of vocal study in Lynn and Boston, Conley made his first professional appearance in a performance of *Robin Hood* by the Boston Light Opera Company. Other performances in oratorios and over the radio followed. His success over WWJ in Detroit attracted the notice of NBC executives, who engaged him to appear in his own program, "NBC Presents Eugene Conley," over its network. He was also engaged to appear as soloist with the NBC Symphony under Toscanini.

After additional study with Ettore Verna in New York, Conley made his opera debut

EUGENE CONLEY

in September 1940, when he appeared as the Duke in *Rigoletto* at the Brooklyn Academy of Music. Though he had to sing this part without rehearsal, he did so well that he was asked to appear for the rest of that season in leading tenor parts. After that, he performed with several other American opera companies, including the San Carlo, the New Opera conducted by Fritz Busch, and the Cincinnati Summer Opera, as well as the Mexican National Opera Company.

During World War II, Conley served in the Army Air Force. He appeared in its production, *Winged Victory,* by Moss Hart. He was also given special permission to appear five times with the San Carlo Opera. After the war, he continued his career in opera with successful appearances with the New York City Opera and the New Orleans Opera.

During the 1947-1948 season he toured Europe as guest performer with several leading opera companies. He was the first American since 1939 to appear in a leading role at the Stockholm Royal Opera; and at the Opéra-Comique he was acclaimed for his interpretation of Rodolfo in *La Bohème.* His outstanding success in Europe came in January 1950 when he made his La Scala debut in *I Puritani,* revived expressly for him, and the first time that an American appeared in the leading male role in Italy. So popular did he become that he had to sing the role ten times that season. He returned to La Scala the following year to inaugurate its regular season with *I Vespri Siciliani;* once again Conley made history by being the first American-born, American-trained singer to help inaugurate a La Scala season.

Meanwhile, on January 25, 1950, he made his debut at the Metropolitan Opera in *Faust.* "It takes an American to come here and show us again how a tenor should sing," reported *Time* magazine. After that Conley appeared at the Metropolitan Opera in the leading tenor parts of the Italian and French repertory, as well as in the American première of Stravinsky's *The Rake's Progress.* He has also been heard with the San Francisco Opera, and the New Orleans Opera, as well as in the major European opera houses. His appearances in concerts, with symphony orchestra, and over radio and television have also been frequent. In 1953 he sang in the *Missa Solemnis* under Toscanini over the NBC network (recorded by Victor). He appeared in the motion picture *Of Men and Music,* and sang for the sound track of *Faust,* filmed in Rome in 1950.

On March 9, 1948, Conley married Winifred Heidt, a contralto with whom he has since appeared in joint recitals and opera performances. They have a New York apartment and a fifty-acre farm in Flemington, New Jersey. Conley has retained his boyhood interest in, and aptitude for, sports, though he now confines himself mostly to swimming, sailing, and regular workouts in a gymnasium. Less strenuous pursuits include cooking and photography.

CONNER, NADINE, soprano, was born in Compton, near Los Angeles, California, on February 20, 1914. Her ambition originally was to become a pianist, and for several years she took lessons with local teachers. In high school she turned to dramatics. While there, she began studying voice, first with Horatio Cogswell, then with Amado Fernandez, making such progress that she won a scholarship in music for the University of Southern California. As a university student, she made several appearances over radio station KHJ which had such audience appeal that she was soon given a regular program of her own. She devoted seven years to radio work, ultimately appearing on important sponsored programs, including the "Coca-Cola Hour," which gave her star billing.

In 1939 she married Laurance Heacock, a Compton surgeon who had operated on her for appendicitis. He influenced her to turn to opera. When Albert Coates founded the Los Angeles Opera Company in 1939, she joined that organization and stayed with it two years. One of her appearances was seen by Bruno Walter, who suggested she audition for the Metropolitan Opera. That audition proved successful. She made her Metropolitan Opera debut on December 22, 1941, as Pamina in *The Magic Flute,* Bruno Walter conducting. "She sang her role with remarkable poise," reported Francis D. Perkins in the New York *Herald Tribune,* "and she interpreted the character with an appropriate sense of youth and wistfulness."

Since she has been a principal soprano of the Metropolitan Opera she has appeared in a variety of roles, including Rosina in *The Barber of Seville,* Zerlina in *Don Giovanni,* Mimi in *La Bohème,* Gilda in *Rigoletto,* Gretel in *Hänsel und Gretel,* Micaela in *Carmen,* Marguerite in *Faust,* Sophie in *Der Rosenkavalier,* and Mélisande in *Pelléas et Mélisande.* After her appearance as Marguerite on February 25, 1954, the New York *Herald Tribune* described her performance as follows: "Her pure clear-toned voice is just exactly right for this role. She gauged her tonal and expressive degrees to perfection, and her impersonation, both vocally and in her acting, seemed one of the most satisfactory Marguerites the Met has had."

NADINE CONNER

She appeared as Micaela in the performance of *Carmen* which was televised from the stage of the Metropolitan Opera on a closed circuit to motion picture theatres throughout the United States on December 11, 1952; and she appeared as Mimi when the Metropolitan Opera later presented *La Bohème* in English in a telecast performance on the "Omnibus" program.

Her performances on top radio and television programs, in recitals, and as soloist with major orchestras have been numerous. She was also seen in the motion picture *Of Men and Music.* In 1953 she made her first tour of Europe, acclaimed at the Holland Music Festival for her performance in *The Marriage of Figaro.*

Nadine Conner maintains a permanent home in the city of her birth, but also a duplex penthouse apartment in New York City. She has two children. Her favorite recreation is to make pack trips with her husband in the Sierras and to go fishing in mountain streams. Other interests include painting, cooking, and caring for her pet fish. She designs most of the costumes for her opera appearances, and at one time was voted by the Fashion Institute one of the world's best-dressed women.

The COOLIDGE STRING QUARTET. For its earlier history, see *Living Musicians*, 1940.

* * *

The Quartet discontinued concert appearances after World War II. Nicolai Berezowsky, second violinist, died in New York City on August 26, 1953.

COPELAND, GEORGE, pianist. See *Living Musicians,* 1940.

COPPOLA, PIERO, conductor. See *Living Musicians,* 1940.

CORDON, NORMAN, bass-baritone. For his earlier career, see *Living Musicians,* 1940.

* * *

Cordon left the Metropolitan Opera after the 1945-1946 season and devoted himself to concert appearances.

CORIGLIANO, JOHN, violinist. For his earlier career, see *Living Musicians,* 1940.

* * *

Corigliano succeeded Mishel Piastro as concertmaster of the New York Philharmonic-Symphony in 1943.

CORTOT, ALFRED, pianist. See *Living Musicians,* 1940.

COURBOIN, CHARLES MARIE, organist. See *Living Musicians,* 1940.

CROOKS, RICHARD, tenor. For his earlier career, see *Living Musicians,* 1940.

* * *

Crooks left the Metropolitan Opera after the 1942-1943 season, and went into retirement in 1946.

CULP, JULIA, mezzo-soprano. For her earlier career, see *Living Musicians,* 1940.

* * *

Culp returned to her native land, Holland, in 1938 where she henceforth lived in semi-retirement. On the occasion of her seventieth birthday, in October 1950, she was the recipient of many public honors.

CURZON, CLIFFORD, pianist, was born in London on May 18, 1907. His father, an antique dealer, was a music lover who encouraged his son's musical activities. Clifford began taking violin lessons when he was five, but one year later turned to the piano. When he was twelve he was enrolled in the Royal Academy of Music in London, the youngest pupil ever admitted there. Three years later, at the Academy, he began study with his first important piano teacher, Charles Reddie, with whom he made such progress that he won not only two scholarships but every prize open to pianists, including the coveted McFarren Gold Medal. Later piano study took place with Tobias Matthay and Katharine Goodson.

He made his first public appearance in 1923 when he was one of three pianists performing the Bach Concerto for Three Pianos at a Queen's Hall Promenade Concert directed by Sir Henry J. Wood. In 1925 he began concertizing in England, and in the same year he joined the faculty of the Royal College of Music, where he remained until 1937 when he was made Fellow of the Academy.

A concert by Artur Schnabel convinced him that he needed more study. For two years he worked under Schnabel in Berlin. After that he went to Paris where he studied with Wanda Landowska and Nadia Boulanger. In Paris, on July 16, 1931, he married an American pianist, Lucille Wallace, who had been his fellow-student with Schnabel. Lucille Wallace has since become a harpsichordist, and occasionally appears in joint concerts with her husband.

Meanwhile, in 1930, Curzon resumed his concert career with recitals and appearances with leading orchestras throughout Europe. In 1936 he toured Europe with Lionel Tertis

CLIFFORD CURZON

in viola sonata recitals, and two years later he toured as solo pianist under the auspices of the British Council.

His American debut took place at Town Hall, New York, on February 26, 1939. A few weeks later, on March 10, he appeared as soloist with the New York Philharmonic-Symphony under Alexander Smallens in a program made up of three concertos. He made such a favorable impression that Arthur Judson signed him to tour the country the following season. The outbreak of World War II prevented his return. Curzon remained in England during the war years playing for troops and civilians.

He was able to return to the United States in 1947, his first appearance taking place on November 30 with the New York Philharmonic-Symphony under Mitropoulos in the Tchaikovsky B-flat minor Concerto. "This writer can remember only one previous performance, that of Rachmaninoff, which approached Mr. Curzon's incandescent intensity, technical perfection, and beauty of tonal investiture," wrote Jerome D. Bohm in the New York *Herald Tribune*. After Curzon's recital in New York on December 20, Noel Straus wrote in the New York *Times*: "Curzon must be reckoned among the greatest keyboard artists of his time."

His appearance in America and Europe since 1947 have placed him in the front rank of contemporary pianists. He is, as Olin Downes wrote in the New York *Times,* "an artist of true humbleness and a consecrated devotion to his task . . . one of the most remarkable pianists and musicians now before the public."

DAMROSCH, WALTER, conductor. For his earlier career, see *Living Musicians,* 1940.

* * *

Damrosch retired as conductor of the NBC Music Appreciation program in 1942, and as musical adviser of NBC in 1947. He died in New York City on December 22, 1950.

DAVIS, AGNES, soprano. See *Living Musicians,* 1940.

DAVIS, ELLABELLE, soprano, was born in New Rochelle, New York, where her parents ran a grocery store. Though she loved music, took some vocal lessons, and sang continually (performing solos with the high school glee club), Ellabelle had little hope of becoming a professional singer. She studied, instead, to be a dressmaker. In 1941 she

ELLABELLE DAVIS

found a job as dressmaker to Louise Crane, daughter of a former governor of Massachusetts and United States senator. One day, while adjusting the hemline of her employer's dress, Ellabelle began singing softly to herself an aria from *Louise.* Louise Crane thus first became aware of Ellabelle's singing talent, and soon made it possible for her vocal studies to continue in New York City.

Ellabelle Davis made her first professional appearance in New York City in 1941, at a "Coffee Concert" at the Museum of Modern Art in New York City, of which Miss Crane was a patron. In the fall of 1942, when Davis gave a recital at Town Hall, New York, Virgil Thomson wrote in the New York *Herald Tribune* that "so sumptuous a soprano voice, impeccably schooled and nowhere wanting in power, combined with a platform presence both handsome and gracious, is indeed welcome in our concert routine."

Despite the good notices won by her debut recital, Davis did not achieve any measure of success until, in August 1946, she was "discovered" in South America by Eugene Ormandy, conductor of the Philadelphia Orchestra. At that time, Davis was rehearsing with her accompanist on the stage of the Teatro Gran Rex in Buenos Aires when Ormandy happened to stroll into the theatre. He was so impressed by her singing that he went up to her and, in broken Spanish, asked if she would be interested to come to the United States as his discovery. In perfect English, Davis replied that she was American, that she had already given concerts in the United States. Ormandy invited her to appear as soloist with the Philadelphia Orchestra. Her appearance with that orchestra on November 22, 1946, was a major success.

In 1947 she made further ambitious forward strides in her career. On March 7, she appeared as soloist with the Boston Symphony under Koussevitzky in the world première of Lukas Foss' *The Song of Songs,* a work dedicated to her. Many of the Boston critics felt that much of the powerful effect achieved by the music was due to the compellingly attractive voice of the soloist. (Davis repeated this performance at the Berkshire Music Festival in the summer of 1950.) Later the same year, Davis became the first Negro artist to sing a title role in a major opera house when she appeared in the title role of *Aida* at the Opera Nacional in Mexico City.

In 1948-1949, Ellabelle Davis made her first tour of Europe. In Norway she was acclaimed as "a new Jenny Lind, a sensation of the age." An American news syndicate reported from Vienna that her performance in that city "brought cheers from a highly critical audience . . . and exploded, possibly for all time, the myth of America's musical illiteracy." Since then Ellabelle Davis has made many successful appearances in recitals and as soloist with major orchestras in Europe and the United States, and in opera in South America.

DEERING, HENRI, pianist. For his earlier career, see *Living Musicians,* 1940.

* * *

From 1938 to 1940 Deering was on the music faculty of Adelphi College in Garden City, Long Island. Since then, besides making concert appearances, he has been teaching privately in New York City and, during summers, holding classes at Middlebury College in Vermont.

DEFAUW, DÉSIRÉ, conductor. For his earlier career, see *Living Musicians,* 1940.

* * *

Between 1943 and 1947 Defauw was principal conductor of the Chicago Symphony Orchestra. After leaving Chicago, he became principal conductor of the Grand Rapids (Michigan) Symphony and the Bloomington (Indiana) Normal Symphony Orchestra.

DE GOGORZA, EMILIO EDOARDO. See GOGORZA, EMILIO EDOARDO DE.

DE LAMARTER, ERIC, conductor. For his earlier career, see *Living Musicians,* 1940.

* * *

De Lamarter died in Orlando, Florida, on May 17, 1953.

DEL MONACO, MARIO, tenor, was born in Florence, Italy, on July 27, 1915. Both parents were musical and they directed him toward music very early in his life. When Mario was seven he knew that he would some day be an opera singer. In Pesaro, where he spent his boyhood because his father worked there as a city official, he attended the Conservatory. He was still only in his boyhood when he made his opera debut, appearing in Massenet's *Narciso* in Mondolfo.

After a few months of music study he became discouraged by his slow progress and he abandoned it. He now began to study singing by himself, mostly by listening to phonograph records and studying opera scores. This practice continued for several years. Not until he was nineteen did he make a second attempt at formal study, after winning a scholarship for the Rossini Conservatory in Pesaro. But once again the period of instruction proved brief; after half a year he returned to his records and scores.

His professional debut took place in Milan when he was twenty-five—on January 1, 1941, when he appeared as Pinkerton in *Madama Butterfly.* But his career was still not yet to

MARIO DEL MONACO

Del Monaco: dĕl mô'nä-kō

be fully launched. Because of the war he had to serve for several years in the army. But after the war, his return to opera resulted in important appearances throughout Italy. He scored his first important successes at La Scala in Milan, then was heard in over thirty leading tenor roles in such leading opera houses as the San Carlo in Naples, the Teatro Reale in Rome, Covent Garden in London, and with major opera companies in Barcelona, Lisbon and Stockholm. In 1946 he was acclaimed in Mexico and at the Teatro Colón in Buenos Aires and the Teatro Municipal in Rio de Janeiro.

His American debut, as Radames in *Aida,* took place with the San Francisco Opera in the fall of 1950. Rudolf Bing, general manager of the Metropolitan Opera, heard him there and engaged him for his company. Del Monaco's Metropolitan Opera debut followed on November 27, 1951, when he appeared as Des Grieux in *Manon Lescaut.* Arthur Berger wrote in the New York *Herald Tribune* that he was "the proud possessor of a fresh and powerful voice . . . and he had the added asset of an animated and by no means reticent personality."

The following season, Del Monaco became a regular member of the Metropolitan Opera company. He was now sometimes severely criticized both for singing too loudly and for overacting. But when he returned to the stage of the Metropolitan Opera in 1953-1954, after a season's hiatus, he had remedied these faults and was the possessor of what Virgil Thomson described in the *Herald Tribune* as "one of the purest tenor voices lately encountered."

Both in this country and abroad, Del Monaco has proved himself to be one of the most important Italian tenors to come to prominence since the end of World War II. Besides those already mentioned, his most successful roles have been Otello, Andrea Chenier, Cavaradossi in *Tosca,* Ernani, Don José in *Carmen,* Canio in *Pagliacci,* Don Alvaro in *La Forza del Destino,* Edgardo in *Lucia di Lammermoor,* and Manrico in *Il Trovatore.*

Del Monaco is married to Rina Fedora, a former professional singer. They have two sons and maintain their permanent home in Milan, where Del Monaco pursues his favorite hobby of collecting Chinese art.

DE LOS ANGELES, VICTORIA. See ANGELES, VICTORIA DE LOS.

DE LUCA, GIUSEPPE. See LUCA, GIUSEPPE DE.

DE SABATA, VICTOR. See SABATA, VICTOR DE.

DESSOFF, MARGARETE, conductor. For her earlier career, see *Living Musicians,* 1940.

* * *

Dessoff died in Locarno, Switzerland, on November 27, 1944.

DICKSON, DONALD, dramatic tenor (formerly baritone) was born in Cleveland, Ohio, on November 13, 1915. Though the members of his family gave him no direction, since they were not musical, he manifested an interest in good music from childhood on. When he was fifteen, while attending public school, he started taking vocal lessons with Warren Whitney. Four years later he auditioned for Artur Rodzinski, then the musical director of the Cleveland Orchestra. "You don't know what you are doing, or why," Rodzinski told him, "but, nevertheless, what you are doing is precisely right." Rodzinski now began taking a personal interest in him and coached him.

Dickson made his professional debut in his nineteenth year by appearing with the Cleveland Orchestra under Rodzinski in a concert presentation of *The Merry Wives of Windsor,* performing the role of Ford. For the next three years he continued appearing in concert performances of operas given by the Cleve-

DONALD DICKSON

land Orchestra—sometimes in tenor, sometimes in baritone roles.

Two scholarships brought him to New York and enabled him to continue his vocal training with Ella Toedt at the Institute of Musical Art and to undertake the study of harmony, music history, and languages at the Juilliard Graduate School. He was selected to create the title role in Albert Stoessel's opera *Garrick* at the Juilliard Graduate School early in 1937. He made such a good impression that he was signed by the Metropolitan Opera for its spring season, making his debut there on May 3, 1937, as Valentine in *Faust*. Olin Downes reported in the New York *Times:* "He has a fine voice, unmistakable sincerity and dramatic talent. The tone has warmth and mettle, too. Dickson does not merely sing. He welds text and tone together. By means of accentuation, nuance and a sense of declamation he stirs his listeners and conveys the composer's full intention to them." During this spring-season Dickson also appeared in the world première of Walter Damrosch's *The Man Without a Country*.

Dickson remained at the Metropolitan Opera two seasons. He was subsequently heard in principal baritone roles at the San Francisco Opera, the Philadelphia La Scala, the Chicago Opera, and the Chautauqua Opera. At the same time he began a long and distinguished career over the radio, becoming one of radio's most popular serious-music performers. He appeared for thirty weeks or more on each of about half a dozen major sponsored programs; on the Chase and Sanborn Hour he was the singing star for three and a half years. He was also seen and heard in the motion picture *Up in Arms,* starring Danny Kaye.

Dickson has made numerous appearances throughout the country in recitals and with symphony orchestras, filling about 150 engagements a year. Despite his success in virtually every field of singing, he has continued to study assiduously: with Lotte Lehmann and Margaret Matzenauer, in California, from 1939 to 1945; and, in New York, with Paul Althouse from 1950 to 1952.

Dickson sang in the baritone range up to April 1956. Since then he has been appearing as a tenor. His tenor debut took place on August 3, 1956, with the Chautauqua Opera when he was seen as Canio in *Pagliacci*. A few days later he sang the part of Otello in the Verdi opera, presented in a concert version by the Chautauqua Symphony. Later concert appearances throughout the country, and on the stage at the San Antonio Opera, served to reintroduce him to his audiences in his new voice range.

DILLING, MILDRED, harpist. See *Living Musicians,* 1940.

DI STEFANO, GIUSEPPE, tenor, was born in Sicily in 1921. He was trained for the priesthood, but when he reached his sixteenth year he decided against entering the church and went to work at various jobs. His study of singing began with Luigi Montesano just before the outbreak of World War II. The war interrupted these studies. Conscripted into the Italian army, Di Stefano served in the infantry, was captured, but managed to escape to Switzerland where he was interned. Despite this internment, he was permitted to sing at concerts and over the radio.

When the war was over, Di Stefano returned to Italy. He spent ten months of intensive study with Montesano to prepare himself for a career in opera. His opera debut took place at the Reggio Emilia in April 1946. He was so successful that he was engaged by La Scala, where he made his first appearance in March 1947.

His American debut took place at the Metropolitan Opera on February 25, 1948, as the Duke in *Rigoletto*. "There is no doubt," said the New York *Times*, "that the young

GIUSEPPE DI STEFANO

Di Stefano: dē stä′fä-nō

man scored in a big way. Mr. Di Stefano has a lyric voice of natural beauty. It is probably the purest and freshest Italian tenor in the company." During the next few seasons, Di Stefano appeared in twelve leading tenor roles, strengthening the good impression he made during his debut. He was also heard in Mexico City and Rio de Janeiro. In the latter city, the long-standing rules against encores had to be broken because of the vociferous demand that he repeat one of the arias.

During the 1955-1956 season, Di Stefano returned to the Metropolitan Opera after an absence of three years. Before this return, he won the coveted Mantua Award in Italy as the best tenor of the year, and was given an ovation during his first appearances at the Lyric Theatre in Chicago.

While in the United States, Di Stefano fell in love with Maria Girolami, a voice student and daughter of an engineer employed by 20th Century-Fox. They were married in New York City on May 23, 1949, and have two children. They divide their year between Italy and the United States, with a home in Tenafly, New Jersey, a villa in Ravenna, and a town house in Milan.

DIXON, DEAN, conductor, was born in New York City on January 10, 1915. Though his mother, a native of Barbados, had planned a medical career for him, she allowed him to indulge his passion for music. He was only a baby when he heard his first concert, in Carnegie Hall. At the age of four he started studying the violin and depite his aversion to formal exercises, made excellent progress because of his extraordinary musical aptitude and memory and his ear for perfect pitch. While attending De Witt Clinton High School he impressed Harry Jennison, head of the music department, who persuaded him to consider music as a career. When Dixon was graduated from high school in 1932, he went to the Institute of Musical Art, continuing his academic education at Columbia College. Later on, he took postgraduate courses at Columbia University for his master's degree and doctorate, and for three years he studied conducting on a fellowship at the Juilliard Graduate School.

His career as conductor began in 1932 when he organized an orchestra in a Harlem branch of the YMCA. Starting with only a handful of musicians, he built an orchestra until it comprised seventy members, using his own money to buy music and instruments. In 1937 a group of social-minded women helped to subsidize the orchestra. Now known as the Dean Dixon Symphony Orchestra, it gave a

Courtesy of Musical Courier

DEAN DIXON

regular series of concerts in New York each year. His work with this organization was so noteworthy that it attracted the interest and enthusiasm of several notables, including Mrs. Eleanor Roosevelt, who invited him to direct several concerts under her personal sponsorship.

He combined this activity with his own orchestra with guest appearances at Town Hall and with various minor orchestras. In 1940 he organized and became conductor of the National Youth Administration Orchestra. Samuel Chotzinoff, music director of NBC, engaged him to lead two guest performances with the NBC Symphony in June 1941. This was his first appearance with a major orchestra, and he made such a brilliant impression that he was invited to conduct the NBC Symphony for several performances the following January. He was also called for guest appearances with the New York Philharmonic-Symphony, the Philadelphia Orchestra, and the Lewisohn Stadium Orchestra. Thus he became the first Negro ever to direct major American orchestras. From 1944 to 1949 he was the principal conductor of the American Youth Orchestra. On May 8, 1948, he received the Alice M. Ditson Award for outstanding contributions to American music. The citation read: "Both as artist and citizen he has brought distinction to the American scene."

Since then, Dixon has settled in Paris and has concentrated his activity as conductor on the European musical scene, directing major organizations in Europe, as well as the Israel Philharmonic in 1950 and 1951. He has been indefatigable in presenting American music to European audiences.

DOBBS, MATTIWILDA, soprano, was born in Atlanta, Georgia, on July 11, 1925. She was the fifth of six children, the daughter of a railroad mail clerk who succeeded in seeing all of his children go through college. At the age of seven, Mattiwilda began taking piano lessons. Several years later she sang in the choir of the First Congregational Church in Atlanta; while attending Spelman College, she studied voice with Naomi Maise and Willis James. After graduation from college in 1946 (she was class valedictorian), she was taken by her father to New York for additional musical training. For four years she studied with Lotte Leonard; at the same time she received a master's degree in Spanish at Teachers College, Columbia University.

She made her first concert appearance in 1947 at the music and drama festival at the University of Mexico. In that year she won the Marian Anderson Scholarship, and the following year other scholarships to study opera at the Mannes School in New York and at the Berkshire Music Center in Lenox, Massachusetts. The award of the Jay Hay Whitney Opportunity Fellowship, amounting to $3,000, enabled her to go to Paris in 1950 to study with Pierre Bernac. In October of that year she won first prize in the International Competition in Geneva, even though she

MATTIWILDA DOBBS

had to appear with a leg badly sprained the night before. A concert appearance in Paris followed. This was attended by S. Hurok, the impresario, who then and there signed her to a contract. Under Hurok's management, she made her first tour of Europe in 1951-1952, appearing in recitals and with symphony orchestras. She attracted attention at the Holland Music Festival in the summer of 1952 in the leading soprano role in Stravinsky's *Le Rossignol.*

On March 4, 1953, she made her debut at La Scala in Milan as Elvira in Rossini's *L'Italiana in Algeri.* This was the first time a Negro sang a leading role at this historic theatre. Two months later she was heard as Zerbinetta in *Ariadne auf Naxos* at Glyndebourne. She returned to Glyndebourne in 1956 to appear as Queen of the Night in *The Magic Flute.* Her successes brought her a contract for Covent Garden, where during the season of 1953-1954 she appeared successfully as Gilda in *Rigoletto,* the Queen in Rimsky-Korsakov's *Le Coq d'Or,* and the Forest Bird in *Siegfried.*

Her American debut took place at Town Hall, New York on March 8, 1954, when she was heard as Zerbinetta in a concert performance of *Ariadne auf Naxos* by the Little Orchestra Society under Thomas Scherman. Olin Downes said in the New York *Times:* "She immediately proved herself to be one of the most gifted bravura singers now before the public. . . . Miss Dobbs has more than exceptional virtuosity in song. She has temperament and charm . . . and [is] a coloratura of exceptional range."

In July 1954 she appeared in a gala performance of *Le Coq d'Or,* at Covent Garden, given in honor of King Gustav II and Queen Louise of Sweden, and attended by Queen Elizabeth II of England. Dobbs made this appearance despite the fact that only four days earlier she had been stricken by tragedy: the sudden death of her husband, Louis Rodriguez, a journalist whom she had married one year earlier. Following this appearance, she was given the Swedish decoration of the Order of the North Star.

Her first world tour took place in 1955, culminating with her American opera debut at the San Francisco Opera on October 13, in *Le Coq d'Or.* As had been the case at La Scala, this was the first time a Negro appeared in a major role at the San Francisco Opera. Reporting this event for the New York *Times,* Howard Taubman wrote: "This is not the biggest nor the most exciting part in the coloratura catalogue, but Miss Dobbs, once her early nervousness had worn off, made the most of its opportunities. There is brilliance in her voice, and plenty of flexibility. . . . The voice is well schooled enough for most coloratura roles."

A few months later, on January 30, 1956, after her recital in Town Hall, New York. Mr. Taubman wrote again: "There was no question of the intelligence and sensitivity of Miss Dobbs' singing. . . . She is an artist." Towards the end of the same year, on November 9, 1956, she made her debut at the Metropolitan Opera, as Gilda in *Rigoletto*. "She rose to the occasion admirably," reported Mr. Taubman. "The young soprano has a voice of substance and quality. . . . All told, a fine debut. It may even be that greatness is within the girl's reach."

DOBROWEN, ISSAI, conductor. For his earlier career, see *Living Musicians, 1940.*

* * *

Between 1949 and 1951 Dobrowen conducted Russian operas at La Scala in Milan. He died in Oslo, Norway, on December 9, 1953.

DOE, DORIS, contralto. See *Living Musicians, 1940.*

DOHNÁNYI, ERNST VON, pianist and conductor. For his earlier career, see *Living Musicians, 1940.*

* * *

Dohnányi settled in the United States in 1948, making his home in Tallahassee, Florida, where he joined the music faculty of the Florida State College.

DOKTOR, PAUL, violist, was born in Vienna on March 28, 1919, the son of Karl Doktor, a celebrated violist who founded, and for thirty-five years played in, the Busch Quartet. Paul was originally intended for the violin rather than the viola. When he was five, he began taking violin lessons from his father; during his boyhood he often participated in chamber-music performances at home. After several years of study with his father, Paul entered the Academy of Music in Vienna, where he completed a five-year course in two years. Following his graduation, he joined the violin section of the Adolf Busch Chamber Orchestra, with which he toured Europe.

Chance made him change from violin to viola. At a concert by the Busch Quartet in Zurich, he was called upon to substitute for

PAUL DOKTOR

his father in a performance of a Mendelssohn Quintet. This concert went off so well that when the Busch Quartet played in London, he was again invited to perform the viola, this time in a Mozart Quintet. The winning of first prize at the International Music Competition in Geneva in 1942—the first time the prize went to a violist—was the final influence in converting him to the viola. From then on, in his public appearances he concentrated on the viola, reserving the violin only for chamber-music concerts at home.

Paul Doktor came to the United States in 1947, established permanent residence in this country, and became a citizen. His American debut took place in March 1948 with a concert at the Library of Congress in Washington, D.C. "Not for many years," reported the Washington *Times-Herald*, "has such a competent master of the viola been heard in American concert halls." Soon after this debut, Doktor was chosen by Quincy Porter to introduce his Concerto for Viola and Orchestra; this performance took place on May 16, 1948, in New York City at the American Music Festival held at Columbia University.

In 1948 Doktor was appointed to the faculty of the School of Music of the University of Michigan, where for three years he taught viola and chamber music and played the viola in a resident string quartet. In 1951 he left the University to devote himself to concert work. Since then he has each winter toured the United States in sonata recitals and as guest soloist with major orchestras. Each year, in the summer and fall, he has toured Europe, performing at many major European music events, including the Salzburg Festival. "No one can play his instrument, possess a more complete technique, and have a richer and varied sonority, and more beautiful phrasing. He is comparable to Kreisler in his best years," reported a music critic of the *Nouvelles Littéraires* in Paris in 1955.

Doktor is now a resident of New York City, where he is a member of the faculty of the Mannes School. During the summer he conducts a master class in viola at the International Summer Academy at the Mozarteum in Salzburg.

The DOLMETSCH FAMILY. See *Living Musicians*, 1940.

DORATI, ANTAL, conductor, was born in Budapest on April 9, 1906. Both parents were musicians. His father was a violinist in the Budapest Philharmonic Orchestra, and his mother a teacher of the piano. At an early age Antal was directed to music study, which was completed in 1924 at the Budapest Academy where his teachers had included Béla Bartók and Zoltán Kodály. Dorati was the youngest person in the history of the Academy to receive a degree. Immediately after he left the Academy he was appointed to the staff of the Budapest Royal Opera as coach, assistant conductor, and arranger. For

ANTAL DORATI

Dorati: dō-rä′tē

two years, while holding this post, he traveled twice a week to Vienna to attend the University.

In 1928 Fritz Busch appointed him as his assistant at the Dresden Opera. Dorati stayed there only one season, receiving in 1929 an appointment as musical director and principal conductor of the Münster Municipal Theatre. During his three years in Münster he appeared extensively as guest conductor of major symphony orchestras and opera companies in Germany, Hungary, and Czechoslovakia.

After conducting a series of opera broadcasts over the French National Radio in Paris in 1933, Dorati was appointed principal conductor of the Ballet Russe de Monte Carlo. He held this post for a decade, directing performances throughout Europe and the United States, and in 1937 at the Florence May Music Festival. In December 1937 he made his American debut as symphony conductor when Hans Kindler invited him for a guest concert with the National Symphony in Washington, D.C. in an all-Beethoven program. Between 1939 and 1941 he toured Australia.

In 1941 he made the United States his permanent home, becoming an American citizen six years later. Between 1941 and 1945 he was the musical director of the American Ballet Theatre, and in 1941 and 1942 director of the New Opera Company in New York. At the same time he appeared as guest conductor of several major American orchestras.

When the Dallas Symphony Orchestra was reorganized in 1945, Dorati was appointed musical director. Under his dynamic leadership, this orchestra assumed a position of importance among American symphony orchestras. Dorati extended the annual schedule from forty-two to eighty-four concerts; he inaugurated extensive tours and broadcasts; he introduced vital choral festivals and cycles of orchestral literature; he made it a practice not only to emphasize performances of new music but even to commission important American composers to write new works for him, among these being Morton Gould, Walter Piston, and Paul Hindemith. John Sherman, the Dallas music critic, described Dorati's regime as "a love affair of four breathless seasons."

In 1949 Dimitri Mitropoulos resigned as musical director of the Minneapolis Symphony. Dorati was called to replace him as conductor—a position he held with such distinction that six years later he was given the title of musical director. In the summer of

1953 he made successful guest appearances in South America and Sweden; in the latter country he directed the Stockholm Philharmonic in a concert celebrating the seven hundredth anniversary of the founding of the city.

Dorati married his childhood sweetheart, Klara Korody, in Dresden on July 14, 1929. They have a daughter, Tonina. In his youth, Dorati enjoyed playing hockey and riding horseback, but his principal hobby now is sketching, in which he sometimes has his daughter as a companion. About the art of conducting he has said: "Each time you conduct it is a spiritual rebirth. You unload your strength, nerves, feelings, everything. You are permitted again and again to relive a great moment."

DORFMANN, ANIA, pianist. See *Living Musicians,* 1940.

DOUTHITT, WILFRED. See GRA-VEURE, LOUIS

DRAGONETTE, JESSICA, soprano. For earlier career, see *Living Musicians,* 1940.

* * *

For her contributions to the war effort, during World War II, Dragonette was decorated with Army and Navy Wings and with a silver medal from the United States Treasury Department. She has written her autobiography, entitled *Faith Is My Song* (1951).

DUPRÉ, MARCEL, organist. For his earlier career, see *Living Musicians,* 1940.

* * *

Dupré made extensive tours of the United States in 1946 and 1948, and during this period he conducted master classes in organ at the University of Chicago. In 1947 he was appointed director of the American Conservatory at Fontainebleau, France, and held this post for a year.

DUSHKIN, SAMUEL, violinist. See *Living Musicians,* 1940.

EAMES, EMMA, soprano. For her earlier career, see *Living Musicians,* 1940.

* * *

Eames died in New York City on June 13, 1952.

EASTON, FLORENCE, soprano. For her earlier career, see *Living Musicians,* 1940.

* * *

Easton died in New York City on August 14, 1954.

ECHANIZ, JOSÉ, pianist and conductor. For his earlier career, see *Living Musicians,* 1940.

* * *

Echaniz was appointed conductor of the Grand Rapids (Michigan) Symphony Orchestra in 1948.

EDDY, NELSON, baritone. See *Living Musicians,* 1940.

EHLERS, ALICE, harpsichordist. See *Living Musicians,* 1940.

EISENBERG, MAURICE, cellist. For his earlier career, see *Living Musicians,* 1940.

* * *

Until 1949, Eisenberg was professor of the Casals Class at the École Normale de Musique in Paris. Since 1953 he has been the head of the cello department at the Longy School of Music in Cambridge, Massachusetts, and artistic director of the International Cello Centre in London.

ELMAN, MISCHA. See *Living Musicians,* 1940.

ENESCO, GEORGES, violinist and conductor. For his earlier career, see *Living Musicians,* 1940.

* * *

Enesco spent the years of World War II on his large farm in Sinai, Rumania, near Bucharest. When the Soviets took over his country, they made an exception in his case to their general practice of confiscating all the farms; he was allowed to keep one third of his. After an absence of almost a decade, Enesco returned to the United States in 1946 for a five-month tour as conductor and violinist. During this visit, on March 31, 1947, he received the Grand Order of Loyal Service for services to Rumanian music from Mihai Ralea, Rumanian Ambassador to the United States. Enesco died in Paris on May 4, 1955.

ENGEL, A. LEHMAN, conductor. For his earlier career, see *Living Musicians,* 1940.

* * *

During World War II, Engel served in the Navy for four years, a period in which he wrote music for several Navy films. Since the end of the war, Engel has been active as a conductor of musical-comedy productions on Broadway.

EREDE, ALBERTO, conductor, was born in Genoa, Italy, on November 8, 1908. His father, a physician, led him to music at an early age. When he was four, Alberto began studying both the violin and the piano. His first attempt at composition came a year later, the occasion being the death of his music teacher.

In 1927 Erede was graduated from the Milan Conservatory. During a visit to Switzerland he met Felix Weingartner, who encouraged him to become a conductor. Erede studied first wtih Weingartner, then with Fritz Busch in Dresden.

His debut as conductor took place at the Turin Opera where he led the entire *Ring* cycle. Recognition came a few years later— at the Glyndebourne Festival in 1934. Erede continued to conduct opera at Glyndebourne for five years, distinguishing himself for his classic style, particularly in the operas of Mozart. During this period, between 1935 and 1938, he was also the principal conductor of the Salzburg Opera Guild. It was with the latter company that he first came to the United States, making his American debut in 1937. In the same year he also led guest performances with the NBC Symphony. Two years later he was engaged by NBC to direct

the première of Menotti's radio opera, *The Old Maid and the Thief,* given a concert performance over the NBC network on April 12, 1939.

In 1945 Erede was appointed principal conductor of the Italian Radio Company Orchestra in Turin. One year later he became musical director of the New London Opera Company at the Cambridge Theatre in London. In this post he conducted six opera telecasts. In May of the same year he was back at Glyndebourne after an absence of six years. Between 1946 and 1950 he appeared throughout Europe as guest of leading opera companies, including La Scala in Milan, San Carlo in Naples, the Vienna State Opera, and the Teatro La Fenice in Venice.

When Rudolf Bing became general manager of the Metropolitan Opera in 1950 he engaged Erede as a conductor. (They had formerly worked together at Glyndebourne.) Erede made his Metropolitan Opera debut on November 11, 1950, in *La Traviata,* and has remained a principal conductor since that time. His repertory embraces over seventy-five works, including such unusual operas as Monteverdi's *The Coronation of Poppea* and Stravinsky's *The Rake's Progress.* He is also a successful symphony conductor who has mastered over two hundred works in the symphonic and choral repertory and has appeared as a guest of several major American orchestras.

Erede's hobbies include mountain climbing and going to horse races even though he seldom makes a wager.

ERICOURT, DANIEL, pianist. See *Living Musicians,* 1940.

FALKNER, KEITH, baritone. See *Living Musicians,* 1940.

FARRAR, GERALDINE, soprano. See *Living Musicians,* 1940.

FARRELL, EILEEN, dramatic soprano, was born in Willimantic, Connecticut. Her parents, of Irish descent, were headliners on the vaudeville circuit, billed as "The Singing O'Farrells." Her mother, who was a teacher of singing at Storrs College, gave Eileen her first voice lessons. After the family settled in Woonsocket, Rhode Island, Eileen appeared as soloist in church and school performances. For a while, however, she thought of a career in the visual arts, and after graduating from high school went on to art school,

ALBERTO EREDE

Erede: ĕ-rä′dĕ

EILEEN FARRELL

where she suddenly decided to specialize in music. She subsequently undertook an intensive period of study with Merle Alcock and then with Eleanor McLellan.

Her professional career began in 1942, when she impersonated Rosa Ponselle in a "March of Time" broadcast over NBC. This led to an audition with the Columbia Broadcasting System which, in turn, resulted in an engagement for a weekly program entitled "Songs of the Centuries." During the next few years, Farrell appeared on many important radio programs, including one on which she was starred, "Eileen Farrell Presents." She was subsequently also a frequent guest on television programs, after making her television debut on the Milton Berle program in 1950.

She made her first extensive concert tour of America in 1947-1948, and her first South American tour in 1949. Success on the concert stage came on October 24, 1950, when a recital in Carnegie Hall established her among the most gifted dramatic sopranos to emerge since World War II. The New York Times wrote: "This was great singing. The big notes soared out thrillingly, only to be followed with pianissimos of ravishing softness as the mood changed. The effortless production, the swells and diminuendos on single breaths, the purity of sound—all these were notable, and yet everything was subordinate to the interpretation, which was truly felt from the heart."

The full extent of her versatility became evident during that season when she made a total of sixty-one appearances in five separate engagements with the New York Philharmonic-Symphony Orchestra—more often than any other artist in the history of that organization. During this period she was soloist with the orchestra during its tradition-breaking engagement at the Roxy Theatre in New York, where she was heard fifty-five times in two weeks. Later the same season she appeared with the New York Philharmonic-Symphony in the American première of Milhaud's *Les Choëphores,* in Alban Berg's *Wozzeck,* and in an all-Wagner program. Her personal triumph as Marie in *Wozzeck* resulted in her recording that part for Columbia Records. Farrell has also appeared extensively with other major American orchestras. Toscanini selected her to sing in Beethoven's Ninth Symphony over NBC, a performance that was recorded by Victor. In the film biography of Marjorie Lawrence, *Interrupted Melody,* Farrell sang all the vocal selections for the sound track.

Farrell is married to Robert Reagan, a New York police officer. With their two children, they share a home in Staten Island, New York.

FERRIER, KATHLEEN, contralto, was born in Higher Walton, Lancashire, on April 12, 1912. When still a child, she went to live in Blackburn, where her father, a schoolmaster, became headmaster of a boys' school. While attending the public schools there, she studied piano and sang in the local church choir and in nearby festivals. When she was eleven she won first prize in a piano competition, and from 1927 to 1936 she worked as a piano accompanist. She had no thought of becoming a singer until 1938, when, on a challenge and a bet, she entered a vocal competition in Carlisle and won first prize. This encouraged her to begin vocal study. While doing this, and filling some minor engagements as a singer, she supported herself by working as a telephone operator.

In 1940 she became a pupil of J. E. Hutchinson in Newcastle-on-Tyne. During this period she was heard by Sir Malcolm Sargent, the eminent conductor, who urged her to go to London and provided her with influential letters of recommendation. She arrived in London in December 1942, studied for a period with Roy Henderson, and soon began appearing in recitals and as soloist with choral groups. Her first important appearance took place in 1943 when she ap-

KATHLEEN FERRIER

peared as soloist in the *Messiah* at Westminster Abbey. Other appearances during the war years were in public auditoriums and other gathering places to help bolster civilian morale.

Soon after World War II, she was selected for a leading role in Benjamin Britten's opera *The Rape of Lucretia*, which had its première at Glyndebourne on July 12, 1946 (the first performance at Glyndebourne after the war). She then made about sixty appearances in that opera at Glyndebourne, Covent Garden, and other places in England and Scotland. Her distinguished performance led to her engagement as Orfeo in Gluck's *Orfeo ed Euridice* at Glyndebourne in 1947, a performance in which she scored her first triumph. Dyneley Hussey spoke of her "regal and beautiful presence" and of the beauty and power of her voice. She repeated her success as Orfeo that summer at the Edinburgh Festival.

Attracting the interest of Bruno Walter, she was engaged to appear under his direction at the Edinburgh Festival in the summer of 1947 in Mahler's *Das Lied von der Erde*. It was in the same Mahler work, and under the same conductor, that she made her American debut as soloist with the New York Philharmonic-Symphony, on January 15, 1948. Herbert F. Peyser, writing in *Musical America*, reported that her voice was one "of unusual quality and texture, singularly vibrant and substantial." In later appearances in the United States she was further ac-

claimed not only for the beauty of her voice but also for her sensitive musicianship and profound interpretative insight. Among these appearances were her American debut recital, Town Hall, New York on March 28, 1949, and in the same month her first American performance of Orfeo. Her growing artistry as a recitalist led Bruno Walter to serve as her accompanist when she subsequently gave a song recital in New York; this was only the second time that Bruno Walter appeared as accompanist, the first time having been for Lotte Lehmann.

Meanwhile, in 1948, she toured Scandinavia for the first time, and in 1949 (besides appearing in the United States) she was heard in Canada, Cuba, England, and at the Holland Music Festival, where, on July 14, she appeared in the world première of Britten's *Spring Symphony*.

Ferrier died after a long and painful illness in London on October 9, 1953, at the age of forty-one.

FEUERMANN, EMANUEL, cellist. For his earlier career, see *Living Musicians,* 1940.

* * *

Feuermann died in New York City on May 25, 1942.

FIEDLER, ARTHUR, conductor. For his earlier career, see *Living Musicians,* 1940.

* * *

Fiedler was made Chevalier of the Legion of Honor of France in 1954.

FIRKUSNY, RUDOLF, pianist, was born in Napajedla, Czechoslovakia, on February 11, 1912. He began studying the piano by himself when he was only three. One year later he acquired his first teacher, and at six came under the influence and personal instruction of one of Czechoslovakia's foremost composers, Leos Janáček. Janáček had him enrolled in the Brünn Conservatory when he was eight. There the boy received a comprehensive training under Ruzena Kuzova, Josef Suk, and Janáček. On June 14, 1920, Firkusny made his concert debut as soloist with the Prague Philharmonic.

His professional career was launched in Vienna in 1923 and continued for a few years with appearances in different parts of Europe. He did not achieve any notable success. Provided with funds by the Czechoslovakian government, through the influence of his friend and musical godfather, Thomas

Firkusny: fĕr-kōōsh'nĕ

RUDOLF FIRKUSNY

Masaryk, Firkusny returned to piano study. From 1927 to 1929 he attended the Master School in Prague, where his principal teachers were Vilem Kurz and Rudolf Karel. In 1933 he began studying privately with Artur Schnabel.

After returning to the European concert stage, Firkusny performed in the United States in 1938 but was not well received. When World War II broke out, he settled in Paris, where he gave many benefit concerts for the Czechoslovakian government. After Hitler invaded Paris, Firkusny fled to Portugal, then made his way to the United States, where he made another brief tour. This time there were critics to speak well of him; one of them said that whereas he had been "much too young" three years earlier, he was now playing "with the poise and maturity of a master." A tour of South America took place in 1943, and an extensive tour of Europe in 1946. It was during the latter period, particularly at the Prague Music Festival, that Firkusny scored his first major successes.

After the Iron Curtain descended on his native land, Firkusny became *persona non grata* with the new regime, because of his past personal ties with the Masaryk family. He now made the United States his permanent home, and he subsequently became a citizen and acquired two residences, an apartment in New York City, and a house in Staatsburg, New York.

Success in America began in 1949, when he played in fifty cities and was everywhere

hailed for his sensitive and poetic interpretations of the classic repertory and for the delicacy of his style. As Albert Goldberg wrote in the Los Angeles *Times*: "He is one pianist who never strives for effect. He states for the composer simply, directly, and respectfully, intruding his own personality only when such comment is suitable and in good taste."

His appearances in recitals and with major orchestras have been frequent throughout the world of music since 1949. He has distinguished himself in modern music as well as in the classical and romantic repertory—especially in the music of his native land. He has given world premières of new concertos by Bohuslav Martinu, Howard Hanson, and Gian-Carlo Menotti, among others.

FISCHER, EDWIN, pianist. See *Living Musicians*, 1940.

FISCHER-DIESKAU, DIETRICH, baritone, was born in Berlin, on May 28, 1925. Both parents were musical. It was from his mother that Dietrich inherited his love of *Lieder*. His study of voice, however, did not begin until he was sixteen—when George Walter introduced him to oratorio literature and to the cantatas of Bach. Dietrich then enrolled in the Berlin Hochschule für Musik for intensive musical training, principally with Professor Weissenborn. His studies were terminated with the outbreak of World War II. Mustered into the Nazi army in 1943, he saw action, was captured, and for two years was interned in a prison camp. There he gave some concerts, and continued his music study by listening to recordings.

He began his professional career after the war. His debut took place in Freiburg, Germany, in 1947, when he appeared as soloist in Brahms' *A German Requiem*, substituting for a baritone who became suddenly indisposed. A year later he was engaged as a principal baritone of the Berlin Municipal Opera. During the next few years he distinguished himself there in both the German and the Italian repertory; his best roles included Wolfram in *Tannhäuser*, the Count in *The Marriage of Figaro*, Jokanaan in *Salome* and Valentine in *Faust*. During this period he also appeared with outstanding success at the Bayreuth and Edinburgh Festivals.

His world fame, however, came not through his operatic appearances (excellent though these were) but from his recitals. His concerts in Europe after 1950 placed him with the foremost interpreters of *Lieder* of

Fischer-Dieskau: fĭsh'ĕr dēs'kou

Courtesy of Musical Courier
DIETRICH FISCHER-DIESKAU

our generation. When he sang the complete cycles of Schubert's *Die Schöne Müllerin* and *Die Winterreise* in London in 1950 and 1951, he brought back to English critics memories of other celebrated *Lieder* singers, including Elena Gerhardt and Lotte Lehmann in her prime.

His American debut took place in Cincinnati on April 15, 1955, when he appeared as soloist with the Cincinnati Symphony in a Bach cantata and Brahms' *A German Requiem.* Reporting this debut for *Musical America,* Mary Leighton wrote: "Mr. Fischer-Dieskau's voice was remarkably sonorous, his singing masterful in matters of diction, phrasing, breath control and profundity of interpretation. He impressed me as a singer of the first magnitude." About three weeks later, on May 2, he made his New York debut in a recital that comprised the complete *Die Winterreise* cycle. "He performed the considerable feat of holding the audience's interest and close attention throughout," said the New York *Times.* "Not every singer, however gifted, is capable of this feat. . . . Herr Fischer-Dieskau, in doing so, proved himself a vocalist of very unusual attainments."

Fischer-Dieskau has since made several more tours of the United States, besides appearing throughout Europe in opera and recitals. His wife is a cellist whom he met when both were students at the Berlin Hoch-

schule; they were married in 1949, and have a son. Fischer-Dieskau is an ardent collector of recordings.

FISHER, SUSANNE, soprano. See *Living Musicians,* 1940.

FLAGSTAD, KIRSTEN, soprano. For her earlier career, see *Living Musicians,* 1940.

* * *

In April 1941 Flagstad left America to return to her native land, Norway, even though it was then occupied by the Nazis. Her insistence on going home, when it meant living with the Nazis, made her the object of considerable criticism in the free world. Her position was made even more difficult by the fact that her husband was a notorious Quisling. (After the war he was prosecuted for treason, found guilty, and saved from execution only by his sudden death in prison.)

When the war ended, and Flagstad resumed her career in America, there was considerable opposition to her return, despite her insistence that she had never cooperated with the Nazis in any way. The Metropolitan Opera refused to reengage her, and she was turned down for recitals in several cities, and by a major recording company. When she made her first American reappearance—with a recital in Boston on April 6, 1947—there were pickets outside the hall. There were also pickets in Chicago and New York when she performed; and in Philadelphia stench bombs were released in the auditorium. However there was no question about the quality of her art. Reporting her Boston concert, Virgil Thomson wrote in the New York *Herald Tribune:* "She sang like an angel. . . . Never in the writer's concertgoing lifetime . . . has there been available any other vocal artistry of such sumptuous natural acoustics, such perfect technical control and such sound musicianship."

This opposition to Flagstad, however, soon died down—and then was completely forgotten. She made her American return to opera with electrifying performances with the San Francisco Opera in 1949. A year later she was back with the Metropolitan Opera company. Her last appearance with the Metropolitan, and her last opera appearance in America, took place in *Alcestis* in the spring of 1952. In March 1955 she returned to the United States to make two appearances with the Symphony of the Air (formerly the NBC Symphony) in New York in all-Wagner concerts. She has also made intermittent appearances in Norway and in London. In the latter city, during 1952 and the Coronation year of 1953, she was seen in Purcell's *Dido and Aeneas.*

FLEISHER, LEON, pianist, was born in San Francisco on July 23, 1928. His father was a fashion designer; his mother had been a student of singing. When he was still a child he began studying the piano with Lev Shorr. At seven he gave a recital in San Francisco. Three years later Artur Schnabel heard him and, despite his lifelong distaste for prodigies, accepted him as a pupil. For six months Fleisher lived and studied with Schnabel at his studio at Lake Como.

Just before World War II, Fleisher returned to the United States, where he continued to prepare himself for concert work. In 1943 he appeared as soloist with the San Francisco Symphony conducted by Monteux, and one year after that was heard with the New York Philharmonic-Symphony. He followed these performances with appearances throughout the United States both in recitals and as soloist with orchestras; everywhere he played he was acclaimed as one of the most gifted new pianists to emerge since the war.

In 1950 he went to Paris for more study as well as for some concert appearances. In May 1952 he entered the Belgian International Music Competition, competing with seventy other pianists from all parts of the world. In the preliminary round his playing received such prolonged applause that the presiding judge had to ring a bell to restore order. In the final round, Fleisher played the Brahms Concerto in D minor. Despite a mishap (one of the strings of his piano snapped) he was selected by the thirteen judges as the winner of the first prize—$3,000 and appearances with major European orchestras.

He returned to the United States in 1954 for a tour of the country that included recitals in most of the principal cities together with guest performances with fourteen leading orchestras. He has, wrote a Cleveland critic, "all the requirements of a concert star of the . first water. He uses his prodigious technical mastery with an expressive sense—delicacy as well as power—that is remarkable." A Rochester (New York) critic wrote: "He is a tremendously powerful virtuoso with a technical equipment of prodigious authority, and he knows, too, how to make the piano sing. The Boston critic Cyrus Durgin reported: "His technique . . . is prodigious; his musical intelligence is keen, and he possesses the admirable quality of expressive individuality."

Besides his appearances in all parts of this country, Fleisher has concertized successfully in France, Belgium, Holland, Scandinavia, Italy, and Germany.

Away from the piano, he is most interested in swimming, ping-pong, and reading. His tastes in literature range from James Joyce and John Dewey to Ellery Queen.

FLESCH, CARL, violinist. For his earlier career, see *Living Musicians,* 1940.

* * *

Flesch died in Lucerne, Switzerland, on November 14, 1944.

FOURNIER, PIERRE, cellist, was born in Paris on June 24, 1906. His grandfather was the noted sculptor of several famous Parisian monuments and statues, including the Pont Alexandre III spanning the Seine; his father served as general in the French army during World War I, and subsequently was governor of Corsica.

Pierre's father wanted him to prepare for a military career, but his mother, a fine amateur pianist, encouraged him to follow a natural bent for music and gave him lessons on the piano at an early age. When Pierre was nine he became a victim of poliomyelitis, which made it impossible for him to use the piano pedals. He consequently adopted a new instrument—the cello—and made it his spe-

LEON FLEISHER

Fournier: fōōr-nyä′

PIERRE FOURNIER

cialty. His principal musical education took place at the Paris Conservatory, and was concluded privately with André Hekking.

After serving as a member of several orchestras and chamber-music ensembles in Paris, Fournier made his concert debut by appearing as soloist with the Colonne Orchestra in the late 1930's. Within a short time, and by the time World War II erupted in Europe, he was heard in most European countries—such a favorite in Germany that in 1939 he had to give thirty-two consecutive concerts in Berlin alone.

From 1937 to 1939 Fournier served as professor of the cello and of chamber music at the École Normale de Musique in Paris; in 1941 he became professor of the cello at the Paris Conservatory, a post held eight years. His career as virtuoso, interrupted during the war, was resumed in 1945 when he gave his first concerts in England. Besides appearing in that country in recitals and as soloist with orchestras, Fournier also joined Szigeti, Schnabel, and Primrose in distinguished chamber-music concerts over BBC.

In 1948 Fournier made his first tour of the United States where he became an immediate favorite. "Pierre Fournier," wrote Cyrus Durgin in the Boston *Globe,* "is a very great cellist and an exceptional musician. . . . Technical virtuosity, mastery of style are all blended and directed toward making music. The tone is satiny. The phrasing has utmost grace. Such is the combined mastery and

superior perception of this artist that everything was set forth with equal excellence." Virgil Thomson wrote in the New York *Herold Tribune:* "I do not know his superior among living cellists, nor any . . . who give one more profoundly the feeling of having been present at music-making."

One year later, Fournier made his first tour of South America. He also appeared extensively throughout Europe, between 1948 and 1950, with performances at major festivals at Edinburgh, Salzburg, and Lucerne.

Since 1950 Fournier has played throughout the world of music. In 1957, for example, he made his seventh tour of the United States, his third of Latin America, his second of the Orient — besides giving numerous performances throughout Europe. Indicative of his position in French music is the fact that two celebrated French writers dedicated books to him. In one of these, Colette said that Fournier "sings better than anything sings"; in another, André Gide spoke of "vivid memories of unforgettable musical moments." Fournier was honored by the French government in 1953 when he was made Chevalier of the Legion of Honor.

Fournier has an extensive repertory that embraces not only the classical and romantic literature for the cello, but early works of the seventeenth and eighteenth centuries by masters like Couperin and Karl Philipp Emanuel Bach, and modern music. He has given notable performances of contemporary works by Ernest Bloch, Virgil Thomson, Bohuslav Martinu, and Francis Poulenc among others; several of these works were compositions which were written for him and which he introduced.

FRANCESCATTI, ZINO, violinist, was born in Marseilles, France, on August 9, 1905. Both of his parents were professional violinists. His father had studied with Paganini's only direct pupil, Camilio Sivori. His mother had been his father's pupil when she fell in love with her teacher and married him.

Early in life Zino was taught the violin by his father, proving to be such a remarkable prodigy that when he was only five he made his first public appearance. At ten he was acclaimed for a performance of the Beethoven Violin Concerto, and at twenty he scored a sensation when he made his Paris debut as soloist with the Paris Conservatory Orchestra. By the time he made his debut in the United States he had been heard

Francescatti: frän-chĕs-kä′tē

ZINO FRANCESCATTI

throughout Europe and South America and had achieved recognition as one of Europe's foremost violinists.

His debut in the United States took place on November 8, 1939, when he appeared as soloist with the New York Philharmonic-Symphony Orchestra in a performance of the original edition of Paganini's Concerto in D. After that, he toured this country each season, appearing extensively not only in recitals, but also over the radio (more than fifty times with the Telephone Hour) and as soloist with all the major orchestras. He has appeared over sixty times with the Philadelphia Orchestra, and over fifty times with the New York Philharmonic-Symphony.

"His playing," as the New York *Times* reported, "opens new realms of sound." The New York *Herald Tribune* has written: "His perfection, in fact, has become a habit. Virtuosity and musicianship and all the fractional distinctions between the two are his to deal with as he chooses."

Francescatti has followed family tradition by marrying a violinist, Yolande Potel de la Brière, who, however, has sacrificed her own career to devote herself to her husband. When not on tour, the Francescattis occupy a rambling house in the Berkshires which they call "Fiddletop." Francescatti has been honored by his native country by being named Officer of the Legion of Honor.

FRECCIA, MASSIMO, conductor. For his earlier career, see *Living Musicians,* 1940.

* * *

Freccia was the principal conductor of the New Orleans Philharmonic from 1944 to 1952. In 1952 he succeeded Reginald Stewart as principal conductor of the Baltimore Symphony Orchestra.

FREMSTAD, OLIVE, soprano. For her earlier career, see *Living Musicians,* 1940.

* * *

Fremstad died in Irvington-on-the-Hudson, New York, on April 21, 1951.

FRIED, OSKAR, conductor. See *Living Musicians,* 1940.

FRIEDBERG, CARL RUDOLPH HERMAN, pianist. For his earlier career, see *Living Musicians,* 1940.

* * *

In the fall of 1949, Friedberg's former pupils organized the Carl Friedberg Association to provide scholarships to gifted young pianists. Friedberg died in Merano, Italy, on September 9, 1955.

FRIEDMAN, IGNAZ, pianist. For his earlier career, see *Living Musicians,* 1940.

* * *

Friedman settled in Sydney, Australia, in 1940 and died there on January 26, 1948.

FRIJSH, POVLA, soprano. See *Living Musicians,* 1940.

FRISKIN, JAMES, pianist. See *Living Musicians,* 1940.

FUCHS, JOSEPH, violinist, was born in New York City on April 26, 1905. When he was four years old he broke his left arm in a fall. To help strengthen his muscles, he was made to practice the violin by his father, an amateur violinist. In his sixth year, Joseph began formal study with Louis Svcenski, violist of the Kneisel Quartet, and when he was eleven he entered the Institute of Musical Art, where he remained a little over seven years, a pupil of Franz Kneisel. Soon after his graduation from the Institute, Fuchs received the Morris Loeb Memorial Prize, enabling him to travel in Europe. In 1927, though he was only twenty-two, he was appointed concertmaster of the Cleveland Or-

JOSEPH FUCHS

chestra, with which he remained twelve seasons, often appearing as soloist in major concertos.

The arm injury sustained in early childhood began to affect him again, and by 1939 he found he was unable to continue playing the violin. Examined by many physicians and neurologists, Fuchs was discovered to be suffering from a splinter, negligently left in his arm from his childhood injury, which was rubbing a nerve in the elbow. Surgery was required, and for a period after that it seemed that Fuchs' career was over. When strength started returning to his arm, Fuchs began painstakingly to retrain his hand so that its one-time flexibility might return. This proved to be a long, and at times painful, process, but in 1943 he was able to give a recital in Town Hall, New York, which he now considers as his official debut as virtuoso. This performance proved so successful that Fuchs was now able to concertize extensively throughout the United States, both in recitals and as soloist with major orchestras. Beginning with 1954 he made several tours of Europe. On April 6, 1954, he scored such a major success at the Rome International Festival that he was asked to return for two more performances the following month. Reporting from Rome, Virgil Thomson wrote in the New York *Herald Tribune*: "The most remarkable execution for tone, technique, and musical authority has been the playing of Joseph Fuchs. Europe has not heard violin playing of this power and quality for many months."

After additional concerts that year in Italy, Switzerland, Luxembourg, and Paris, Fuchs was heard as soloist at the Casals Festival in Prades, France; of his Prades appearance Casals said: "His performance will always remain for me a memory of great music-making."

In 1956 Fuchs was invited to perform in London the ten sonatas for violin and piano by Beethoven. He was so well received that he was asked to return the following year to London to repeat the series. He has also given all the Beethoven sonatas in Boston, and has recorded them for Decca.

In the summer of 1957 Fuchs toured South America for seven weeks through the International Exchange Program of the American National Theatre and Academy. On these programs he included many works by Americans. He has been an ardent propagandist for contemporary music everywhere, having given either world or American premières of major works by Nikolai Lopatnikoff, Ben Weber, Bohuslav Martinu, and Mario Pergallo, among others.

Fuchs' sister, Lillian, is a concert violist; and their brother, Harry, is a cellist. Joseph Fuchs has often appeared with his sister in joint recitals and in duo-performances with major symphony orchestras.

FURTWÄNGLER, WILHELM, conductor. For his earlier career, see *Living Musicians*, 1940.

* * *

After World War II, attempts were made to bring Furtwängler back to the United States, first as a conductor of the New York Philharmonic-Symphony, then of the Chicago Symphony Orchestra. In both cases, the invitations to Furtwängler were rescinded because of the public clamor against a musician who had been so intimately associated with the Nazi regime. Furtwängler insisted, however, that he had never supported Nazi racial theories, and at his denazification trial, witnesses recalled many acts of courage. In 1947 he was cleared of charges of active collaboration by a four-power commission. Continuing to dominate European musical life, he held the office of music director for both the Berlin Philharmonic and the Berlin State Opera; made memorable appearances at the major European festivals, including Bayreuth, Salzburg, and Lucerne; and was a guest with most of the great European orchestras and opera companies.

In 1954 it was announced that Furtwängler would finally return to the United States as the conductor of the Berlin Philharmonic Orchestra, on its first American tour. His death in Eberstein, Germany, on November 30, 1954, frustrated these plans. When the Berlin Philharmonic visited this country in 1955 it was led by Herbert von Karajan, who subsequently inherited Furtwängler's posts with both the Berlin Philharmonic and the Berlin State Opera.

GALLI-CAMPI, AMRI, soprano. See *Living Musicians,* 1940.

GALLI-CURCI, AMELITA, soprano. For her earlier career, see *Living Musicians,* 1940.

* * *

In 1936 Galli-Curci went into retirement at Rancho Santa Fe in California, where she became a follower of a Hindu mystic, Paramhansa Yogananda.

GANZ, RUDOLPH, pianist. For his earlier career, see *Living Musicians,* 1940.

* * *

Ganz conducted the Young People's Concerts of the New York Philharmonic-Symphony and the San Francisco Symphony until 1949. In 1954 he resigned as president of the Chicago Musical College, having held this post for twenty-one years; since then he has been president emeritus. On the occasion of his eightieth birthday, an old banquet hall in Chicago was converted into a concert auditorium and named the Rudolph Ganz Recital Hall.

GARBOUSOVA, RAYA, cellist. See *Living Musicians,* 1940.

GARDEN, MARY, soprano. For her earlier career, see *Living Musicians,* 1940.

* * *

After World War II, Garden made several lecture tours of the United States. She also collaborated with Louis Biancolli in a bestselling autobiography, *Mary Garden's Story* (1951).

GARDNER, SAMUEL, violinist. See *Living Musicians,* 1940.

GAUBERT, PHILIPPE, flutist and conductor. For his earlier career, see *Living Musicians,* 1940.

* * *

Gaubert died in Paris on July 10, 1941.

GAUTHIER, EVA, contralto. See *Living Musicians,* 1940.

GEORGESCU, GEORGES, conductor. See *Living Musicians,* 1940.

GERHARDT, ELENA, soprano. For her earlier career, see *Living Musicians,* 1940.

* * *

After the rise of the Nazi regime in Germany, Gerhardt settled in London, where she devoted herself to teaching a few selected pupils and to writing her autobiography, *Recital* (1953).

GHIONE, FRANCO, conductor. For his earlier career, see *Living Musicians,* 1940.

* * *

Since 1940 Ghione has been principal conductor of the Italian repertory at the Teatro Colón in Buenos Aires. He has also directed performances at the Municipal Theatre in Rio de Janeiro.

GIANNINI, DUSOLINA, soprano. See *Living Musicians,* 1940.

GIESEKING, WALTER, pianist. For his earlier career, see *Living Musicians,* 1940.

* * *

Gieseking remained in Germany throughout the years of World War II. After the war, he was blacklisted by the American Military Government in Germany, but in 1947 this decision was reversed. He now began playing for American soldiers and gave concerts throughout Europe.

Booked to tour the United States early in 1949, after an eleven-year absence, he was, upon arrival, subjected to an investigation by the Immigration Service and the Department of Justice. Rather than face these developments, he canceled the tour and returned to Europe. For the next four years he played extensively both in Europe and in the Far East. He was finally permitted to return to the United States in 1953, and gave his first American concert since the war on April 22. Olin Downes, reviewing his performance for the New York *Times,* remarked that while there was a deterioration in his physical prowess, this did not condition "the distinction, and beauty of his style, or his gifts as an interpreter and colorist." After this return, Gieseking toured the United States several times.

In December 1955 Gieseking was in a bus accident in Germany in which his wife was killed and he himself suffered a brain concussion. He recovered from this accident and was able to resume his concert appearances. Late in October 1956, while in London for a recording session, he was hospitalized for an emergency operation. He died of a heart attack soon after this operation, on October 26.

GIGLI, BENIAMINO, tenor. For his earlier career, see *Living Musicians*, 1940.

* * *

Gigli's alleged collaboration with the Nazi-Fascist Axis during World War II—charges of which he was later cleared—alienated many of his American admirers. His position as one of the world's leading tenors in the foremost European opera houses, however, remained secure. When Gigli returned to the United States for his first American tour since the war, in the spring of 1955, he was given a magnificent welcome.

GILELS, EMIL, Soviet pianist, was born in Odessa on October 19, 1916. "There were no professional musicians in my family," he told an interviewer. "However, my family was quite musical in an amateur way, performing on the piano, and there was much singing and playing in our home." He was six years old when he started taking piano lessons with Jacob Tkach. At nine he made a first public appearance, and four years after that made a formal debut in Odessa. After seven years with Tkach, he began studying with Bertha Ringold. "Everything I was taught about playing," he has said, "I learned from

Lipnitzki, Paris
EMIL GILELS

Gilels: gē'lĕls

her." In 1931 he entered in the All-Ukrainian Piano Contest but failed to win a single prize.

In 1932 he was enrolled in the Odessa Conservatory. In his first year there he played for Artur Rubinstein, who was in Odessa for a concert appearance. "I remember as if it happened yesterday," Rubinstein told Victor Seroff, who in turn reported the conversation in the *Saturday Review.* "There was a boy—short, with a mass of red hair and freckles, who played. . . . I can't describe it. . . . All I can say is—if he ever comes here I might as well pack my bags and go." Rubinstein suggested to Gilels that he enter the All-Union Musicians Competition for pianists in Moscow. Gilels did so in 1933 and won first prize.

After leaving the Odessa Conservatory in 1935, Gilels went to the Moscow Conservatory, where he studied with Professors Neuhaus and Goldovski. In 1936 he played in an international competition for pianists held in Vienna and captured second prize. But two years later, at the world-famous Ysaÿe Competition in Brussels, he received the first prize among pianists.

He now entered upon an active concert career with performances throughout the Soviet Union. At the same time he first engaged in another activity which since then has been a major preoccupation—teaching. In 1936 he was appointed assistant to Professor Neuhaus at the Moscow Conservatory. He has remained one of the leading teachers of the Conservatory, with a schedule that now includes two classes a week in piano technique and four private pupils.

The Soviet Union planned to send him to the United States in 1939 to play in the Soviet Pavilion at the New York World's Fair. But the outbreak of war in Europe aborted this plan. During the war, Gilels continued his teaching activity while concertizing both at the front line for Soviet soldiers and in occupied cities. In 1946 he received the Stalin Prize of 100,000 rubles for his achievements as a concert artist. Somewhat later he was the recipient of two other high honors: the Order of the Red Banner of Labor, and the Order of the Sign of Honor.

After the war, in 1948, Gilels scored a personal triumph at the Third International Spring Festival in Prague. In his first recital there he played a rather conventional program, but, as Seroff recalls, "before he finished the first part . . . it was obvious that we were in the presence of an extraordinary musical talent with supreme powers at his command."

Despite the lowering of the Iron Curtain, Gilels was permitted by the Soviet government to make appearances outside his own country.

In 1951 he was one of eleven artists sent by his country to the Florence May Music Festival. One year later he toured Scandinavia, and in 1954 he played in the Berlin Embassy during the Berlin Conference of Foreign Ministers. Besides his appearances in Europe, he filled about fifty engagements a year in his native land.

Reports of his phenomenal technique and digital control, and his supreme artistry, reached the United States long before Gilels arrived in this country; these reports were supplemented by recordings in which he revealed himself to be an interpretative artist of first importance. After a decision had been reached at the Geneva Convention of 1955 for an exchange of culture between the Soviet Union and the United States—and through the personal efforts of Yehudi Menuhin with our State Department—Emil Gilels was invited to the United States for a tour. He made his American debut in Philadelphia on December 3, 1955, as soloist with the Philadelphia Orchestra under Ormandy in the Tchaikovsky Concerto in B-flat minor. He was the first Soviet artist to appear in this country since 1921. He created a sensation. Max de Schaunsee wrote in the Philadelphia *Bulletin* that he had "rarely heard playing of such beauty." When Gilels repeated this performance in New York City one day later, Howard Taubman said in the New York *Times*: "He is a virtuoso in the grand line. . . . Mr. Gilels has everything that it takes to be a top-grade pianist. His tone is as solid as his physique with its peasant sturdiness. His fingers have boundless agility and control. He can make the piano sing, and he can cause it to thunder; it bends to his will. Best of all, he is a musician of personality."

After giving a series of concerts throughout the United States and in Mexico, Gilels returned to the Soviet Union early in 1956. But he was back on this continent in March and April for a five-week coast-to-coast tour of Canada.

Gilels, who is one of three pianists to hold the coveted title of People's Artist of the U.S.S.R., married Farizet Khutzyostova in 1947. At the time she was a student at the Moscow Conservatory. They have one child, a daughter, Elyena. Gilels' older sister, Elisaveta, is a distinguished concert violinist, and is married to still another concert violinist, Leonid Kogan, winner of first prize at the Brussels Ysaÿe competition.

GINSTER, RIA, soprano. For her earlier career, see *Living Musicians*, 1940.

* * *

Ginster was appointed head of the vocal department of the Zurich Conservatory, in Switzerland, in 1938. Since then Zurich has been her permanent home.

GLAZ, HERTHA, contralto. For her earlier career, see *Living Musicians*, 1940.

* * *

Glaz made a highly successful debut at the Metropolitan Opera on December 25, 1942, as Amneris in *Aida*. Up to the 1955-1956 season, she appeared there in a varied repertory, enjoying particular success in German operas.

GOBBI, TITO, baritone, was born in Bassano del Grapa, near Venice, on October 24, 1915. His father was a successful business man. As a boy, Tito suffered from an asthmatic condition which led his father to place him under the guidance of a physical-education instructor. Tito developed so well under him that by eighteen he became an excellent athlete himself, particularly adept at skiing, mountain climbing, and cycling. In his boyhood, Gobbi showed so little talent for singing that he was dismissed from the school choir because, as he recalls, "my teacher said I had too loud a voice, and disturbed too much." He was directed to law, which he studied at the University of Padua. In his late teens, one of his friends strongly advised him to begin vocal lessons. From 1933 to 1938 he studied with Giulio Crimi, making such progress that all thoughts of pursuing the practice of law were permanently discarded. In 1938 he won first prize among 330 competitors in an international voice competition in Vienna. In the same year, he made his opera debut at the Adriano Theatre in Rome as the elder Germont in *La Traviata*. His first major success came in Rome in Wolf-Ferrari's *Le Donne Curiose*. Since then, and up to the present time, he has been a principal baritone of the Rome Opera and since 1942 of La Scala as well.

His first appearance outside Italy took place in 1947, when he was invited to appear with the Stockholm Opera. One year later, he made his American debut at the San Francisco Opera. After that, his popularity became as great in cities throughout the rest of Europe as it was in Italy. He scored a triumph at the Salzburg Festival in 1950 when he appeared as *Don Giovanni* under Wilhelm Furtwängler's direction. He has also gathered success after success in such major music centers as

Gobbi: gôb′bē

TITO GOBBI

London, Wiesbaden, Zurich, Barcelona, Lisbon, Los Angeles, and Chicago, and has been highly praised in tours of Egypt, Israel, South America, and South Africa.

Gobbi made his debut at the Metropolitan Opera as Scarpia in *Tosca* on January 13, 1956. Jay Harrison wrote in the *Herald Tribune* that his characterization was "without doubt, hesitation or question, the finest this writer has ever seen." In the New York *Times,* Howard Taubman said: "As an interpreter of Scarpia he is an expert. He understands the cruel police chief with his suave, smiling surface. He plays him for all he is worth, and he is a good enough musician to give point and emphasis to the musical aspects of a powerful role."

Gobbi's repertory includes over ninety baritone roles. His own favorites are Tonio in *Pagliacci;* Scarpia; Michele in *Il Tabarro;* Amonasro in *Aida;* and the title roles in *Simon Boccanegra, Nabucco, Falstaff, Wozzeck,* and *Rigoletto.*

His outstanding acting ability has made him almost as famous in motion pictures as in the opera house. He has been seen in more than twenty-five films (in four languages), including screen versions of *Rigoletto, The Barber of Seville, La Forza del Destino,* and *Pagliacci.*

In 1937 Gobbi was married to Tilde de Rensis, daughter of a musicologist; they have a daughter. They maintain two houses, one in Rome, and a little cottage at a seaside near the city. Gobbi has retained his early interest in sports, and he has an additional interest,

painting, in which he demonstrates considerable talent. When he is in London he shares a studio with Leonard Boden, whose portrait of Gobbi as Scarpia hangs in the London Royal Academy.

GOGORZA, EMILIO EDOARDO DE, baritone. For his earlier career, see *Living Musicians,* 1940.

* * *

De Gogorza resigned as head of the vocal department of the Curtis Institute in Philadelphia in 1940, and died in New York City on May 10, 1949.

GOLDBERG, SIMON, violinist. For his earlier career, see *Living Musicians,* 1940.

* * *

Goldberg was en route to the United States, following a tour of the Orient, when war broke out between Japan and the United States in December 1941. He and his wife became prisoners of the Japanese, and were interned for almost three years. He finally reached the United States in 1947 and resumed his concert activity both in this country and abroad.

GOLDMAN, EDWIN FRANKO, conductor. For his earlier career, see *Living Musicians,* 1940.

* * *

Goldman led his last band concert at the Central Park Mall on August 15, 1955. He died in New York City on February 21, 1956.

GOLDSAND, ROBERT, pianist. See *Living Musicians,* 1940.

GOLDSTEIN, ELLA, pianist, was born in Harbin, Manchuria, on January 30, 1927. Her father was a professional violinist and conductor who had come from his native Russia to settle in China. Her mother was an excellent pianist. When Ella was five years old she began taking piano lessons with her mother, and at nine she made a public appearance. Her success as a prodigy brought her a contract to tour China and Japan, following which she made several highly acclaimed appearances in Palestine.

A period of additional study at the Amsterdam Conservatory in Holland preceded numerous performances throughout Europe, both in recitals and as guest artist with symphony orchestras. When war broke out in Europe Ella Goldstein went to live in Palestine. During the war years she was

ELLA GOLDSTEIN

Golschmann retired as musical director of the St. Louis Symphony Orchestra in the fall of 1955, after his twenty-fifth season with that organization. Subsequently he filled guest engagements with that orchestra and with various symphonic organizations in Europe.

GOMEZ, VICENTE, guitarist. See *Living Musicians,* 1940.

GOOSSENS, EUGENE, conductor. For his earlier career, see *Living Musicians,* 1940.

* * *

Goossens resigned as principal conductor of the Cincinnati Symphony Orchestra in 1946. One year later he settled in Sydney, Australia, where he became conductor of the Sydney Symphony and the New South Wales Conservatory. He resigned from both posts in 1956.

GOOSSENS, LEON, oboist. See *Living Musicians,* 1940.

The GORDON STRING QUARTET. For its earlier history, see *Living Musicians,* 1940.

* * *

The Quartet was disbanded after the death of its founder and first violinist, Jacques Gordon—in Hartford, Connecticut, on September 15, 1948.

GORIN, IGOR, baritone. For his earlier career, see *Living Musicians,* 1940.

* * *

Gorin was awarded the ASCAP Gold Medal for his contributions to American music on June 5, 1957.

GORODNITZKI, SASCHA, pianist. See *Living Musicians,* 1940.

GOULD, GLENN, pianist, was born in Toronto, Canada, on September 25, 1932. His entire musical education took place at the Royal Conservatory of Music (where he studied the piano with Alberto Guerrero). He was graduated in 1950 with the highest honors ever given by that institution. Meanwhile, on January 14, 1947, he made an impressive debut by appearing as soloist with the Toronto Symphony Orchestra, under Sir Ernest MacMillan, in Beethoven's Fourth Piano Concerto.

When Gould made his American debut in Washington, D.C., in January 1955, Paul

heard in concerts in Palestine, throughout the Near East, and in South Africa. "Ella Goldstein," wrote Gershon Swet in the Jerusalem *Haarez,* "has all the qualities of an eminent pianist." During this period she continued her piano study in Palestine with Leo Kestenberg.

Ella Goldstein made her American debut with a recital at Town Hall, New York, early in 1947. She made such a good impression that Serge Koussevitzky invited her to appear that summer at the Berkshire Music Festival, where she was heard in the Tchaikovsky Concerto in B-flat minor on July 29; since this concert was broadcast on a national hookup program, her fame was instantly spread throughout the country. After 1947 Ella Goldstein was often heard in this country and abroad. After one of her appearances in New York, the New York *Times* said of her: "The climax of audience enthusiasm came with the conclusion of Rachmaninoff's Third Piano Concerto, rousingly played by Ella Goldstein. . . . The surging and romantic Rachmaninoff work proved well suited to her gifts."

Ella Goldstein won first prize in the Ferrucio Busoni competition held in Bolzano, Italy, in September 1953.

GOLSCHMANN, VLADIMIR, conductor. For his earlier career, see *Living Musicians,* 1940.

* * *

GLENN GOULD

Hume wrote in the Washington *Post:* "It is unlikely that the year 1955 will bring us a finer piano recital. . . . We know of no pianist anything like him of any age." Though this appearance was followed by an equally impressive concert in New York City, Glenn Gould's fame can be said to have been established through a recording—Bach's *Goldberg Variations,* released by Columbia Records. *Time* magazine described the recording session as follows: "The frail-looking young pianist walked into the recording studio one day last June (1955), wearing beret, coat, muffler and gloves, carrying two large bottles of spring water to drink, five small bottles of pills, and his own piano chair. Before he started to play, he soaked his hands and arms in hot water. Then he began a week's stint. . . . Sometimes he sang as he played, and when he finished a 'take' that particularly pleased him, he jumped up with a gleeful 'Wow!' But when a piano note sagged by a hair, a tuner was called instantly. And when the pianist made the same mistake three times, he announced desperately he must be suffering from a mental block."

"Here, unquestionably, is Something: a young pianist who can take such a seemingly mechanical sequence as the Bach elaborations . . . and make an absorbing, wholly interesting experience of it. . . . Gould not only has all the finger discipline that can be taught, but also the kind of darting finesse that cannot. In other words, along with learning the mechanics of his instrument thoroughly,

Gould has been imbued with a considerable sense of what to do with them." Thus wrote Irving Kolodin in his review of the recording in the *Saturday Review.*

On July 9, 1956, an entire program was given over to Gould at the Second Annual Music Festival in Stratford, Ontario, where he appeared in the triple role of composer, conductor, and pianist. He conducted Schoenberg's *Ode to Napoleon,* played piano works by Alban Berg and Ernst Krenek, and was represented as composer by a new one-movement quartet.

His first extensive tour took place during the 1956-1957 season when he was heard throughout the United States and Canada both in recitals and appearances as guest with leading orchestras. His European debut took place in the spring of 1957 when he made three appearances with the Berlin Philharmonic Orchestra under Karajan. In May he went to the Soviet Union for performances in Moscow and Leningrad, becoming the first North American concert pianist to be invited by that government. Soon after this he performed at the Vienna International Music Festival.

In reviewing Gould's recital in New York on November 16, 1956, a critic for the New York *Herald Tribune* described him as "astounding." He added: "One does not expect such extraordinary control of resources from a comparative youngster, nor such precision and refinement of thinking."

GRAARUD, GUNNAR, tenor. See *Living Musicians,* 1940.

GRADOVA, GITTA. See *Living Musicians,* 1940.

GRAFFMAN, GARY, pianist, was born in New York City in October 1928. His piano study began in his fourth year. Four years later he received a scholarship for the Curtis Institute in Philadelphia, where for ten years he studied piano with Isabelle Vengerova. Even before he was graduated from the Institute in 1946, he began making public appearances.

Recognition, however, first came in 1947, when he was the first winner in the recently organized Rachmaninoff Fund Contest. This entitled him to a recording contract with RCA Victor, a nation-wide tour in recitals, and appearances with major orchestras. As an immediate result of winning this award, Graffman was presented as soloist of the Philadelphia Orchestra under Ormandy in

GARY GRAFFMAN

Rachmaninoff's Second Piano Concerto on March 28, 1947. One day later he appeared with the same orchestra and in the same work in a nation-wide broadcast over the Columbia Broadcasting System. The authority of his musicianship and the spaciousness of his playing won him accolades from the Philadelphia critics.

In 1948 the Rachmaninoff Fund presented Graffman with a Special Award providing him with the opportunity to give his first New York recital, at Carnegie Hall. On this occasion, Olin Downes wrote in the New York *Times:* "This is a young pianist with a true and communicative temperament, an admirably schooled musician, and a virtuoso who can give a representative performance before any audience in the world."

The awards from the Rachmaninoff Fund were not the only ones received by this artist. In 1949 he was presented with the Leventritt Award, enabling him to appear as soloist with the New York Philharmonic-Symphony, the Cleveland Orchestra, and the Buffalo Philharmonic. One year later he received a Fulbright Fellowship, which provided him with the means to study for a year in Europe.

Since then his concert appearances in America and Europe have been extensive. In the spring of 1953 he toured with the Little Orchestra Society of New York, performing five different concertos. He made his debut in England on October 31, 1956, as soloist with the London Philharmonic Orchestra in

Prokofiev's C major Concerto. This appearance was followed by other successful performances in England, Sweden, Spain, Czechoslovakia, and Switzerland. In the same year he also completed a fifteen-concert tour of South America.

GRAINGER, PERCY, pianist. See *Living Musicians,* 1940.

GRANDJANY, MARCEL, harpist. For his earlier career, see *Living Musicians,* 1940.

* * *

In 1956 Grandjany became head of the newly organized harp department at the Manhattan School of Music in New York City.

GRAVEURE, LOUIS, baritone and tenor. For his earlier career, see *Living Musicians,* 1940.

* * *

In the late 1940's the discovery was made through the acquisition of Graveure's birth certificate that his real name was Wilfred Douthitt and that he had been born in London on March 18, 1888—facts which he had until then consistently concealed. As Wilfred Douthitt, he had sung in an operetta, *The Lilac Domino,* produced in New York in 1914. After the close of that production, he disappeared, returning one year later as a concert baritone named Louis Graveure who said he was of Belgian birth.

During the Nazi regime and up to the outbreak of World War II, he lived in Germany. In June 1940 he was on his way to the United States on a French boat when he was evacuated at Bordeaux by the British consul. This gave rise for the first time to the suspicion that he was a British and not a Belgian subject. He remained in England throughout the war. He returned to the United States in June 1947, still refusing to divulge his true identity, which, however, became known and was made public soon afterwards.

The GRILLER STRING QUARTET. See *Living Musicians,* 1940.

GRUMIAUX, ARTHUR, violinist, was born in the village of Villers-Perwin, in Belgium, on March 21, 1921. When his grandfather, an excellent musician, noticed that the boy had perfect pitch, he presented the child with a violin and began teaching him the elements of music. Arthur was five years old at the time. A half year later he appeared in a public concert. When he was

Grumiaux: grü-myō′

ARTHUR GRUMIAUX

After the war, Grumiaux resumed his career. He now toured Europe extensively, and was praised for the sensitivity and refinement of his playing as well as for his penetrating musicianship. He appeared with outstanding success in Great Britain, Scandinavia, Italy, France, Spain, and Switzerland, playing with virtually all the major European orchestras under their principal conductors. He was also heard at such outstanding music festivals as those in Prague, Strasbourg, and Aix-en-Provence.

His American debut took place at the Peabody Conservatory in Baltimore, on January 18, 1952. Reporting his performance for the Baltimore *News-Post*, Helen Penniman described "the magnificent texture of his tone . . . like the latent shades in changeable silk," and his "admirable solo work, aside from the spirited sentiment of the interpretation." On February 1, he appeared with the Boston Symphony under Ernest Ansermet, playing a Mozart concerto. Cyrus Durgin wrote in the Boston *Globe* that his playing was "sheer beauty in rhythm and phrasing, sweet and rich of tone, and absolutely perfect as to style." A comprehensive tour of America followed with recitals in principal cities and thirteen performances with major orchestras. A second tour in 1952-1953 was even more extensive, and included performances with seven major orchestras.

His wife, the former Amanda Webb, is also a violinist; they live in a secluded part of Brussels. Grumiaux's diversions include reading books on history, cooking, playing chamber music, and amateur photography.

eleven he was graduated from the Conservatory of Charleroi. He subsequently attended the Brussels Conservatory, where he studied the violin with Alfred Dubois. He studied privately with Jean Absil (counterpoint and fugue), and with Georges Enesco (violin) in Paris. While pursuing these musical studies he received numerous awards pointing to his remarkable talent, among these being the Prix Vieuxtemps and that of the Belgian National Competition. He also pursued academic study at the Episcopal College, majoring in literature, languages, and history.

His first appearance as a mature artist took place just before World War II when he performed Vieuxtemps's Fifth Violin Concerto over the radio. Alphonse Onnou, a member of the celebrated Pro Arte Quartet, heard that broadcast and used his influence to get the Brussels Philharmonic to engage him as soloist. With Charles Munch conducting, Grumiaux performed the Mendelssohn Concerto, for which he was acclaimed. This was, however, his last public appearance in several years. During the difficult years between 1940 and 1945 when Belgium was occupied by the Nazis, Grumiaux played the violin in a string quartet and taught music at the Brussels Conservatory. The Nazis offered him the post of concertmaster with the Dresden Philharmonic, but he refused to accept it and went into hiding. When Belgium was liberated he played for the Allied troops at the front, then toured the United Kingdom, performing for war workers.

GUARRERA, FRANK, baritone, was born in Philadelphia. "I have always loved music," he says, "but became especially interested in singing when I was twelve years old and joined a church choir." In his seventeenth year, while attending high school, he applied for a scholarship to the Curtis Institute of Music. He won it, becoming the youngest member to be admitted to the vocal department. At the Curtis Institute he studied with Richard Bonelli and Mme. Euphemie Giannini-Gregory. At the same time he completed his high school education at night.

His studies were interrupted in 1943 when he joined the Navy. But after two and a half years of service, he returned to the Curtis Institute to complete his music studies. While still attending the Institute, he appeared in *Idomeneo* at the Berkshire Music Festival in Tanglewood, and made his debut with the New York City Opera Company on

October 25, 1947, as Silvio in *Pagliacci*. He also competed in the Metropolitan Auditions of the Air. In the preliminaries he sang Ford's monologue from *Falstaff*, a broadcast heard by Toscanini, who was greatly impressed. Guarrera tells the rest of the story: "Mr. Pelletier called me to the studio and asked me if I would be willing to study part of a new role, then come back in two weeks and sing for 'somebody' who might use me. He gave me a role in an opera I had never heard, Boïto's *Nerone*. Two weeks later when I came back, Mr. Pelletier said, 'Now we'll take a cab over to NBC and you will sing for Toscanini.' This was the first time I had any idea who the 'somebody' was. It's lucky I hadn't known it for two weeks, or I might have been too nervous. As it was, I didn't have much time to get frightened. When the Maestro heard me, he was very kind. He asked if I'd be willing to learn the rest of the role and go to Milan with him in the summer to sing at La Scala for the Boïto festival at which he was conducting."

In May 1948 Guarrera received first place in the Metropolitan Auditions of the Air. A few days later he was graduated from the Curtis Institute, and just one day after this graduation he flew to Milan to appear with Toscanini. "Intensive rehearsals began at once," Guarrera recalls. "Two days later I lost my voice completely! You can imagine how terrible I felt. I was sent to the local doctor who gave me several kinds of different pills. Then, Herva Nelli, whom Toscanini was also presenting at the Festival, discovered an American doctor for me. He told me to go to bed for twenty-four hours and get some rest. This worked. I got up the next day, and came through all right. I have never seen such a brilliant affair as the opening night at La Scala. When Maestro Toscanini appeared on the podium there was thunderous applause that lasted for ten minutes."

Guarrera's success was so great that he was urged by the management to stay on and sing some more roles at La Scala. The following fall, on December 14, 1948, he made his debut at the Metropolitan Opera as Escamillo in *Carmen*. He has since then appeared at the Metropolitan Opera in about twenty major baritone roles, and has been acclaimed particularly for his interpretations of Figaro in *The Barber of Seville*, Count Almaviva in *The Marriage of Figaro*, Count di Luna in *Il Trovatore*, Escamillo in *Carmen*, and the title role in *Rigoletto*. He has also been heard frequently over television. "Guarrera is out-

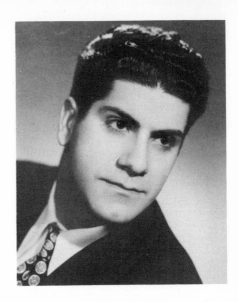

FRANK GUARRERA

standing," wrote Olin Downes in the New York *Times* in July 1953. "Superb in every way—gallant, romantic, proud of bearing, singularly successful."

In 1944 Guarrera married Adeline di Cintio, a childhood friend; they have a daughter, Valerie. Guarrera's diversions include tennis and fishing.

GUEDEN, HILDE, soprano, was born in Vienna on September 15, 1923. She is of Austrian, Italian, and Hungarian ancestry. Her grandfather had been a noted tragedian; her mother, a professional actress; her father, a member of a well-known Italian-Austrian banking family. Her musical education began at the piano when she was seven, and when she was fourteen she began to study voice. In her sixteenth year, she attracted the attention of the Viennese operetta composer Robert Stolz, who gave her a part in his play, *Goodbye, Goodbye*. Though she became an immediate favorite in Vienna, she had no intention of devoting herself to operettas. During the run of the Stolz play she studied dramatics at the Max Reinhardt School and ballet with the prima ballerina of the Vienna State Opera.

After *Goodbye, Goodbye*, she was starred in another operetta, *Hearts of Stone*, her last appearance on the Viennese popular stage before World War II. When the Nazis took over Austria, she escaped to Switzerland. There she sang for Robert Denzler, director of the Zurich Opera, who engaged her im-

Gueden: gü'dĕn

HILDE GUEDEN

mediately. She made her grand-opera debut in Zurich in 1939 as Cherubino in *The Marriage of Figaro.* She stayed two years with the Zurich Opera, appearing in many coloratura and lyric roles.

In 1941 she was compelled to return to Austria to straighten out some family difficulties. Now unable to leave Austria or Nazi Germany, she went on to Munich, where she appeared successfully as Zerlina in *Don Giovanni,* Clemens Krauss conducting. While appearing in *Così Fan Tutte,* she was heard by Richard Strauss, who visited her in her dressing room after the performance to persuade her to study the role of Sophie in his opera, *Der Rosenkavalier.* In December 1942 she made her Italian debut at the Royal Opera in Rome in that very role. Unwilling to sing any longer under Nazi auspices, she stayed on in Italy. But when Italy was occupied by the Nazis, she retired temporarily from opera, and went into seclusion, first in Venice, then in a small town near Milan.

After the war she was invited to the Salzburg Festival, where, in 1946, she scored a major success in *Don Giovanni.* She has been heard there frequently since that time. In 1947 she joined the companies of the Vienna State Opera and La Scala as leading soprano, dividing her season between them. In 1950 she received the honorary appointment of Kammersängerin of the Vienna State Opera, the youngest singer thus honored. Meanwhile, she was acclaimed in Holland, London, Paris,

Nice, Brussels, Glyndebourne, and at the Edinburgh Festival.

She made her American debut at the Metropolitan Opera on November 15, 1951, as Gilda in *Rigoletto.* She was so well received by both audience and critics that she was retained as a principal soprano of the company from then on. While her specialty is Mozart, she has also been heard in the French and Italian repertory, and has appeared in such important modern operas as Kurt Weill's *Mahagonny,* Blacher's *Romeo and Juliet* (in which she created the part of Juliet), Britten's *The Rape of Lucretia,* Stravinsky's *The Rake's Progress* (creating the principal soprano role for the American première), and Hindemith's *Mathis der Maler.* She has also performed frequently in recitals and over radio and television. In June and July 1957 she made her first appearances in South America, scoring major successes at the Teatro Colón in Buenos Aires as Gilda in *Rigoletto* and in the leading role in *L'Elisir d'Amore.*

GUI, VITTORIO, conductor. For his earlier career, see *Living Musicians,* 1940.

* * *

In 1938, Gui became principal conductor at Covent Garden. Upon the death of Fritz Busch in 1951, Gui succeeded him as musical director of the Glyndebourne Opera Company, with which organization he had for several years been giving brilliant performances.

GUILBERT, YVETTE, diseuse and cantatrice. For her earlier career, see *Living Musicians,* 1940.

* * *

Guilbert died in Aix-en-Provence, France, on February 2, 1944.

GULDA, FRIEDRICH, pianist, was born in Vienna on May 16, 1930. His father was the principal of a Vienna high school who, when the Nazis came to power in Austria, went into retirement because of his pronounced anti-Nazi views. In his seventh year, Friedrich began studying the piano with Professor F. Pazofsky, and from his twelfth to his seventeenth years he studied with B. Seidlhofer at the Vienna State Academy of Music. He was only sixteen when he entered the International Competition of Music held at Geneva, winning first prize among seventy-eight pianists. This was followed by his first public appearance which was so successful

Gulda: gōōl′dȧ

FRIEDRICH GULDA

stature had entered the field of jazz professionally. Commenting on his performance, John S. Wilson wrote in the New York *Times:* "The only obvious carry-over from his classical training is his easy command of his instrument. There are none of the 'long hair' derivations that some jazz pianists work into their performances with apparent pride. . . . When he plays jazz, he concentrates on jazz. His playing is evidence that he believes jazz is worthy of his best abilities. . . . And his playing is also evidence that he is one of the very few classically trained musicians who is both aware of that essential characteristic of a jazz performance, phrasing, and capable of using it effectively."

As if to point up the dichotomy of Gulda's career, in the summer of 1956 Gulda appeared as a jazz performer at the Newport Jazz Festival, in Rhode Island, and performed the complete cycle of Beethoven's sonatas in Milan, Italy.

Gulda is married to an Italian actress whom he met while he was touring Argentina. They have a son who was born on the 200th anniversary of Mozart's birth and who was, consequently, named David Wolfgang.

GURNEY, JOHN, basso. See *Living Musicians,* 1940.

HACKETT, CHARLES, tenor. For his earlier career, see *Living Musicians,* 1940.

* * *

Hackett died in New York City on January 1, 1942.

HALE, RICHARD, baritone. See *Living Musicians,* 1940.

HALSTEAD, MARGARET, dramatic soprano. See *Living Musicians,* 1940.

HAMBOURG, MARK, pianist. See *Living Musicians,* 1940.

HANNIKAINEN, TAUNO, conductor, was born in Jyväskaylä, south Finland, on February 26, 1896. He came from a family of musicians. His father was a violinist and composer who founded the first music journal in the Finnish language; his mother was a singer and teacher; three of his brothers became professional musicians.

Tauno attended the Lyceum in his native city until he was eighteen, and from 1914 to 1917 he specialized in the cello, organ, and piano at the Sibelius Academy. His studies

that he was invited by Ernest Ansermet to perform the Beethoven Fourth Piano Concerto with the Orchestre de la Suisse Romande. Recitals in major European cities followed, culminating with appearances at the Prague Music Festival in 1947 and the Festival of Vienna in 1948. Since then he has been heard in all the major music centers of Europe, acclaimed particularly for his penetrating interpretations of Beethoven's piano literature. He also made extensive recordings which first made him known to the American public.

He came to the United States for the first time in 1950, making his American debut at Carnegie Hall in January of that year. "I have no hesitation in saying," wrote Louis Biancolli in the New York *World-Telegram and Sun,* "that young Gulda's appearance was the most sensational keyboard debut since that of Vladimir Horowitz." A tour of the country followed.

During his first visit to New York, Gulda, a jazz enthusiast, paid a visit to Birdland, the night club where Duke Ellington was performing. "It was a terrific experience," he confessed. From then on, he was fired with the ambition to perform jazz music professionally. His ambition was realized six and a half years later, on June 21, 1956, when he started a two-week engagement at Birdland, leading a sextet of jazz musicians in programs made up of jazz, some of it of his own composition. This is believed to have been the first time that an artist of Gulda's

Hannikainen: hä′nē-kī-nĕn

Courtesy of Musical Courier

TAUNO HANNIKAINEN

were interrupted when Finland became involved in war and revolution. In this struggle, Hannikainen was so active that he subsequently received the Civil War medal.

After the war, Hannikainen joined two of his brothers in forming a trio which gave concerts in Finland and on the Continent. After a period of playing the cello in the Helsinki Orchestra, Hannikainen was appointed assistant conductor of the Finnish State Opera in Helsinki, and in 1922 was elevated to the post of principal conductor. During this period he continued his study of music: cello with André Hekking and Pablo Casals in Paris, composition in Berlin and Vienna.

In 1927 he was appointed conductor of the Abö Symphony Orchestra, and from 1929 to 1940 served as principal conductor of the Turku Symphony. While holding the latter post he appeared as guest conductor throughout Scandinavia and in many other European cities.

In 1938 he was invited by the Finnish government to conduct a special concert in the United States commemorating the 300th anniversary of the settling of Delaware by the Finns. It was on this occasion that he made his American debut, on June 30. Two years later he returned to this country on an invitation by Serge Koussevitzky to conduct five concerts of the Boston Symphony. He was so well received that he was asked to lead concerts at the Robin Hood Dell in Phila-

delphia and several performances of the Detroit Symphony.

In 1942 Hannikainen was appointed permanent conductor of the Duluth Symphony Orchestra. He remained there five years. During the war period he made frequent appearances raising money for Finnish, Norwegian, and British war relief. He was also heard as guest conductor of several major American symphony orchestras. Between 1947 and 1950 he conducted the Chicago Civic Orchestra and in 1948 he was appointed assistant conductor of the Chicago Symphony. In 1951, his appointment as principal conductor of the Helsinki Symphony Orchestra (originally made in 1941) was renewed; his all-Sibelius concerts and festivals with this organization attracted world attention.

The New York *Times,* discussing his conducting, has spoken of his "complete poise and control, the balancing of all elements, power held long in reserve for shattering climaxes, and reigning over all, a sovereign nobility."

In 1953 Hannikainen was honored with the decoration of Commander of the Order of the Finnish Lion. His wife, Anne Arvica Niskanen, is an opera soprano whom he married in 1933. Their adopted son, Eero, is a chemical engineer who makes his home in Whittier, California.

HANSON, HOWARD, conductor. For his earlier career, see *Living Musicians,* 1940.

* * *

On May 12, 1945, Hanson received the Ditson Award for his services to American music; and in April 1946 he was awarded the George Foster Peabody Award.

HARRELL, MACK, baritone, was born in Celeste, Texas, on October 8, 1909. As a boy he suffered an attack of paralysis, from which he recovered but which prevented him from engaging in sports. Music proved a substitute. Hearing some recordings of Fritz Kreisler fired him with the ambition to become a concert violinist. In his twelfth year he started the study of the violin, and one year later made a few local appearances. He also became interested in singing. "My vocal career," he recalls, "began at the age of eight when I invented the Mack Harrell method of singing. Galli-Curci, Caruso, Gigli, and John McCormack were my teachers—and what other singer could make that boast? I played their records over and over again on our old phonograph. I must have sounded

Harrell: hăr'ĕl

MACK HARRELL

Colomb and *Les Choëphores*, and Ravel's *L'Heure Espagnole*.

During the next three years he made numerous concert appearances and in' 1937 toured Europe for the first time. After his return from abroad he made important guest appearances with the Boston Symphony under Koussevitzky and the Philadelphia Orchestra under Ormandy; gave a concert at the White House; and made a successful New York debut at Town Hall in October 1938.

Early in 1939, Harrell won the Metropolitan Auditions of the Air. His Metropolitan Opera debut took place on December 16, 1939, when he appeared as Biterolf in *Tannhäuser*. Since then he has been seen at the Metropolitan in principal baritone roles in the French, Italian and German repertories. He has also been heard with the San Francisco Opera, and at leading American and European festivals.

His wife still appears occasionally on the concert stage as a violinist, sometimes in joint recitals with her husband. They live in an old Dutch house in Larchmont, New York, with their three children. Harrell's diversions include cooking, and playing the violin in chamber-music performances.

pretty funny because I knew no foreign languages, yet I tried to sing arias in French, German, and Italian, reproducing the sounds phonetically."

He continued his music study at the University of Oklahoma where, during three years of undergraduate life, he supported himself by playing the violin in theatre orchestras. He left the University when he won a scholarship to study violin with Emanuel Zetlin at the Music Settlement in Philadelphia. One day he sang a small solo part at a glee-club concert. After the performance, a young lady approached him, introduced herself as Marjorie Fulton, a violin student, and told him he had "a voice in a million." Marjorie Fulton, with whom Harrell soon fell in love, and later married, induced him to give up the violin for singing. Harrell now studied voice with Robert Lawrence Weer in Philadelphia, and three years later with Mme. Schoen-René at the Juilliard School of Music.

Harrell made his first important public appearance in 1935 as soloist with the New York Philharmonic-Symphony, in a concert performance of Rimsky-Korsakov's *Snow Maiden*. This inaugurated a long and fruitful association; since that time Harrell has appeared more often with the New York Philharmonic than any other featured singer. He has been heard in such notable events as the concert performances of Berg's *Wozzeck*, Monteverdi's *Orfeo*, Milhaud's *Christophe*

HARRISON, GUY FRASER, conductor. For his earlier career, see *Living Musicians*, 1940.

* * *

Harrison became principal conductor of the Oklahoma Symphony Orchestra in 1951, and four years later its musical director.

HARSHAW, MARGARET, dramatic soprano, was born in Philadelphia of Scottish-Irish parentage. Her vocal studies were begun in her native city where, while attending high school, she won the Eisteddfod singing contest sponsored by the city. After leaving school she made a few concert and opera appearances with minor companies while supporting herself by working for the telephone company. The winning of the first prize at the Biennial Auditions of the National Federation of Music Clubs, in 1935, was a turning point. "The auditions came at a decisive time in my life," she reveals, "really a crossroad in my career. I was bored and discouraged with the repetition of my daily working routine. The contest I felt would force me to a decision, either to admit that I was beating my head against the musical wall, and that it was worth it, or else that

MARGARET HARSHAW

I should forget the whole idea of a professional career."

Her prize money enabled her to give up some of her outside work and concentrate on music study and concert work. She made some notable appearances in 1935 and 1936, including one at the Robin Hood Dell in a performance of Manuel de Falla's *El Amor Brujo,* and several others with the Rochester Philharmonic and the Lewisohn Stadium Orchestra in New York., This last appearance led, in 1936, to a scholarship for the Juilliard School of Music, where for the next few years she studied voice with Mme. Schoen-René.

By 1942 she was so completely discouraged by her inability to make any headway as a singer that she decided to give up all thoughts of a professional career. Having in the meantime been married to Oskar Eichna and become the mother of two children, she now decided to devote herself to her family. Just then she received a call from Wilfred Pelletier to appear at the Metropolitan Auditions of the Air. She won first prize, and received a contract for the Metropolitan Opera.

When she made her Metropolitan Opera debut, on November 25, 1942, it was as a contralto—in the role of the Second Norn in *Götterdämmerung.* For the next nine years she continued singing contralto roles at the Metropolitan, her best being Amneris in *Aida,* Azucena in *Il Trovatore,* La Cieca in *La Gioconda,* and Erda, Waltraute, Ortrud, Venus, Fricka, and Brangäne in the Wagner

repertory. In 1948 she appeared successfully at the Paris Opéra as Dalila in *Samson et Dalila,* Brangäne in *Tristan und Isolde,* and Amneris.

By 1950 Harshaw was convinced that she was ready to assume dramatic soprano roles. She made her first appearance in the new voice on November 22, 1950, when she was seen as Senta in *The Flying Dutchman.* Since that time she has sung all the leading dramatic soprano roles in the Wagner repertory, and has been acclaimed as one of the most important Wagnerian sopranos to appear since Flagstad and Traubel departed from the opera stage. "It now seems evident," wrote Olin Downes in the New York *Times,* after hearing her as Brünnhilde in *Die Walküre,* "that the greater the Wagnerian role the more remarkable Miss Harshaw proves to be in it. . . . Her vocal range is unconditionally that of the dramatic soprano and her high B's came clear and true. But that is a detail. What was wonderful was the tenderness, the depth and subtlety of her scene with Wotan and the sweeping drama of the ensuing passage with Siegmund. We speak comparing her performances with those, for instance, of the Flagstads and the Traubels of the past. In neither of these interpretations was there such a wealth of feeling and significance of statement, such dramatic communication, coupled on occasion, with intimacy and depth of feeling."

Harshaw has also been acclaimed in Europe. When, in October 1953, she was invited by Covent Garden to open the season, she became the first American singer to do so in a stellar role. For several seasons after that she returned to Covent Garden to sing each year the three Brünnhilde roles in two complete *Ring* cycle performances. In July 1954 she sang Donna Anna ten times in *Don Giovanni* at the Glyndebourne Festival. And in September 1954 she sang the three Brünnhilde roles in the *Ring* cycle presented by the Berlin Stadtische Oper in West Germany. Her appearances as soloist with the major orchestras of the world, and at American music festivals, have been extensive.

The HART HOUSE QUARTET. For its earlier career, see *Living Musicians,* 1940.

* * *

Boris Hambourg, cellist of the Quartet, died in Toronto, Canada, on November 24, 1955.

HARTMANN, CARL, tenor. See *Living Musicians,* 1940.

HARTY, SIR HAMILTON, conductor. for his earlier career, see *Living Musicians,* 1940.

* * *

Harty died in Hove, Ireland, on February 19, 1941.

HASSELMANS, LOUIS, conductor. See *Living Musicians,* 1940.

HAWKINS, OSIE, baritone, was born in Phoenix City, Alabama, on August 16, 1913. Both parents were musical—his father ran a music store in nearby Columbus, Georgia— and encouraged him in his musical inclinations. While he attended public school in Phoenix City, Osie sang as a boy soprano in the choir of the First Presbyterian Church in Columbus. After his voice changed to a baritone, he continued singing at the church and with the high school glee club.

After graduation from high school, Hawkins worked as a salesman for a men's clothing store in Columbus. Between 1932 and 1941, while still working as a salesman, he served as the cantor of Temple B'nai Israel, and once a week went to Atlanta to study voice with Margaret Hecht.

When the Metropolitan Opera visited Atlanta, Margaret Hecht arranged for Hawkins to audition for two of her friends, Frank St. Leger and Erich Leinsdorf, respectively coach and conductor of the Metropolitan Opera. Both were sufficiently impressed by Hawkins to arrange for him to get a Metropolitan Opera scholarship, the first this organization had ever given. Now able to give up his job, Hawkins concentrated on music study and made several appearances in concerts and oratorio performances throughout the southeastern states.

Hawkins made his debut at the Metropolitan Opera House on January 22, 1942, in the role of Donner in *Das Rheingold.* He continued to appear in minor roles for the rest of the season. But when the Metropolitan Opera went on tour that spring, Hawkins was twice called upon to substitute for Herbert Janssen, once as Kurvenal in *Tristan und Isolde,* the second time as Wotan in *Die Walküre.* Though on each occasion he had to appear without rehearsals, he gave impressive performances.

The following season he sang twenty-one roles and two seasons later he appeared in forty different parts. His specialty was the Wagnerian repertory, in which he was now assuming major baritone roles, but he was also heard successfully in Italian and French

OSIE HAWKINS

operas. He combined a commanding stage presence and notable histrionic abilities with a voice and musicianship that have earned the respect of leading critics. He has since then been a principal member of the Metropolitan Opera company—making on the average of about fifty appearances a season. He has also appeared with other opera companies and has been heard in concerts and on the radio.

HAYES, ROLAND, tenor. See *Living Musicians,* 1940.

HAYWARD, THOMAS, tenor, was born in Kansas City, Missouri. He is descended from a long line of American ancestors dating back to the Revolutionary War. Though his mother was a successful teacher of singing— and though he himself appeared as boy contralto in radio broadcasts when he was only nine—a musical career was not considered for him for a long time. At first he thought of being a doctor, and began studies preparing him for medical school. When he abandoned medicine, he changed to business school, hoping to engage in commerce. But in his seventeenth year he appeared in an amateur musical production in his native city. His success made him consider for the first time the possibility of becoming a professional singer, particularly when a local radio station offered him a four-year contract. He now began his study of voice with Edna Forsythe. While pursuing his musical education, he sang over

THOMAS HAYWARD

the radio, on the concert stage, and with the Kansas City Civic Opera Company.

During World War II he was employed in a Missouri war plant, where for nine months he helped manufacture machine-gun bullets. Ill health finally compelled him to abandon this work. After recuperating he returned to professional singing. One day, Jeanette MacDonald heard him sing and urged him to go to New York City for more vocal study. He arrived in New York on September 1, 1943, and at once began to study with Frank La Forge. One year later, on November 10, 1944, he made a successful New York appearance in a joint recital with the violinist Mishel Piastro. In the same year he entered the Metropolitan Auditions of the Air, but failed to win. But he did succeed in joining the New York City Opera Company, with which he appeared during the next year in leading tenor roles in *Cavalleria Rusticana, Manon Lescaut,* and *The Gypsy Baron.*

In 1945 he once again entered the Metropolitan Auditions of the Air, this time winning first prize. As a result he was able to make his debut at the Metropolitan Opera—on December 4, 1945, as Tybalt in *Romeo and Juliet.* He was well received. He has since that time been a permanent member of the company, appearing in leading tenor roles in French and Italian repertory. He has also appeared extensively throughout the country in performances of operettas and in concerts; he has sung on important radio programs, including the Cities Service Program, the Bell

Telephone Hour, the Chicago Theatre of the Air, and the "Serenade to America" program; and he has been a guest artist with major opera companies.

He lives in New York City with his wife and son, Thomas Hayward, Jr. His pastimes include fencing, boxing, fishing, collecting recordings of famous opera stars, and going to the movies. One of his most precious possessions is a ring once worn by Caruso.

HEIFETZ, JASCHA, violinist. See *Living Musicians,* 1940.

HEKKING, GERARD, cellist. For his earlier career, see *Living Musicians,* 1940.

* * *

Hekking died in Paris on June 5, 1942.

HEMPEL, FRIEDA, soprano. For her earlier career, see *Living Musicians,* 1940.

* * *

Hempel gave her last recital at Town Hall, New York, on November 7, 1951. Four years later, on October 7, 1955, she died in Berlin.

HENDERS, HARRIET, soprano. See *Living Musicians,* 1940.

HENDL, WALTER, conductor, was born in West New York, New Jersey, on January 12, 1917. His first musical experiences came when he was about sixteen and some of his musical friends started taking him to concerts. Though until then he had been primarily interested in chemistry, these initial musical contacts—particularly a recital by Josef Hofmann—made such a deep impression on him that he began studying the piano. In 1933 he became a pupil of Clarence Adler. Two years later he won the New Jersey State Music Contest sponsored by the Griffith Foundation, and one year after that received a scholarship for the Curtis Institute for piano study with David Saperton. In 1939 he was also the recipient of a conducting fellowship with Fritz Reiner; it was a Beethoven concert conducted by Reiner at the Lewisohn Stadium that first fired Hendl with the ambition of becoming a conductor.

From 1939 to 1941 Hendl taught music at Sarah Lawrence College in Bronxville, New York. In 1941 and again in 1942 he received scholarships for the study of conducting with Serge Koussevitzky at Tanglewood in Lenox, Massachusetts.

The war interrupted his music study. In the autumn of 1942 he served in the Army Air

Force Ferry Command. In line of duty he incurred a back injury which sent him to various army hospitals for seven months. For a while, convinced that this injury would keep him permanently from a professional musical career, he was greatly discouraged. To cheer him up, a Red Cross nurse told him of a small group which was producing a new play for Broadway and suggested to Hendl that he write music for it. Hendl followed this suggestion. The play, *Dark of the Moon,* opened on Broadway with Hendl's music.

Shortly after his return to civilian life, Hendl was invited by Fritz Reiner to be guest soloist with the CBS Symphony Orchestra. Soon after this Hendl appeared both as piano soloist and as guest conductor of Fritz Reiner's orchestra, the Pittsburgh Symphony. In the summer of 1945 he also appeared as guest conductor of the Boston Pops Orchestra.

In 1945 Hendl heard that there was an opening for an assistant conductor to Artur Rodzinski with the New York Philharmonic-Symphony. He wrote a letter to Rodzinski applying for the job and detailing his qualifications, and he was engaged; this was probably the only instance in which such an important musical post was filled through an application sent by the mails. Two weeks after he was appointed, Hendl was suddenly called upon to substitute for Rodzinski, then ailing. His Philharmonic debut in December was acclaimed. A few weeks after that he appeared again with the New York Philharmonic, this time as a piano soloist in the Gershwin Piano Concerto, substituting for the indisposed Oscar Levant.

Hendl remained a conductor with the New York Philharmonic-Symphony through the 1947-1948 season. In 1949 he was appointed musical director of the Dallas Symphony. His first two concerts with that organization were so successful that he was immediately signed to a three-year contract. He has since then held this post with great distinction.

In the summer of 1950 Hendl was sent to South America on a cultural mission for Braniff International Airways, conducting numerous concerts and making a first-hand survey of South American music. In the summer of 1951 Hendl, sponsored by the Alice M. Ditson Fund, went to Europe to make records for the American Recording Society. Two years later he received the Alice M. Ditson Award of Columbia University for "distinguished services to American music."

Besides conducting his own orchestra in Dallas, Hendl has appeared in guest per-

WALTER HENDL

formances in Europe and the Philippines. In the summer of 1953 he was appointed musical director of the Chautauqua (New York) Symphony Orchestra; his concerts broke all attendance records in the then eight-year history of this organization. Hendl's posts in both Chautauqua and Dallas make him the only conductor in America to be head of two major symphony orchestras. In 1955 Hendl was one of the conductors of the Symphony of the Air (formerly the NBC Symphony) during its tour of the Orient.

HENRIOT, NICOLE, pianist, was born in Paris. She was seven years old when she entered the Paris Conservatory, and fifteen when she made an impressive debut as soloist with the Pasdeloup Orchestra in Paris. Engagements in Paris and Brussels, both in recitals and as soloist with major orchestras, put her in the vanguard of younger French performing artists when World War II broke out. During the war she engaged in the activities of the French Underground. The Gestapo raided her home the morning after D-day, and she still bears the scars from the beating inflicted upon her at the time. But, before the Nazis arrived, she had succeeded in destroying all the secret papers hidden by her brother, an active member of the Resistance. For her services during the war period she was subsequently decorated with the Badge of the Commandos of Africa, an honor received by few civilians.

Henriot: än-ryō′

NICOLE HENRIOT

After the war she returned to the concert stage. She was the first French pianist to appear in England after the cessation of hostilities. An extensive tour followed, covering Holland, Belgium, Portugal, Czechoslovakia, Austria, Switzerland, Scandinavia, Egypt, Algeria, Israel, and Turkey. She made her American debut on January 29, 1948, when she appeared as soloist with the New York Philharmonic-Symphony under Charles Munch in Schumann's Concerto in A minor. Virgil Thomson, writing in the New York *Herald Tribune,* was impressed by both her "technical authority" and "musical thought, which is of a depth and freshness to which we are little accustomed these days." When she appeared for the first time with the Boston Symphony in Boston, on February 25, 1949, in the Liszt Concerto in E-flat, Rudolph Elie of the Boston *Herald* described the event as "the most triumphant debut a young pianist had ever in my experience achieved in Symphony Hall."

Since 1949 Henriot has toured the United States several times, performing both in recitals and as guest of major orchestras. When the Boston Symphony under Munch presented a French program in Washington, D.C., on March 31, 1951, in which she performed Ravel's Concerto in G major, the audience included both President Eisenhower and President Auriol of France. "The twenty-five-year-old blond . . . really stole the show," reported James G. Deane in the Washington *Sunday Star.* She received such

an ovation that she had to repeat the last movement. In 1952 she was heard for the first time at the Berkshire Music Festival at Tanglewood and over the American radio networks.

She has performed extensively throughout the world of music. In 1955, besides appearing in the United States, she performed the European première of Prokofiev's Second Piano Concerto and was acclaimed in Istanbul and at the International Festival in Prague.

HERTZ, ALFRED, conductor. For his earlier career, see *Living Musicians,* 1940.

* * *

Hertz died in San Francisco on April 17, 1942.

HESS, DAME MYRA, pianist. For her earlier career, see *Living Musicians,* 1940.

* * *

In 1941, Hess was made Dame Commander of the Order of the British Cross by George VI of England for her services to her country. By the time the war ended, she had arranged 1,698 concerts in England—concerts in which over a thousand artists had participated and which had been attended by over ten million music lovers. On October 12, 1946, she made a triumphant return to the American concert stage—at Town Tall, New York—after an absence of seven and a half years.

HILSBERG, ALEXANDER, violinist and conductor, was born Alexander Hillersberg in Warsaw, Poland (then Russia), on April 24, 1900. He was a child prodigy, giving violin recitals when he was only nine. His first extensive musical training came from Leopold Auer at the St. Petersburg Conservatory, which he entered in his tenth year; there he was a fellow student of Jascha Heifetz, who has since then been one of his closest friends. Hilsberg remained at the Conservatory until the first outbreak of Revolution in 1917. In the fall of that year he went to Tomsk, western Siberia, where for a year he taught violin at the Conservatory. Then, discouraged by the regimentation of the new regime, Hilsberg left Russia for China to settle in Harbin, Manchukuo. There, for four years, he played in a string quartet, on one occasion performing for the President of the Chinese Republic in Peking.

In 1923 Heifetz—then on a world tour—went to China for a concert and persuaded

C. Bennette Moore

ALEXANDER HILSBERG

Hilsberg to emigrate to America. Hilsberg arrived in the United States in late fall of that year and began concertizing. In 1926 a twenty-year association with the Philadelphia Orchestra was launched: first as violinist; then, beginning in 1931, as concertmaster; and from 1945 on as associate conductor. During this period Hilsberg joined the faculty of the Curtis Institute, and in 1947 he became head of the orchestra department and conductor of the Curtis Symphony.

His debut as conductor took place in the summer of 1935 at the Lewisohn Stadium in New York. That same summer he also conducted a concert at the Robin Hood Dell in Philadelphia. After 1945 he led some of the regular subscription concerts of the Philadelphia Orchestra. In 1946, when Eugene Ormandy, the musical director of the Philadelphia Orchestra, had to cancel some of his appearances because of ill health, Hilsberg substituted for him. His first appearance in this connection came in New York during a visit of the orchestra. Olin Downes then said of him in the New York *Times* that his performance was "sheer virtuosity in every detail . . . in tone qualities as rich and glowing as a stained glass window."

Since 1946 Hilsberg has often appeared as guest conductor not only of the Philadelphia Orchestra but also of many other major American symphonic organizations. He has also conducted at important festivals in Worcester and Ann Arbor.

In 1951 Hilsberg made several appearances with the New Orleans Symphony Orchestra. These were so successful that a year later, when the regular conductor of this orchestra resigned, Hilsberg was chosen his successor. In this office Hilsberg has proved a vital force in developing the musical culture of the city. He has extended the symphony season from twenty to twenty-five weeks; established a chorus of 135 voices, which sometimes appears with the orchestra in performances of choral masterworks; and instituted broadcasts for school children which are heard by 600,000 young people throughout the state of Louisiana.

HINES, JEROME, bass, was born Jerome Heinz in Hollywood, California, on November 8, 1921. His father was a motion-picture producer. Jerome liked singing from boyhood on, but as a student at the Bancroft Junior High School he was dismissed from the 'glee club because he "had no voice." While attending Fairfax High School, he began to study the piano. Then, after a year at the University of California in Los Angeles —which he entered in 1937, and where he majored in mathematics and chemistry—he sang for Edwin Lester, executive director of the Los Angeles Civic Light Opera Association. Lester advised intensive music study, and Hines became a pupil of Gennaro Curci. Up to the time of Curci's death in 1955, that master was Hines' vocal teacher; his only other coach has been Samuel Margolis of New York.

In April 1940, while attending the University, Hines made his professional debut by appearing in Gilbert and Sullivan's *Pinafore*, performed by the Los Angeles Light Opera Association. (It was on this occasion that he changed his name to Hines.) On October 1941 he made his debut with the San Francisco Opera as Biterolf in *Tannhäuser*; in 1942 he made his bow with the San Carlo Opera as Ramfis in *Aida* and appeared as soloist with the Los Angeles Philharmonic and the Hollywood Bowl Orchestra; and in 1943 he played minor parts with the Opera Association of the Golden West.

He was graduated from the University in June 1943. From 1944 to 1945 he worked as a chemist with the Union Oil Company of Los Angeles. During this period he installed a chemical laboratory in his own home and did research in operational mathematics. Then, convinced anew that his future lay with music, he joined the New Orleans Opera Company, where he stayed a year. He won

JEROME HINES

the Caruso Award of $1,000, and soon after, on March 16, 1946, he auditioned for the Metropolitan Opera, receiving a contract one day later. That summer, before his Metropolitan debut, he made impressive appearances at the Central City Opera in Colorado in *The Abduction from the Seraglio*.

His debut at the Metropolitan Opera took place on November 21, 1946, in a minor part in *Boris Godunov*. It was not long before he was graduated to leading basso roles—becoming the first American to sing principal bass parts at the Metropolitan Opera since Herbert Witherspoon. Hines has since that time been seen in about thirty major roles, including Boris Godunov, Ramfis in *Aida*, Don Giovanni, King Mark in *Tristan und Isolde*, Gurnemanz in *Parsifal*, and Padre Guardino in *La Forza del Destino*. He is the first American to have sung the title roles of *Boris Godunov* and Boïto's *Mefistofele* with a major opera company; and he is the first American in thirty-nine years to have appeared in the part of King Mark at the Metropolitan Opera.

"Mr. Hines has made steady progress in his career at the Metropolitan" wrote Howard Taubman in the New York *Times* when Hines made his first appearance there as Don Giovanni, on March 10, 1955. "He has always had a fine, sonorous voice, and he has worked hard to rivet his control of it and make it subject to his musical purpose. Each season he has been able to assume larger responsibilities. . . . He sang last night with color, smoothness and flexibility."

Besides his appearances at the Metropolitan Opera, Hines has been heard as a guest with other major American opera companies, in concerts, and on leading radio and television programs. He has also scored major successes at the festivals in Glyndebourne, Edinburgh, and Munich.

Hines married an opera singer, Lucia Evangelista, on July 23, 1952. They met while singing together at the Cincinnati Summer Opera. With their two children, they live in South Orange, New Jersey. Chemistry and mathematics remain major interests, together with psychology and hypnosis.

HIRAOKA, YOICHI, xylophonist. See *Living Musicians*, 1940.

HOFMANN, JOSEF, pianist. For his earlier career, see *Living Musicians*, 1940.

* * *

Hofmann's last appearance on the concert stage took place at Carnegie Hall, New York, on January 16, 1946. After that he went into retirement in California. He died in Los Angeles on February 16, 1957.

HOFMANN, LUDWIG, bass-baritone. See *Living Musicians*, 1940.

HOMER, LOUISE, contralto. For her earlier career, see *Living Musicians*, 1940.

* * *

Homer died in Winter Park, Florida, on May 6, 1947.

HOROWITZ, VLADIMIR, pianist. See *Living Musicians*, 1940.

HUBERMAN, BRONISLAW, violinist. For his earlier career, see *Living Musicians*, 1940.

* * *

Huberman's last public appearance was as soloist with the New York Philharmonic-Symphony Orchestra in December 1945. He died in Nant-sur-Corsier, Switzerland, on June 16, 1947.

HUBERT, MARCEL, cellist. See *Living Musicians*, 1940.

HUEHN, JULIUS, baritone. For his earlier career, see *Living Musicians*, 1940.

* * *

Huehn left the Metropolitan Opera after the 1945-1946 season.

HÜSCH, GERHARD, baritone. See *Living Musicians*, 1940.

HUTCHESON, ERNEST, pianist. For his earlier career, see *Living Musicians*, 1940.

* * *

Hutcheson died in New York City on February 9, 1951.

INGHELBRECHT, DÉSIRÉ ÉMILE, conductor. For his earlier career, see *Living Musicians*, 1940.

* * *

After World War II, Inghelbrecht became principal conductor of the Paris Opéra.

ISTOMIN, EUGENE, pianist, was born in New York City on November 26, 1925. His first teacher was Kariena Siloti, who prepared him for the Curtis Institute of Music, where for several years he studied piano with Rudolf Serkin and Mieczyslaw Horszowski. Two important awards in 1943 led to concert appearances. The first was the Philadelphia Youth Contest award, which brought him an appearance with the Philadelphia Orchestra under Ormandy in Chopin's F minor Concerto. The second was the Leventritt Award, through which means he made his New York debut as soloist with the New York Philharmonic-Symphony under Rodzinski in the Brahms B-flat major Concerto. On both occasions he was highly praised. His concert career now launched, he appeared as guest performer with many other major American orchestras, besides giving recitals.

He made his first European tour in 1950, playing with leading orchestras in France, appearing in recitals in Italy and Switzerland, and participating in the Pablo Casals Festival in Prades, France. During the next few years he continued to appear at the annual Casals Festivals in France, often in chamber-music performances with Casals himself; in 1957 he was one of the soloists appearing at the Pablo Casals Festival in San Juan, Puerto Rico. Howard Taubman reported in the New York *Times* from Prades: "Istomin proved to be a revelation. His piano sang; not once did he forget that he was part of an intimate chamber-music group." Pablo Casals said of him: "He is destined for a great career."

Since 1950 Istomin has toured both America and Europe extensively. In 1956 he made a thirty-concert tour of the Far East, including fifteen appearances under the joint aus-

EUGENE ISTOMIN

pices of the International Exchange Program of the American National Theatre and Academy and the Sangyo Keizai Shibun.

The New York *Post* critic said of Istomin: "He plays in the grand manner. He warmed his phrases to such a degree that the sun itself could not have done any better." The New York *Daily News* reviewer wrote: "He plays with the virtuosity of a thoroughly drilled technician and the musical sensitivity of an intuitive artist."

ITURBI, AMPARO, pianist. See *Living Musicians*, 1940.

ITURBI, JOSÉ, pianist and conductor. For his earlier career, see *Living Musicians*, 1940.

* * *

Iturbi resigned as musical director of the Rochester Philharmonic Orchestra in 1947. Since then he has appeared as guest conductor of several major orchestras in Europe and America and performed extensively as pianist.

JAGEL, FREDERICK, tenor. See *Living Musicians*, 1940.

JAMES, PHILIP, conductor. See *Living Musicians*, 1940.

JANIS, BYRON, pianist, was born in Pittsburgh in 1927. His musical talent first became evident in kindergarten when, while

Istomin: ĭs-tō'mĭn

BYRON JANIS

playing a toy xylophone for his teacher, he revealed perfect pitch. The teacher urged his parents to have him take piano lessons. When Byron was nine years old he made his debut in a recital in his native city. Joseph Lhevinne, the noted pianist, heard him and advised the boy to go to New York to continue his music study with Adele Marcus at the Chatham Square Music School. While doing this, he also received an academic education at the Columbia Grammar School.

Samuel Chotzinoff, musical head of NBC and the director of the Chatham Music School, soon became the boy's unofficial sponsor. In 1942, he arranged for Janis to appear with the NBC Symphony Orchestra, Frank Black conducting, and to give a series of recitals over that radio network. During this period Janis was also heard as soloist with the Pittsburgh Symphony. Vladimir Horowitz, who was in the audience, approached him after the concert, offering to guide his career and give direction to his musical development; this was the first time Horowitz had made such an offer to a young musician.

When Adele Marcus joined the faculty of the Hockaday Music School in Dallas, Texas, the Janis family moved there so that his studies with that teacher might not be terminated. Janis made a return appearance with the NBC Symphony in 1943. Soon after this he toured with the Pittsburgh Symphony, and made guest appearances with other leading American orchestras including the Boston Symphony and the Philadelphia Orchestra. His New

York recital debut, at Carnegie Hall on October 29, 1948, was acclaimed. "Not for a long time," wrote Olin Downes in the New York *Times*, "had this writer heard such a talent." When, on January 27, 1949, Janis appeared as soloist with the New York Philharmonic-Symphony under Stokowski in the Gershwin Concerto, Irving Kolodin wrote in the New York *Sun*: "He is certainly the finest pianist we have ever heard in this score." Two years later, the music critic of the New York *Herald Tribune* said: "There is nothing in the literature for the piano which lies beyond the reach of his technical powers."

In 1948 Janis made his first tour of South America, and three years later his first tour of Europe. During a second European tour, in 1953, following a successful recital at the Festival Hall in London, he was married to June Dickson Wright of London, daughter of the senior surgeon of St. Mary's Hospital. Janis is a sports enthusiast. He plays tennis well, likes to ride horseback, and is a devoted rooter for the Pittsburgh baseball team.

JANSSEN, HERBERT, baritone. See *Living Musicians,* 1940.

JANSSEN, WERNER, conductor. For his earlier career, see *Living Musicians,* 1940.

* * *

From 1946 to 1947 Janssen was conductor of the Portland (Oregon) Symphony Orchestra, and from 1952 to 1954 of the San Diego (California) Symphony. Since 1940 he has also directed the Janssen Symphony, which he founded.

JEPSON, HELEN, soprano. For her earlier career, see *Living Musicians,* 1940.

* * *

Jepson left the Metropolitan Opera after the 1946-1947 season. Since 1948 she has lectured about the Metropolitan Opera and has been a member of the music faculty of the Fairleigh-Dickinson College in New Jersey.

JERITZA, MARIA, soprano. See *Living Musicians,* 1940.

JESSNER, IRENE, soprano. See *Living Musicians,* 1940.

JOHNSON, EDWARD, tenor and opera manager. For his earlier career, see *Living Musicians,* 1940.

* * *

Johnson resigned as general manager of the Metropolitan Opera in 1950, and was succeeded by Rudolf Bing. His fifteen-year regime was commemorated on February 28, 1950, with a gala evening in his honor; an opera pageant presented some of the company's most eminent singers in roles from twelve of the most important operas performed during the Johnson era.

JOHNSON, THOR, conductor, was born in Wisconsin Rapids, Wisconsin, on June 10, 1913, the son of a Moravian minister. He was four years old when his father was transferred to Winston-Salem, North Carolina. There Thor attended the public schools and began taking music lessons privately. He was only thirteen when he organized an orchestra of seventeen members. "It was lots of fun," he recalls. "We played a Bach work, the Schubert *Rosamunde* Overture, movements of Haydn symphonies. Sometimes our relatives and friends came—and it turned into a concert." He also led concerts of his high-school orchestra.

He attended the University of North Carolina from which he was graduated in 1934 with a Phi Beta Kappa key. During his years in college he continued his musical activity by conducting the Carolina Ensemble, which gave about a hundred concerts in four years, and by serving as associate conductor to Lamar Stringfield with the North Carolina Symphony Orchestra.

After receiving a master's degree in music from the University of Michigan (where once again he founded and led an orchestra), he was enabled by the Beebe Foundation Scholarship to go to Europe and study conducting: with Felix Weingartner and Bruno Walter, and with Nicolai Malko at the Mozarteum in Salzburg; and with Hermann Abendroth at the Leipzig Conservatory. He returned to the United States in 1937, joining the faculty of the University of Michigan as assistant professor of music. During this period he served an extensive and valuable apprenticeship as conductor. He founded the Little Symphony of Ann Arbor, which under his direction gave performances in twenty-eight states; founded and directed the Asheville Mozart Festival and led the University Music Society May Festivals; served as conductor of the Grand Rapids Symphony and the Michigan University Symphony. During the summers of 1940 and 1941 he studied conducting with Serge Koussevitzky at the Berkshire Music Center in Lenox, Massachusetts.

Soon after Pearl Harbor he enlisted in the United States Army and became a warrant

THOR JOHNSON

officer band leader. While in uniform he organized at Fort Monmouth the first soldier symphony orchestra; its performances were so noteworthy that for the first time Johnson began to achieve national prominence. He was now invited to appear as guest conductor of important orchestras in New York, Chicago, Philadelphia and Boston, with the approval of the Army. He was also sent by the Army to England in 1946 to conduct the American University Symphony Orchestra, organized at the United States Army base at Shrivenham.

After being separated from the Army, in 1946, he was appointed director of the Juilliard School of Music Orchestra. His conducting was so outstanding that it attracted the attention of the directors of the Cincinnati Symphony Orchestra. When, in December 1946, Eugene Goossens suffered pneumonia while on tour with the Cincinnati Symphony, they wired Johnson to come and substitute for him. He arrived for his first performance only a few minutes before concert time, and without rehearsal (and with only a single change in program) gave such a remarkable demonstration that he received an ovation not only from the audience but from the men in the orchestra. He led the Cincinnati Symphony for the rest of the tour, and for several performances in Cincinnati itself, strengthening the good impression he had made at his debut. After the 1946-1947 season, Eugene Goossens resigned as musical director of the Cincinnati Symphony. The directors telephoned Koussevitzky that they were thinking of engaging Johnson as Goossens' successor and asked for his opinion on the matter. "In five years," said Koussevitzky, "Johnson will be among the great." This was all the endorsement they needed. Johnson was hired, and he has remained the musical director of the orchestra since that time. He has grown, as Koussevitzky prophesied, into one of the foremost American conductors of our time, a musician of authority and scholarship, and a conductor who has a command of his men and of his music. He has proved himself particularly brilliant in modern compositions. In his first decade in Cincinnati he has led fifty-two world premières (twenty-six of these being works which he commissioned for his orchestra) and twenty-one United States premières. He has also appeared as guest conductor of many other American orchestras, and he has performed at virtually all major festivals in the United States, some of which he has helped to found. In 1949, for example, he was heard at seven major American festivals. In 1955 he was invited to conduct some of the concerts of the Symphony of the Air during its tour of Asia.

JONAS, MARYLA, pianist, was born in Warsaw, Poland, in 1911. She began the study of the piano in childhood, and in her ninth year made her debut as soloist with the Warsaw Philharmonic in a performance of a Mozart concerto. Two years later, Paderewski became interested in her and gave her lessons. A recital in Berlin when she was fifteen

MARYLA JONAS

marked the beginning of her career as a concert artist, bringing her a contract to tour Germany. After studying three additional years with Emile Sauer — and winning the Chopin Prize in 1932 and the Beethoven Prize of Vienna in 1933—she toured all of Europe, acclaimed as one of the leading women pianists of the day. Particularly successful was a series of Mozart recitals in Salzburg in 1938. Her personal life was equally fortunate. In 1939 she married a Polish criminologist and settled in a handsome apartment in Warsaw, where they lived happily for several months.

Then Nazi Germany attacked Poland—and tragedy descended on the young artist. Within a short period her husband, father, mother, and a brother were all killed by the Nazis. She herself was interned in a concentration camp when she refused to go to Germany to concertize. In this camp, a German officer—who had once heard her play—helped arrange for her escape, and advised her to find refuge in the Brazilian Embassy in Berlin. She had to make a three-hundred-mile trip to Berlin by foot, hiding in thickets, sleeping in the woods, and eating whatever she could find on the way. Finally, at the Brazilian Embassy, an attaché gave her a forged passport with which she fled by way of Lisbon to Rio de Janeiro, there to find a home with one of her sisters.

The horror of the preceding months had left its impact. She was confined to a sanitorium for several months, and when she left it she refused to play the piano any longer. Artur Rubinstein, then touring South America, resorted to a ruse to get her back to the keyboard. One day in 1940, just before one of his own concerts, he invited her to the empty auditorium and begged her to try out a few chords on the piano so that he could test the acoustics. Reluctantly, Jonas complied, and began playing a sonata. This performance revived in her her old passion for music.

Her personal life completely destroyed by the war, she now decided to dedicate herself exclusively to her art. As she later told an interviewer: "Before the war, my whole life was love, husband, flowers, father, mother, happiness. Now it is only music." After an intensive period of study and practice, she returned to the concert stage, giving several recitals in South America and Mexico. On February 25, 1946, she made her North American debut in Carnegie Hall. The hall was half empty, since she was unknown. But Jerome D. Bohm of the New York *Herald Tribune* described her as the foremost woman pianist since Teresa Carreño, with the result that her next appearance, on March 30, was a sell-out. Olin Downes spoke of her in the New York *Times* as "a poet and master of her instrument. She has few equals as an interpreter among the living pianists of the day."

Her reputation now established, Jonas made appearances in fifty cities throughout the country, both in recitals and with symphony orchestras. She also made numerous recordings for Columbia. Afterward she was frequently heard both in this country and in Europe.

Infected by a blood disease in 1952, Maryla Jonas was compelled to withdraw from concert activity for a period of four years. She returned to New York after a five-year absence on December 1, 1956. Edward Downes, reporting the concert for the New York *Times,* found that in the first half of the program she played "a trifle too brilliantly, like an artist who controls the notes but is not yet enough at ease to give the music warmth." But he added that "by the time she reached the development section of the sonata's first movement (Mozart's Sonata, K. 330), she was playing, or rather singing, the phrases with a sensitivity and glow such as one rarely hears today, even among players of the front rank."

JORDÁ, ENRIQUE, conductor, was born in San Sebastián, Spain, on March 24, 1911. Private music study was begun when he was five. At twelve he served as assistant conductor in his parish church, and at sixteen he started writing music for orchestra. In his eighteenth year he went to Paris to study medicine. During this period music was not neglected: he studied harmony and composition with Paul Le Flem, conducting with François Ruhlmann, and organ with Marcel Dupré. After receiving a degree in philosophy and letters, he abandoned the idea of becoming a doctor in order to devote himself exclusively to music, beginning his career in 1933. From 1937 to 1939 he was conductor of the Basque Ballet. He made his debut as symphony conductor in Paris in 1938, and in 1939 he was invited to make guest appearances with the Brussels Symphony.

When war broke out in Europe he returned to his native land. From 1943 to 1945 he was principal conductor of the Madrid Symphony and received recognition as one of the most important conductors to appear in Spain in many years. He was also invited to conduct concerts of the Orquesta Bética, the celebrated Seville orchestra founded and directed by

ENRIQUE JORDÁ

Manuel de Falla. His work with these Spanish organizations brought him the Conde de Carigena, an award from the Spanish Academy of Fine Arts.

In 1945 Jordá left Spain and toured various European countries. He now appeared with such major symphonic organizations as the BBC Symphony, the Paris Conservatory Orchestra, the Hallé Orchestra, the London Symphony, the Pasdeloup Orchestra, and the Orchestre de la Suisse Romande. Everywhere he conducted, his romantic temperament, command of the orchestra, and vitalized performances won praise. In 1948 he was appointed principal conductor of the Capetown Symphony Orchestra in South Africa. He held that post until 1954.

His North American debut took place with the San Francisco Symphony at the opening concert of the 1952-1953 season. His performances during a four-week period in November were so electrifying that he was invited for a longer engagement the following season. In 1954 he was appointed permanent conductor on a two-year contract, his regime to be launched on November 12; this contract was renewed at its termination. He has combined his successful activity in San Francisco with numerous appearances in Cuba, Australia, South America, and Europe.

Jordá, who now makes his permanent home in San Francisco, is married to an Englishwoman, Audrey, who is an ardent music amateur. They have two daughters. Jordá's main

Jordá: hôr-dä′

interest in sports lies in playing jai-alai; indoors, his principal diversion is reading.

In 1956 he received the Order of Alfonso X from his native land in recognition of his services to music.

JURINAC, SENA, soprano, was born in Travnik, Yugoslavia on October 24, 1921, the daughter of a Croatian physician. While attending elementary and secondary schools in Zagreb, she pursued her musical education at the Zagreb Musical Academy. On October 15, 1942, she made her opera debut with the Zagreb Opera as Mimi in *La Bohème.* During her first season she also gave impressive performances in *Faust, The Marriage of Figaro, Das Rheingold,* and *Parsifal.*

Success came to her at the Vienna State Opera, where she made her debut as Cherubino in *The Marriage of Figaro* on May 1, 1945. In Vienna she was assigned leading soprano and mezzo-soprano roles in an extensive repertory that included leading works by Wagner, Mozart, Richard Strauss, and the principal Italian and French composers, as well as other operas like *Palestrina, The Bartered Bride,* and Gluck's *Orfeo ed Euridice.* To each of her roles she brought a sure dramatic instinct and a magnetic stage presence as well as a voice of compelling beauty and irresistible warmth and charm.

In the summers of 1947 and 1948 she appeared at the Salzburg Festival, and in 1949 she scored major successes at the Florence

SENA JURINAC

Jurinac: yū'rē-näts

May Music Festival and the Edinburgh Festival. In 1949 she also began an association with the Glyndebourne Opera which continued for several years and in which she achieved personal triumphs in the Mozart repertory. One of her most striking achievements as a member of the Glyndebourne Opera was to appear, on different occasions, in each of the two principal soprano roles of *Così Fan Tutte,* those of Dorabella and Fiordiligi, and with equal distinction.

In 1957 Jurinac was engaged by the Metropolitan Opera to assume the leading soprano role in the world première of Samuel Barber's *Vanessa.* But her extensive recordings had previously made her name and art familiar to American music lovers everywhere. Besides her achievements in opera, Jurinac has also won the admiration of the music world for her interpretations of *Lieder* on the concert stage.

KAPELL, WILLIAM, pianist, was born in New York City on September 20, 1922, son of a book shop proprietor.

When he was six, William received his first piano lessons, but since the Kapell family did not own a piano the boy could do no practicing. A $30.00 upright piano was bought for the Kapell home when William was eight. When he was ten he began studying seriously, at the Yorktown Settlement, with Mrs. Dorothea Anderson La Follette, with whom he stayed five years. After only six weeks of lessons with Mrs. La Follette, he won first prize in a contest conducted among the city settlement schools. In 1934 he received a scholarship for the Columbia Grammar School; there, in his senior year, he carried away still another scholarship, this time for the Philadelphia Conservatory, to study the piano with Olga Samaroff. Later piano study took place in 1940-1941 at the Juilliard Graduate School on a fellowship.

In 1940 he won the Youth Contest in Philadelphia, an honor which entitled him to an appearance with the Philadelphia Orchestra. This took place in February of that year, when he was heard in the Saint-Saëns G minor Concerto. In March he won the Naumburg Foundation Award, as a result of which he gave his debut recital at Town Hall, New York, on October 28, 1941. This concert, in turn, brought him the Town Hall Endowment Series Award: an honor bestowed each year on the outstanding Town Hall recitalist of the preceding season under thirty years of age; Kapell turned out to be the youngest artist ever to win this award.

Kapell: kă'pĕl

Courtesy of Musical Courier

WILLIAM KAPELL

Kapell made his first concert tour of the United States in 1942. During that summer he appeared in New York as soloist at the Lewisohn Stadium in the Khatchaturian Piano Concerto, a work with which he was henceforth so intimately identified that friends often called him "Khatchaturian Kapell." He played the work almost thirty times in this country and abroad in half a dozen years, six times with the Boston Symphony under Koussevitzky. In 1943 Kapell received a contract from the Philadelphia Orchestra to appear with that organization, under Ormandy's direction, during the next three seasons; this was the first time the Philadelphia Orchestra had ever made such an arrangement with a soloist. In 1945 he made his first tour of Australia, on an invitation by the Australian Broadcasting Commission—the first American instrumentalist to tour that continent since World War II. One season later he toured South America, and, in 1947, Europe.

Though Kapell won some of his major successes in the modern repertory—particularly in concertos by Khatchaturian, Prokofiev, and Rachmaninoff—he was a sound virtuoso who brought both a brilliant technique and a profound musicianship to the classical and romantic literature. "Mr. Kapell," as Olin Downes wrote in the New York *Times* after one of Kapell's performances, "plays with unlimited fire and élan. . . . There is technique to burn, and in the performance an authority and excitement not

to be resisted. A young musician of exceptional attributes is ablaze at his task."

In 1948 Kapell married Rebecca Anna Lou Nelson, a piano student. They had two children. Kapell was killed on October 29, 1953, when his plane crashed into a mountainside near Half Moon Bay, California. He was returning from a two-month tour of Australia, and he was only three minutes from his final destination—San Francisco—after a trip of 8,600 miles.

KAPPEL, GERTRUDE, dramatic soprano. See *Living Musicians*, 1940.

KARAJAN, HERBERT VON, conductor, was born in Salzburg, Austria, on April 5, 1908. His father, who was of Macedonian extraction, was chief medical officer in Salzburg. A passionate music lover, he directed his son to that art at an early age. Herbert began piano lessons when he was only three and a half, and in his eighth year made a public appearance. From then on it seemed a foregone conclusion he would be trained for a professional career. He attended the Mozarteum in Salzburg, specializing in the piano. "My conception of what could come out of the piano was so exaggerated," he recalls, "that my last piano teacher said one day, 'Try to become a conductor, otherwise you will never be satisfied.' He is the man to whom I am most grateful in my career, Dr. Bernhard Paumgartner, director of the Mozarteum."

He continued his studies at the University of Vienna, where he majored in philosophy and music history, and at the Vienna Academy, where he studied conducting with Frank Schalk. Even before he received a degree, he made his conducting debut in Salzburg in 1927 with an orchestra hired for the purpose by his father. The manager of the Ulm Municipal Theatre heard this concert and engaged him as first conductor of his opera house, a post von Karajan kept until 1934. "Work in Ulm was enormously difficult," explains von Karajan. "The conductor was all in one—coach, chorus master, conductor. My whole time in Ulm was important to me in subsequent years, for I had learned working from the bottom up."

His next assignment was in Aachen, where he became first conductor of its opera company in 1935, and after that general music director of both the opera company and the symphony orchestra. In 1937 the Berlin Philharmonic Orchestra invited him to conduct

Karajan: kä′rä-yän

HERBERT VON KARAJAN

a popular concert. He made such a good impression that he was entrusted with the task of reorganizing the symphony concerts of the Berlin State Opera Orchestra. "It was a wonderful job," he says, "difficult only because I had to divide my time between Aachen and Berlin." Other guest appearances followed in Brussels, Amsterdam, Stockholm, and Copenhagen. In 1938 he directed several performances at La Scala in Milan and at the Florence May Music Festival.

After World War II, the United States Occupation Army in Vienna refused to allow him to conduct because he had been a member of the Nazi Party between 1933 and 1942. He was however cleared by 1947 and permitted to resume his career. He now emerged as one of the most important conductors in Europe, achieving particular renown as conductor of the Vienna Philharmonic Orchestra and as a member of the board of directors of the Salzburg Festival, which he helped to reorganize. In 1948 he was appointed artistic director of the celebrated Gesellschaft der Musikfreunde in Vienna, where his annual series of concerts soon became known as "the von Karajan cycles"; with this organization he made extensive tours of Europe and some remarkable recordings. In 1950 he conducted the International Bach Festival in Vienna, and in 1951 the complete *Ring* cycle in Bayreuth. He also made notable appearances at La Scala and at the Salzburg and Lucerne festivals, besides serving as a conductor of the

London Philharmonia Orchestra, with which he also made extensive tours of Europe and numerous recordings. In 1954 he toured Japan under the auspices of the Japanese radio network, and in the fall of the same year he was principal conductor of the Berlin Philharmonic at the fourth Berlin Cultural Festival.

In 1954 the Berlin Philharmonic was engaged to tour the United States for the first time, under Wilhelm Furtwängler's direction. When Furtwängler died, von Karajan was chosen to replace him. His debut in America, at the head of the Berlin Philharmonic, took place in Washington, D.C., late in February 1955. A few days later, on March 1, he gave his first New York concert at Carnegie Hall. "Mr. von Karajan," reported Howard Taubman in the New York *Times,* "is a conductor of stature. Playing . . . solid familiar fare . . . Mr. von Karajan conducted . . . from memory with very little fuss or furbelows, with a craftsman's knowledge of his business and with an artist's understanding of the music at hand." In the fall of 1955 von Karajan returned to the United States for a second tour, this time at the head of the Philharmonia Orchestra of London.

Herbert von Karajan received a permanent appointment to succeed the late Furtwängler as musical director of the Berlin Philharmonic. (There is some irony in this succession, since Furtwängler and von Karajan were bitter rivals.) In 1956 he also received appointments as artistic director of the Vienna State Opera and of the Salzburg Festival. Among other posts he held were those of principal conductor at La Scala (where he was a member of the board of directors), permanent conductor of the London Philharmonia, and lifetime director of the Vienna Gesellschaft der Musikfreunde.

Von Karajan was married to Anita Gutermann in 1942; this was his second marriage. Of his extra-musical interests he says: "My hobbies are controlled by one major influence and that is my deep love of nature, which I inherited from my father. I am an enthusiastic alpinist and skier, and the days I spend touring the Central Alps (by foot, not by cable) are the greatest joy for me. I also like the sea and spend at least a month cruising on my yacht in the Mediterranean. As I am a technical fan I like everything connected with speed. I have a small racing car which gives me an enormous amount of fun. I also started recently to pilot my own plane; I acquired my license in Switzerland and since then have been flying regularly and with ever-increasing enthusiasm."

KASKAS, ANNA, contralto. For her earlier career, see *Living Musicians,* 1940.

* * *

Kaskas left the Metropolitan Opera after the 1945-1946 season.

KATCHEN, JULIUS, pianist. For his earlier career, see *Living Musicians,* 1940.

* * *

After World War II Katchen made several extended tours of Europe. He was acclaimed at the Prague Spring Festival in 1956, the first American to win approval in that city in a decade.

KATIMS, MILTON, violist and conductor. For his earlier career, see *Living Musicians,* 1940.

* * *

In 1943 Katims was appointed by Toscanini first violist of the NBC Symphony Orchestra, and in 1947 he began conducting that orchestra several times a year. From 1952 on he appeared as guest conductor of the Israel Philharmonic, Buffalo Symphony, Detroit Symphony, Houston Symphony, the orchestra of the Radiodiffusion in Paris, and the Grand Teatro del Liceo in Barcelona. From 1946 to 1954 he was a member of the faculty of the Juilliard School of Music, where he taught a master class in viola. In June 1953 that institution awarded him a Medal of Excellence for outstanding achievement in the field of music. He became permanent conductor of the Seattle Symphony in 1954.

KAYE, MILTON, pianist. See *Living Musicians,* 1940.

KEMPE, RUDOLF, conductor, was born near Dresden, Germany, in 1910. Neither parent was musical. Rudolf was not yet six when he began studying the piano. At twelve he took lessons on the violin, and at fourteen on the oboe. His principal musical education took place at the Orchesterschule der Sächsischen Staatskapelle, presided over by Fritz Busch, in Dresden; it was there that he decided to become a conductor. In 1939 he was engaged as first oboist of the Leipzig Gewandhaus Orchestra. While holding this post

Kempe: kĕm′pĕ

RUDOLF KEMPE

he also held a minor job with the Leipzig Opera and made his debut as conductor by leading a performance of Lortzing's *Wildschütz.*

Determined to pursue a career as a conductor, he resigned his orchestral job with the Gewandhaus in 1948 and assumed the direction of the Chemnitz Opera. His next post was with the Weimar Opera, where he was engaged to direct all new productions, including Sutermeister's *Romeo und Julia.* While performing in Weimar, he also gave guest performances with the Berlin State Opera and appeared as guest conductor of symphony orchestras in Berlin, Leipzig, and Dresden.

In 1949 he was appointed general music director of the Dresden Opera. Three years later he took over the post of musical director of the Bavarian State Opera in Munich. In this period he extended his reputation throughout Europe with guest appearances at La Scala, and in Vienna, Barcelona, and Buenos Aires. He distinguished himself particularly in the operas of Richard Strauss, of which he became recognized as a leading exponent. His first visit to London in 1953, in performances of Strauss' *Arabella* and *Die Liebe der Danae,* was so successful that he was invited to return a few weeks later to conduct both *Salome* and *Elektra* at Covent Garden. One year later he was acclaimed in London for his performance of *Der Rosenkavalier.*

In 1954, immediately after the summer music festival season, Kempe resigned as music director in Munich. He now divided his activity among Covent Garden, the Vienna State Opera, and the Metropolitan Opera. He made his American debut at the Metropolitan Opera on January 26, 1955, in *Tannhäuser* (the Dresden version). "Yesterday's musical interpretation," wrote Francis D. Perkins in the New York *Herald Tribune,* "implied that he is a musician of experience and discernment. Musical proportion was a notable point; this was not a heavy *Tannhäuser;* the vocal and instrumental balance was generally admirable; the orchestra, in good form, never encroached upon solo vocal territory, and the performance revealed fine expressive details as well as fine points of dynamic shading."

Kempe has since appeared regularly at the Metropolitan Opera, where in subsequent seasons he has given notable performances of *Arabella* and *Der Rosenkavalier,* together with the Wagner music dramas. In the spring of 1955 he was hailed at Covent Garden for his performance of the entire *Ring* cycle, and the same summer at the Salzburg Festival for his interpretation of Pfitzner's *Palestrina.*

KENTNER, LOUIS, pianist, was born in Karvin, Silesia, on July 19, 1905. His father was Hungarian, his mother Austrian, neither one of them musicians. Kentner was brought up in Budapest where he received recognition

LOUIS KENTNER

as a child prodigy. "I actually think I could play the piano before I could talk," he once told an interviewer. He was only six when he entered the Budapest Academy of Music, eleven when he appeared in student recitals, and thirteen when he launched his concert career by giving a major recital. He was still in his boyhood when he performed all the Beethoven piano sonatos in a series of concerts in Budapest—a task which he was later to repeat many times in different music centers.

He continued attending the Budapest Academy until 1922—his principal teachers being Hans Koessler, Leo Weiner, and Zoltan Kodály. His studies ended, he pursued his concert career throughout Europe with renewed vigor. During this period he became identified with the music of modern-day Hungary. Kodály wrote for him his *Dances of Marosszek,* which Kentner introduced in 1927. Kentner also performed the world première of Bartók's Second Piano Concerto in 1933, and subsequently was the first to play the Bartók Third Piano Concerto in Europe.

In 1935 Kentner settled in England, henceforth his permanent home; he soon became a British subject. He made numerous appearances in every part of England, distinguishing himself particularly for his monumental cycles of recitals devoted to a single composer. In 1940 he performed not only all the Beethoven sonatas but also all the piano sonatas of Schubert and the complete Bach *Well-Tempered Clavier.* Over the English radio he performed the complete *Années de Pèlerinage* by Liszt, and in Edinburgh all the violin and piano sonatas of Beethoven (with Yehudi Menuhin, who is his brother-in-law). Kentner also became a spokesman for contemporary British music, responsible for the premières of major works by Alan Rawsthorne, William Walton, and Michael Tippett, among others.

In 1954 Kentner toured India with Menuhin, appearing in violin and piano recitals as well as in solo appearances and as guest performer with orchestras. In 1956, during a tour of the Far East, Kentner was heard at a Mozart festival in Iran, when he played for the Shah and Queen. He had, in fact, been heard on four continents and had achieved a world reputation before making his belated debut in the United States. This took place at Town Hall, New York, on November 28, 1956. "His performances were so imaginative and exhilarating," wrote Howard Taubman in the New York *Times,* "that one could not understand why his introduction to this country had been delayed so long. . . . Mr. Kentner's musicianship is solidly complemented by technical gifts of the first order." Paul Henry Lang wrote in the New York *Herald Tribune*: "Mr. Kentner is beyond doubt one of the finest pianists heard here in a long time. His technique and keyboard security are phenomenal, but this surely is the result of perfect rapport between mind and fingers."

KERR, MURIEL, pianist. See *Living Musicians,* 1940.

KIEPURA, JAN, tenor. For his earlier career, see *Living Musicians,* 1940.

* * *

Kiepura left the Metropolitan Opera after the 1941-1942 season. He subsequently appeared in recitals, motion pictures, and operettas.

KINDLER, HANS, cellist and conductor. For his earlier career, see *Living Musicians,* 1940.

* * *

Kindler died in Watch Hill, Rhode Island, on August 30, 1949.

KIPNIS, ALEXANDER, basso. For his earlier career, see *Living Musicians,* 1940.

* * *

Kipnis left the Metropolitan Opera after the 1945-1946 season, and subsequently appeared in recitals and in guest performances with European opera companies.

KIRKPATRICK, RALPH, harpsichordist. For his earlier career, see *Living Musicians,* 1940.

* * *

Since 1944 Kirkpatrick has made several transcontinental tours of the United States, and since 1947 has toured Europe. In 1950 he served as visiting lecturer at Yale University. He has written a definitive biography of Domenico Scarlatti (1953) and made a comprehensive recording of Scarlatti's sonatas for Columbia Records.

KIRSTEN, DOROTHY, soprano, was born in Montclair, New Jersey, on July 6, 1917. She comes from a musical family. Her grandfather had been one of the earliest presidents of the American Federation of Musicians, Local 802; a grand-aunt was known as

DOROTHY KIRSTEN

the "Irish Jenny Lind"; and her mother was an organist and music teacher. While attending Montclair High School, Dorothy Kirsten took lessons in dramatics, dancing, and voice. After her graduation, she worked for the New Jersey Telephone Company in Newark to pay for her music study at the Juilliard School of Music. She was able to give up this job when she received assignments to sing over the radio, including a five-day-a-week feature in 1938. One of her broadcasts was heard by Grace Moore, who decided to finance her career. In March 1939 Kirsten went to Italy, where she studied for more than a year with Astolfo Pescia, who prepared her for the operatic stage. Her intention was to stay in Europe several years, but the outbreak of the war sent her home in 1940.

Back in the United States, she made her concert debut in 1940 at the Court of Peace at New York's World Fair. Her opera debut took place with the Chicago Opera on November 9, 1940, when she was seen in the minor role of Poussette in *Manon*. That season she appeared in fifteen minor parts, but the following year she graduated to such more significant roles as Nedda in *Pagliacci,* Micaela in *Carmen,* and Musetta in *La Bohème* (the last with Grace Moore appearing as Mimi). Her New York opera debut, as Micaela, took place with the San Carlo Opera on May 7, 1942. Between 1942 and 1943 she gave concerts in thirty-eight states, besides appearing as guest artist on many sponsored radio programs. From 1944 to 1946 she sang principal soprano roles with the New York City Opera.

Her debut at the Metropolitan Opera as Mimi in *La Bohème* took place on December 1, 1945. "Her voice showed no hint of debut nerves," wrote Francis D. Perkins in the *Herald Tribune.* "It was satisfying in volume and consistently appealing in quality; her tones were clear and fluently produced, with well-schooled phrasing, and her singing also reflected the emotional flavor of the music." Since that time she has been heard in leading soprano roles of the French and Italian repertory, notably as Violetta in *La Traviata,* Louise, Manon (in the Massenet and Puccini operas), Juliet, and Marguerite in *Faust.* She had been trained for the part of Louise by Gustave Charpentier, the composer of the opera, and she scored a major success in it both at the Metropolitan Opera and at the San Francisco Opera during the 1947-1948 season.

"As pure vocalism," said the New York *Times* after her appearance in Madama Butterfly, "Miss Kirsten's work was a source of unfailing delight. If there had been no more to her performance this would have been enough to be thankful for. But Miss Kirsten was not merely a vocalist. . . . Cio-Cio San became a human being, not a soprano."

Dorothy Kirsten's appearances in the recital hall and on radio and television have been frequent. She has also been seen in several motion pictures, including *Mr. Music,* with Bing Crosby, and *The Great Caruso,* with Mario Lanza.

KLEIBER, ERICH, conductor. For his earlier career, see *Living Musicians, 1940.*

* * *

Between 1936 and 1949 Kleiber was conductor of German opera at the Teatro Colón in Buenos Aires. After 1949 he toured Europe in guest appearances with leading opera companies and at major festivals. In 1952 he was appointed principal conductor of the Berlin State Opera in East Germany. When the opera house in East Berlin was reconstructed in 1955, Kleiber was elevated to the post of music director. But because of governmental interference with his artistic program, Kleiber resigned this post even before the new opera house was opened. He died of a heart attack in Zurich, Switzerland, on January 27, 1956.

KLEMPERER, OTTO, conductor. For his earlier career, see *Living Musicians, 1940.*

* * *

From 1947 to 1950 Klemperer was principal conductor of the Budapest Opera. Since then he has appeared throughout Europe as guest conductor of leading orchestras and opera companies.

KNAPPERTSBUSCH, HANS, conductor. For his earlier career, see *Living Musicians, 1940.*

* * *

After World War II, Knappertsbusch directed successful opera performances in Munich, Bayreuth, Salzburg, Vienna, and other major European music centers.

KNITZER, JOSEPH, violinist. See *Living Musicians, 1940.*

KOLAR, VICTOR, conductor. See *Living Musicians, 1940.*

The KOLISCH QUARTET. See *Living Musicians, 1940.*

KOSHETZ, NINA, soprano. See *Living Musicians, 1940.*

KOSTELANETZ, ANDRE, conductor. See *Living Musicians, 1940.*

KOUSSEVITZKY, SERGE ALEXAN-DROVITCH, conductor. For his earlier career, see *Living Musicians, 1940.*

* * *

In 1941 Koussevitzky founded the Koussevitzky Music Foundation, which commissioned new works from leading composers everywhere. His wife, Natalie, died early in 1942; five years later, Koussevitzky married his niece and secretary, Olga Naumoff. Koussevitzky died in Boston on June 4, 1951, two years after resigning as music director of the Boston Symphony Orchestra.

KRAUSS, CLEMENS HEINRICH, conductor. For his earlier career, see *Living Musicians, 1940.*

* * *

After World War II, Krauss conducted opera performances at the Vienna State Opera, and in Bayreuth, South America, and Mexico. He died in Mexico City on May 16, 1954.

KREISLER, FRITZ, violinist. For his earlier career, see *Living Musicians*, 1940.

* * *

In 1941, while crossing a New York city street, Kreisler was hit by a truck, suffering a fracture of the skull and internal injuries. After a long period of convalescence he was able to return to the concert stage, but some time after the end of World War II he went into complete retirement.

KRIPS, JOSEF, conductor, was born in Vienna on August 8, 1902. His father, who was highly musical, sang in the choir of the Karmeliter Church, which Josef joined in early boyhood. When he was thirteen he began studying the violin. Soon after this, his musical training began in earnest at the Vienna Academy, with Eusebius Mandyczewski and Felix Weingartner; at the same time he pursued his academic education in the local high school.

He was not yet sixteen when he accepted a job as violinist with the Volksoper orchestra, a job which he held for three years. During this time he also joined a touring opera company. "I became their choir conductor, stage manager, harmonium player and, at certain difficult moments, chief of the claque."

In his twenty-first year he was appointed chorus master and conductor at the Volksoper. After three years he went on to Aussig-on-the-Elbe, in Czechoslovakia, to become director of its Opera. One year later, he was appointed music director in Dortmund, Germany, and in 1926 he received an appointment as general musical director in Karlsruhe, one of the youngest musicians ever to fill this important post.

After seven years in Karlsruhe, Krips was engaged as conductor of the Vienna State Opera, where he attracted the attention of European music lovers through his versatility in conducting operas in the German, Italian, and French repertories with equal skill and understanding. In 1935 he began an association with the Salzburg Festival which was to continue up to the present time, and he became a professor at the Vienna Music Academy. All these posts were temporarily relinquished while the Nazis were in power in Austria.

During the war years, Krips worked in a food-processing factory; for eight years he was forbidden to participate in any of the city's musical activities.

But in 1945 he returned to his old post with the Vienna State Opera and now became one of its most important conductors. With that

JOSEF KRIPS

company he toured London in 1947 in a cycle of Mozart operas, and with the Vienna Philharmonic Orchestra he toured all of Europe. He also made significant appearances with the Concertgebouw Orchestra and the Royal Opera of Holland; was appointed principal conductor of the London Symphony Orchestra in 1950, a post he held for five years; and appeared at the Florence May Music Festival in 1949, in a one-week cycle of Mozart operas.

He was invited to the United States in the summer of 1950 to conduct the Chicago Symphony Orchestra at its Ravinia Park festival. But on his arrival he was denied admittance by immigration agents. After two days' detention he decided to return to Europe without waiting for a hearing. Declaring that he had "no politics," he said his difficulties might have arisen from his performances in Russia in 1947. In 1953, however, he was allowed to enter the country. He was appointed musical director of the Cincinnati Festival, and on November 7, 1954, he conducted the Buffalo Philharmonic Orchestra in his first concert as principal conductor and musical director of that organization.

He has combined his activity in this country with extensive appearances in Europe. In June 1955 he conducted several memorable performances with the Vienna State Opera, one of which—that of *Don Giovanni*—was recorded. It was selected by the *Saturday Review* as the best opera recording of the year. In the spring of 1956 he directed an important Beethoven cycle in London, and a few months later a highly acclaimed revival of Handel's *Samson* in Vienna.

On May 28, 1955, Krips received the Bruckner Medal of the Bruckner Society. A few months earlier he had conducted in Berne, Switzerland, the first performance of the original version of Bruckner's Eighth Symphony.

When Krips conducted Bruckner's F minor Mass at the Cincinnati Festival on May 7, 1956, Howard Taubman reported in the New York *Times:* "Mr. Krips . . . is a real conductor. His beat is clear and decisive. He brings not only knowledge of tradition to his work . . . but also a personal point of view."

Krips' American debut as an opera conductor took place in Buffalo on March 16, 1956, when he led a performance of *Don Giovanni.* "The performance was admirable for its continuity, its proportion, and the poise and insight given it by Mr. Krips," reported Berna Bergholtz in *Musical America.*

Krips made his New York debut on December 18, 1956, when he appeared as guest conductor of the Symphony of the Air. "One has to admire," wrote Howard Taubman in the New York *Times,* "the skill with which Mr. Krips drew from it [the orchestra] the kind of performances he wanted."

In 1957 Krips signed a three-year contract with the Vienna State Opera to appear there three months a year.

KRUEGER, KARL, conductor. For his earlier career, see *Living Musicians,* 1940.

* * *

In 1943 Krueger became musical director of the recently reorganized Detroit Symphony Orchestra, holding this post a half a dozen years until the orchestra once again was temporarily disbanded. In 1945, under the auspices of the State Department, he toured South America. One year later he toured Europe, the first American conductor to perform there following World War II. In 1949 he founded and directed the short-lived All-American Art Orchestra.

KUBELIK, JAN, violinist. For his earlier career, see *Living Musicians,* 1940.

* * *

Kubelik died in Prague, Czechoslovakia, on December 5, 1940.

KUBELIK, RAFAEL, conductor, was born in Bychory, Czechoslovakia, on June 29, 1914, the son of the famous violin virtuoso Jan Kubelik. Trained in music by his father

Kubelik: kōō'bĕ-lĕk

Courtesy of Musical Courier

RAFAEL KUBELIK

from the time he was a child, Rafael entered the Prague Conservatory in 1928, and five years later was graduated as violinist, conductor, and composer. Between 1934 and 1936 he was his father's accompanist in tours through Europe and the United States.

In 1936 Rafael Kubelik was appointed acting conductor of the Czech Philharmonic Orchestra. He held this post three years, touring England and Belgium in 1937. From 1939 until the Nazis closed down the theatre in 1941, he was first conductor of the Brünn National Theatre, and from 1942 to 1948 he served as artistic director of the Czech Philharmonic. During the Nazi occupation of Czechoslovakia he consistently refused to cooperate with the enemy.

Immediately after World War II he led concerts in England, Belgium, Scandinavia, Austria, and Poland. Between September 1945 and January 1946 he conducted eight concerts in Moscow, and in 1947 he toured Poland, France, and Switzerland with the Czech Philharmonic.

When the Communists seized control of Czechoslovakia, Kubelik left his native land and settled permanently in London. In the summer of the same year—1948—he conducted the Glyndebourne Opera in *Don Giovanni* at the Edinburgh Festival. One year later he became conductor of the Concertgebouw Orchestra in Amsterdam, and in 1950 he was acclaimed for his performances at the Bach Festival in Zurich and in concerts in South America and Mexico.

He made his American debut as symphony conductor in mid-November 1949, when he appeared with the Chicago Symphony in four concerts. "There can be no doubt that Mr. Kubelik made a distinctly favorable impression," wrote Felix Borowski. Indeed, the impression was so good that towards the end of that year Kubelik was engaged as principal conductor of that orchestra on a two-year contract. When his first appearance in his new post took place in October 1950, Claudia Cassidy said of his performance that "it was clear and fresh and imaginative and understanding." Kubelik became the fifth principal conductor in the fifty-nine-year history of the Chicago Symphony.

When Kubelik appeared with the Chicago Symphony on a visit to New York on March 9, 1953, Howard Taubman wrote in the New York *Times:* "It was clear last night that this conductor is a dynamic leader and a musician of character. There was a driving intensity in all that Mr. Kubelik did. . . . The core of the matter was there—a vivid, personal and glowing concern for the underlying design of the music."

Kubelik resigned from his post in Chicago in 1953. He returned to the United States a year later with the Concertgebouw Orchestra of Amsterdam, then making its first tour of the United States. He conducted forty-three concerts, sharing the podium with Eduard van Beinum. Kubelik was engaged to appear for the first time as guest conductor of the New York Philharmonic-Symphony during the 1957-1958 season.

In 1955 Kubelik was appointed musical director of Covent Garden. He made his bow in this important post on October 17, leading a performance of *Otello*. Reviewing this performance, Cecil Smith wrote in *Musical America:* "Mr. Kubelik showed real understanding of both the dramatic values of the score and its formal construction. . . . The orchestra played cleanly and beautifully; the chorus sang expertly. . . . The minor principals knew their parts more than superficially."

KULLMAN, CHARLES, tenor. For his earlier career, see *Living Musicians,* 1940.

* * *

In 1955 Kullman received an award from the Metropolitan Opera to commemorate his twentieth anniversary as a member of that company. In 1956 he was appointed resident tenor of the Indiana University School of Music.

KUNZ, ERICH, bass-baritone, was born in Vienna on May 20, 1909, the son of an engineer. His music study took place principally with Theodore Lierhammer at the Vienna Academy, following which he made his debut with the Troppau Opera as Osmin in *The Abduction from the Seraglio.* After appearing with other minor German opera companies, he was a member of the Breslau Opera for three years. In 1936 he went to England, where he became an understudy with the Glyndebourne Opera. He soon began to assume some of the minor roles.

He first achieved success at the Vienna State Opera (which he joined in 1941), distinguishing himself in the operas of Mozart and Wagner. He has since been one of the outstanding members of the Vienna State Opera company, and in 1948 received the highest honor Austria could confer on a singer, the title of *Kammersänger.* Meanwhile, in 1942, he appeared for the first time at the Salzburg Festival as Guglielmo in *Così Fan Tutte.* One year later he became the youngest artist to appear in a major role at the Bayreuth Festival when he was heard as Beckmesser in *Die Meistersinger.*

From this point on, his career assumed international significance, as he made many successful appearances with leading opera companies in Budapest, Rome, Naples, Florence, Paris, Brussels, and Buenos Aires. He was also one of the principal performers at the annual Salzburg Festival, and in 1948 at the Edinburgh Festival. In 1947 he toured

ERICH KUNZ

Kunz: ko͞onts

France and England with the Vienna State Opera.

His American debut took place at the Metropolitan Opera on November 26, 1952, as Leporello in *Don Giovanni. Musical America* reported that he had "a flexible, robust voice, and he sang the role . . . very well."

Kunz is married to Friede Kurzbauer, a former ballerina. Their home is in Vienna, where they also like to spend their summers in the Grinzing suburb. Kunz is an enthusiastic gardener, likes to fuss around with the motor of his automobile, and enjoys cooking.

KURENKO, MARIA, soprano. See *Living Musicians,* 1940.

KURTZ, EDMUND, violoncellist, was born in St. Petersburg on December 29, 1908. Though his parents were not musical, two of his brothers became successful musicians. Efrem is a noted conductor ; Arved is a violinist and director of the New York City College of Music.

When Revolution broke out in Russia, the Kurtz family settled in Berlin. There Edmund began the study of the cello with Fritz Espenhagen. After an additional period of study in Leipzig with Julius Klengel, he made his debut in Berlin in 1924. His first successful concert, at the Sala Bach in Rome, led to appearances in other principal Italian cities.

Another period of study followed—with Diran Alexanian in Paris—following which

EDMUND KURTZ

Kurtz undertook his first tour of France, Germany, and Scandinavia. At a recital in the Beethovensaal in Berlin in 1928 he played Saint-Saëns' "The Swan" before an audience that included the celebrated dancer Anna Pavlova. After the concert she went backstage to urge Kurtz to allow her to buy up all his contracts so that he might play "The Swan" for her in all her dance appearances. For two and a half years Kurtz toured with the Pavlova company. His last appearance with that group was in Brussels, immediately after Pavlova's sudden death, when he played "The Swan" to an empty stage.

During his final year with Pavlova, Kurtz joined the Spivakovsky Trio, which became so famous in Europe that in 1932 it was invited to tour Australia in eighty concerts. This marked for Kurtz the beginning of an association with Australia which continued for many years and during which he appeared in recitals and chamber-music performances and held master classes in the cello at the University of Melbourne.

In 1936 aboard ship for Australia, he met a young Australian, Barbara Bellair, with whom he fell in love and whom he married in May of that year. Soon after his marriage, he settled in Chicago, where for eight years he was first cellist of the Chicago Symphony Orchestra. He resigned from this post in 1944 to resume his career as a virtuoso. His American debut as solo cellist took place that same year when he appeared as soloist with the NBC Symphony Orchestra under Toscanini in the Dvořák B minor Concerto. When he appeared in his first New York recital the following January he was hailed by one of the critics as an artist "of challenging importance."

His appearances with symphony orchestras and in recitals have since that time been extensive. Beginning with 1948 he has made annual tours of Europe, and during the 1949-1950 season he made a tour of four continents. He has distinguished himself not only in the classical repertory but also in modern works, being responsible for the world premières of Milhaud's Concerto for Cello and *Élégie* (both written for him and dedicated to him), Honegger's Cello Concerto, and Lopatnikoff's Cello Sonata (Op. 11), and the American première of Khatchaturian's Cello Concerto.

Kurtz, his wife, and their two sons, Antony and John, live in a rambling eighteenth century house in Connecticut which is filled with antiques and old pewterware, of which both Kurtz and his wife are avid collectors. His hobbies include photography and carpentry.

Kurtz: koŏrts

KURTZ, EFREM, conductor. For his earlier career, see *Living Musicians*, 1940.

* * *

From 1943 to 1948, Kurtz was the principal conductor of the Kansas City Philharmonic. In 1948 he became the conductor of the Houston Symphony, and in 1954 conductor of the Liverpool Philharmonic in England. While serving in Liverpool he made major guest appearances with other European orchestras, and with La Scala in Milan. In the spring of 1957 he toured Ireland with the Liverpool Philharmonic.

LAHOLM, EYVIND, tenor. See *Living Musicians*, 1940.

LAMOND, FREDERICK, pianist. For his earlier career, see *Living Musicians*, 1940.

* * *

Lamond died in Stirling, Scotland, on February 21, 1948.

LANDOWSKA, WANDA, harpsichordist and pianist. For her earlier career, see *Living Musicians*, 1940.

* * *

When the Nazis entered Paris in 1940, Landowska abandoned her home at Saint-Leu-La-Forêt, with its precious collection of instruments and a library of over 10,000 volumes. She now established her permanent home in the United States, and gave her first American concert in fourteen years in 1941. In 1951 she made a monumental harpsichord recording for Victor of the complete Bach *Well-Tempered Clavier*.

LANGE, HANS, conductor. For his earlier career, see *Living Musicians*, 1940.

* * *

In 1946 Lange resigned as associate conductor of the Chicago Symphony Orchestra and subsequently assumed direction of the Albuquerque Civic Symphony Orchestra in New Mexico.

LARSEN-TODSEN, NANNY, soprano. For her earlier career, see *Living Musicians*, 1940.

* * *

Until World War II Larsen-Todsen gave guest performances in principal European opera houses, but since that time her appearances have been few and far between.

LASHANSKA, HULDA, soprano. See *Living Musicians*, 1940.

LATEINER, JACOB, pianist, was born in Havana, Cuba, in 1928, of Polish parents. He was four and a half years old when he started taking piano lessons with his mother, continuing them two years later with Jascha Fishermann. At six he gave his first recital, and at eight appeared as soloist with an orchestra conducted by Ernesto Lecuona, both in his native city. In 1939 he and his family settled in Philadelphia, where Jacob attended the Curtis Institute as a pupil of Isabella Vengerova. After five years there he won first prize in the Philadelphia Orchestra Youth Competition, enabling him to appear as soloist with the Philadelphia Orchestra under Eugene Ormandy in December 1945. Earlier the same year he toured the country as accompanist of the violinist Efrem Zimbalist.

Lateiner's professional career as a virtuoso began in 1947 when he appeared as soloist with the Kansas City Philharmonic in a performance of Tchaikovsky's B-flat minor Concerto. A critic of the Kansas City *Times* praised his "astounding technical ability, fine musicianly approach, and easy self-possessed platform presence." During the same year Lateiner also appeared as soloist with the NBC Symphony Orchestra, and at the Berkshire Music Festival, where he was heard in Beethoven's *Emperor* Concerto with the Boston Symphony under Koussevitzky.

Lateiner was graduated from the Curtis Institute in 1947. In his first three seasons as a concert artist he gave over two hundred performances in the United States, Canada, Mexico, and Cuba, besides making extensive tours of Australia and Tasmania. His New York debut took place in December 1948 with a recital which Olin Downes described in the New York *Times* as "astonishing . . . because of the maturity of technique and musicianship in an exceptionally formidable program." In the same year Lateiner became the only pianist selected by the Australian Broadcasting Company for sponsorship in Australia. In Melbourne alone he appeared three times with orchestra and gave four recital programs within ten days.

In 1951 Lateiner became a member of the United States Army. During this period of service, which lasted three years, he was often heard as soloist with the Army Field Band both in the United States and in Europe. His return to the concert stage as a civilian took

JACOB LATEINER

place in January 2, 1954, when he performed Prokofiev's Third Piano Concerto with the New York Philharmonic-Symphony. When, towards the end of the same year, he appeared in a New York recital, Olin Downes wrote: "Everything that he touched had distinction and was imbued with the feeling and thought of a devoted musician."

Lateiner is an avid collector of Greek coins, specimens of fifteenth-century printing, and contemporary graphic arts. Among the unusual items in his collection are a page from the first illustrated edition of Aesop's *Fables* and the last page of a work by St. Thomas Aquinas, both issued in the fifteenth century. Other interests include reading good literature and philosophy, and cooking foreign dishes. His brother Isidore is a concert violinist.

LAUBENTHAL, RUDOLF, tenor. See *Living Musicians,* 1940.

LAUFKOETTER, KARL, tenor. For his earlier career, see *Living Musicians,* 1940.

* * *

Laufkoetter left the Metropolitan Opera after the 1945-1946 season.

LAURI-VOLPI, GIACOMO, tenor. For his earlier career, see *Living Musicians,* 1940.

* * *

Since World War II, Lauri-Volpi has confined his appearances exclusively to Italy. He has written a two-volume autobiography: *L'Equivoco* (1938) and *A Viso Aperto* (1953).

LAWRENCE, MARJORIE, soprano. For her earlier career, see *Living Musicians,* 1940.

* * *

In 1941, Lawrence married Dr. Thomas King, a physician. They went on a honeymoon to Mexico City, where she was scheduled to appear in several Wagner music dramas. During a performance of *Die Walküre* she was stricken by poliomyelitis. For a long time it was feared she would be paralyzed for life. But her own heroism and the devotion and efforts of her husband not only overcame this infirmity but even enabled her to resume her career. Her first appearance following the illness took place at Town Hall, New York, in the fall of 1942, when she appeared seated in a wheelchair throughout the recital. On January 22, 1943, she returned to the stage of the Metropolitan Opera, performing Venus in *Tannhäuser* in a reclining position. A year later she appeared on the same stage as Isolde in a carefully camouflaged wheelchair. In Chicago, on December 11, 1947—in a concert presentation of *Elektra*—she stood throughout a performance for the first time. From then on, she made more and more appearances both in concert and in opera, in this country and abroad. She has told the story of her illness, and recovery in *Interrupted Melody* (1949), which six years after publication was made into a motion picture. In the summer of 1956 she joined the faculty of the Newcomb School of Music of Tulane University in New Orleans.

LAZZARI, VIRGILIO, basso. For his earlier career, see *Living Musicians,* 1940.

* * *

Lazzari made his last appearance at the Metropolitan Opera on December 5, 1950, having appeared there seventeen seasons in twenty-two major basso roles. He died near Rome on October 4, 1953.

LEHMANN, LOTTE, soprano. For her earlier career, see *Living Musicians,* 1940.

* * *

Lehmann made her last appearance at the Metropolitan Opera on March 29, 1945, as the Marschallin in *Der Rosenkavalier.* At a recital in Town Hall, New York, on February 16, 1951, she announced that she was retiring from the concert stage.

LEIDER, FRIDA, soprano. For her earlier career, see *Living Musicians,* 1940.

* * *

Immediately after World War II Leider became a producer for the Berlin State Opera.

LEINSDORF, ERICH, conductor. For his earlier career, see *Living Musicians,* 1940.

* * *

Leinsdorf left the Metropolitan Opera in 1943 to become principal conductor of the Cleveland Orchestra. In 1947 he left Cleveland to assume the office of music director of the Rochester Philharmonic Orchestra, and in the fall of 1956 he was appointed musical director of the New York City Opera Company. He stayed there only a single season. He returned to the Metropolitan Opera, after an absence of over a decade, to appear as guest conductor in a performance of Strauss' *Arabella* on January 7, 1957.

LEMNITZ, TIANA, soprano. See *Living Musicians,* 1940.

The LENER QUARTET. For its earlier history, see *Living Musicians,* 1940.

* * *

The Quartet disbanded just before the outbreak of World War II. Three of its members settled in Mexico. Jenö Lener, the first violinist, lived in New York City, where he participated in chamber-music performances, and where he died on November 4, 1948.

LE ROY, RENÉ, flutist. See *Living Musicians,* 1940.

LEV, RAE, pianist. See *Living Musicians,* 1940.

LEVIN, SYLVAN, conductor. See *Living Musicians,* 1940.

LEVITZKI, MISCHA, pianist. For his earlier career, see *Living Musicians,* 1940.

* * *

Levitzki died in Avon-by-the-Sea, New Jersey, on January 2, 1941.

LHEVINNE, JOSEPH, pianist. For his earlier career, see *Living Musicians,* 1940.

* * *

Lhevinne died in New York City on December 2, 1944.

LIPKIN, SEYMOUR, pianist, was born in Detroit, Michigan, on May 14, 1927. His father, a physician, was intensely musical, and so was his mother. "I was impossibly precocious," Lipkin once told an interviewer. "I began at two by playing the piano along with my mother but an octave higher. At two and a half I knew fifteen pieces by ear with my own improvised accompaniment. A year later, I forsook the kindergarten sandbox for the piano on which I accompanied my playmates in their nursery songs. At four I won a musical quiz, and at five I had an I.Q. of 166—and it's been impossible to live up to it ever since."

Between 1931 and 1939 he studied with local teachers in Detroit. At the same time he attended Northwestern High School. In 1939 he entered the Curtis Institute of Music, where from 1941 to 1947 he was a pupil of Rudolf Serkin, who exerted a tremendous influence on his development. While he attended the Curtis Institute, his academic education was continued at the University of Pennsylvania. He also studied conducting with Serge Koussevitzky at the Berkshire Music Center at Tanglewood, and was opera coach of the Philadelphia Opera in 1943. In 1947-1948 he was an apprentice conductor for the Cleveland Orchestra. Serge Koussevitzky, a few weeks before he died, invited Lipkin to join the conducting faculty of the Berkshire Music Center.

But it was as a pianist that he first won recognition. His first professional appear-

SEYMOUR LIPKIN

ance took place in February 1938 in Detroit, as soloist with the Detroit Civic Orchestra. Important appearances with major symphony orchestras followed. In the spring of 1945 he made a USO tour of Europe with Jascha Heifetz, performing in sixty-five concerts.

He achieved national recognition on April 29, 1948, when he was selected, by unanimous vote of the judges, the winner in a national piano contest sponsored by the Rachmaninoff Fund. His award consisted of a national concert tour under the auspices of two major concert bureaus; guest appearances with more than ten major American orchestras; radio appearances on nationally sponsored programs; a recording contract with RCA Victor. This is believed to be the largest prize won by any pianist in any contest in this country.

Extensive appearances followed. In four seasons he made four coast-to-coast tours of the United States and two successful tours of Europe; he made over sixty appearances in that time with thirty major orchestras. Felix Borowski of the Chicago *Sun Times* described him as "a serious musician as well as a pianist of very uncommon, exceptional gifts." Albert Goldberg wrote in the Los Angeles *Times* that he possessed "an impressive air of authority. He has both power and delicacy." Olin Downes reported in the New York *Times* that "everything he played was significant of musical ideas or a tone picture composed with imaginative as well as structural purpose."

On December 1, 1955, Lipkin conducted the Canadian television première of Leonard Bernstein's one-act opera, *Trouble in Tahiti.*

Lipkin has said that the greatest musical experience of his life was conducting the Curtis Institute Orchestra in Beethoven's *Emperor* Concerto with his teacher, Rudolf Serkin, as soloist.

Outside music, Lipkin's greatest interest is literature. He reads extensively in English, German, French, and Italian. His main hobby is book collecting.

LIPTON, MARTHA, mezzo-soprano, was born in New York City. Her mother was a concert singer who at first had so little faith in Martha's musical talent that she denied her daughter voice lessons. Martha attended the New York City public schools. After graduation from high school she studied stenography and went to work as a secretary for a law firm at $15 a week. She combined work with the study of singing—four nights a week with Melanie Guttman

MARTHA LIPTON

Rice. In her nineteenth year she won a Juilliard Fellowship enabling her to give up working and to concentrate entirely on the study of music, principally with Paul Reimers. But, as she explained to an interviewer, "My career crept. I was often broke. To pay for singing I worked in choruses, on radio, and in church choirs." After two years of such struggle she competed with two thousand others in an annual contest for singers sponsored by the National Federation of Music Clubs. She won first prize: $1,500 in cash and two seasons of concert appearances.

After these two years of concert work she tried out with the Metropolitan Auditions of the Air but failed to place successfully. She did however succeed in getting a hearing with Edward Johnson, then the general manager of the Metropolitan Opera. "I had so little confidence in the result that I went off to the country to forget about it," she reports. "Two months later I got a telegram to come down and sign up."

She made her Metropolitan Opera debut on November 27, 1944 (the opening night of the season), as Siebel in *Faust.* She was well received. Since that time she has been a leading member of the company, having appeared in more than thirty-five important roles, including Carmen, Amneris in *Aida,* Hänsel, Eva in *Die Meistersinger,* Cherubino in *Le Nozze di Figaro,* Brangäne in *Tristan und Isolde,* Emilia in *Otello,* Octavian in *Der Rosenkavalier,* and Mother Goose in Stravinsky's *The Rake's Progress.*

In the summer of 1946 she made her Latin-American debut with appearances at the Teatro Municipal in Rio de Janeiro, and in the summer of 1950 she made her concert debut in Europe. In 1951 she appeared successfully at the Edinburgh Festival, and in 1951 and 1952 at the Holland Music Festival.

"Martha Lipton is a true mezzo," wrote a critic for the New York *Herald Tribune* in 1952, "not merely a soprano whose talents include an ability to descend into the lower vocal regions. Indeed, all her work is predicated on her mezzo color, her mezzo power and the rich and flannel warmth of her low octave tones. Nor is this all. Throughout her range she sings with affirmed technical assurance, and everywhere her activity is that of a crafty and practical performer. . . . Her wise and knowing ways are not alone confined to the mechanics of singing. For Miss Lipton is a musician. That is to say she makes music and does not make lovely sounds for them alone. In sum, Miss Lipton is music's mate. As only the true artist does, she serves it with love and without question."

She has been a frequent performer with major American symphony orchestras besides appearing on numerous occasions on important radio and television programs.

LIST, EMANUEL, bass. For his earlier career, see *Living Musicians,* 1940.

* * *

List left the Metropolitan Opera after the 1951-1952 season.

LIST, EUGENE, pianist. For his earlier career, see *Living Musicians,* 1940.

* * *

In March 1942 List joined the United States Army in the Special Services Division. In 1943 he married the concert violinist, Carroll Glenn (with whom he often appeared in joint recitals after the war). While still in uniform, List became the center of world attention when on July 19, 1945, he performed for President Truman, Stalin, and Prime Minister Churchill at the historic meeting in Potsdam. (President Truman turned the pages of his music.)

Following his separation from the Army, in 1946, List resumed his concert activity with important appearances at the International Festival in Prague and with a tour of seven European countries. Both by himself and in conjunction with his wife he made special concert tours of occupied Germany and Italy at the request of the United States Army. He

and his wife helped organize the American Music Center, with headquarters in Berlin, which operates under the control of the United States and the American Military Government to promote better understanding through music. Besides his many concert appearances in this country and abroad since that time, List has often been heard over the radio and has appeared in a motion picture, *Bachelor's Daughters.*

LJUNGBERG, GÖTA, soprano. For her earlier career, see *Living Musicians,* 1940.

* * *

For several seasons, beginning with 1945, Ljungberg taught singing in New York City. She then returned to her native Sweden, and died there, at Lidingo, near Stockholm, on June 28, 1955.

LOESSER, ARTHUR, pianist. For his earlier career, see *Living Musicians,* 1940.

* * *

Loesser has written two books on music: *Humor in Music* (1942) and *Men, Women and Pianos* (1954). His brother, Frank Loesser, is the famous popular composer who wrote the music for the Broadway musicals *Guys and Dolls* and *The Most Happy Fella.*

The LOEWENGUTT QUARTET. See *Musicians,* 1940.

LONDON, GEORGE, bass-baritone, was born George Burson in Montreal, Canada on May 30, 1921. When his father, a manufacturer of millinery products, suffered a stroke, in 1936, the family moved to and settled in Los Angeles. Since George had no musical ambitions—he had some vague ideas of becoming a lawyer—he received no musical instruction, but attended the public schools. At Hollywood High School, he began appearing in school productions of comic operas and discovered that he liked singing and had a good voice. After his graduation from high school he studied for two years in the opera department of the Los Angeles City College, where he appeared in minor opera roles.

In 1941 Albert Coates selected him to appear in the American première of his opera *Gainsborough* at a concert performance at the Hollywood Bowl. After that London made various appearances with the American Music Theatre (which presented opera in English) and with light opera companies in Los Angeles and San Francisco. In 1943 he made

GEORGE LONDON

his first appearance with the San Francisco Opera in *Rigoletto*.

While appearing with a road company in *The Desert Song* in 1946, London arrived in New York, where he made his concert debut as soloist in Hindemith's *Requiem*, in its première at the New York City Center. Convinced that opera would be his career, he now decided to forgo appearances and concentrate on more study. With borrowed funds he went to Europe in 1947 'and became a pupil of Enrico Rosati. After a year of training he returned to New York and became a member of the Bel Canto Trio (the other two members were Frances Yeend and Mario Lanza), which toured the country for two seasons.

After numerous appearances in concerts and with ensembles London once again set sail for Europe in 1949. In Paris he was coached in operatic roles by Arthur Mahoney, Paola Novikova, and George Doubrovsky. After auditioning successfully with the Vienna State Opera, he made his European opera debut there on September 3, 1949, as Amonasro in *Aida*. He was acclaimed. In a brief period he appeared as Escamillo in *Carmen*, Boris Godounov, Prince Galitzi in *Prince Igor*, and in all the four baritone roles in *The Tales of Hoffmann*. As *Time* magazine reported from Vienna: "In four months he has been the rave of Vienna." Henry Pleasants wrote in the New York *Times*: "He has an extraordinarily beautiful bass baritone, admirably placed, and susceptible of much dramatic coloration. He is also a gifted and

accomplished actor." London has remained a great favorite in Vienna; in 1955 he was given the highest honor Vienna could bestow on an opera singer when he received the honorary title of *Kammersänger*.

George London made his Metropolitan Opera debut on November 13, 1951 (opening night of the season), as Amonasro. Virgil Thomson wrote in the New York *Herald Tribune* that he was "one of the greatest singing actors we have any of us known or remembered." Hardly had the echoes of this success died down when London flew to Europe to make his first appearance at La Scala —as Pizarro in *Fidelio* on January 9, 1952. After that he was heard in seven leading European festivals: Salzburg, Bayreuth, Edinburgh, Glyndebourne, Munich, Aix-en-Provence, and the Holland Music Festival.

London has since appeared in concerts and opera performances throughout the world of music. He has also been a guest performer on important radio and television programs. At the Metropolitan he has been acclaimed for a wide variety of roles, including Don Giovanni, Escamillo, Amfortas in *Parsifal*, Scarpia in *Tosca*, and Boris Godunov. His first appearance in the title role of *Boris Godunov* took place early in 1953 and was an event of particular significance. The opera was being presented for the first time at the Metropolitan Opera in Mussorgsky's original version; it was being given in English; and this was the first time that an American singer appeared in the title role. London received eleven curtain calls. Virgil Thomson wrote: "So fine a bass voice handled with such art, so great a gift for drama, and so subtle a care for diction have not been met up with by this observer since the death of Chaliapin."

London is a large man—six feet two, weighing two hundred pounds. He is a sports enthusiast who keeps his body in trim with daily setting-up exercises. His diversions include social dancing, the movies, jazz, reading detective stories and historical novels, and baseball.

LOWE, JACK. See WHITTEMORE and LOWE

LUBIN, GERMAINE, dramatic soprano. For her earlier career, see *Living Musicians*, 1940.

* * *

Lubin's scheduled debut with the Metropolitan Opera during the 1940-1941 season did not materialize because of the war. She continued her career as principal soprano of the Paris Opéra. After World War II, she made distinguished appearances not only at the Paris Opéra but also in many other leading European opera houses.

LUBOSCHUTZ, LEA, violinist. See *Living Musicians,* 1940.

LUBOSCHUTZ and NEMENOFF, duo-pianists. See *Living Musicians,* 1940.

LUCA, GIUSEPPE DE, baritone. For his earlier career, see *Living Musicians,* 1940.

* * *

Giuseppe de Luca gave his farewell concert in New York City on November 7, 1947—fifty years and a day after his debut. After his retirement he devoted himself to teaching. He died in New York City on August 26, 1950.

LYMPANY, MOURA, pianist, was born in Saltash, England, on August 18, 1916. As a child, she was sent to Belgium for schooling. It was there, in her seventh year, that she started taking piano lessons. She made such excellent progress (at eight she was already playing sonatas by Mozart and Beethoven) that she was sent to the Liége Conservatory, where for a few years she studied with Jules Debefve. In her thirteenth year she became the youngest student ever admitted to the Royal Academy of Music in London. There, under the guidance of Ambrose Coviello, she won the Ada Lewis Scholarship. Two years later she won both the Challon Gold Medal (bestowed upon the best student of the year) and the Hine Gift for composition.

After being graduated with highest honors, she concluded her music study with Paul Weingarten in Vienna and Matthilde Verne and Tobias Matthay in London. During this period she earned her living tutoring students in French and English and accompanying singing teachers during their lessons.

In 1938 she won second prize at the Ysaÿe Piano Competition in Brussels (first prize that year went to Emil Gilels). One of the judges was Artur Rubinstein, who induced his own Parisian manager to take on the young artist. Lympany was thus able to tour Italy, France, Holland, Belgium, and South America.

She was in South America when war broke out in Europe. She canceled all her subsequent engagements and returned to her native

MOURA LYMPANY

land. There, during the war period, she gave concert performances and played for soldiers in hospitals and for war-workers.

In 1945 she and Sir Adrian Boult became the first British artists to perform in Paris after the liberation, and in 1946 she represented Great Britain at the Prague Music Festival. In that year of 1946 she visited the United States on vacation. When she returned to this country two years later, her reputation had preceded her through her successful recordings for London. One of her admirers prevailed upon her to give a concert in Seattle. After making her American debut there, Lympany gave her first New York recital on November 28, 1948. Noel Straus wrote in the New York *Times*: "The handsome, modest musician at once established herself as an artist of decided importance both as technician and interpreter. Miss Lympany's performance had a refreshing and irresistible wholesomeness, a freedom from exaggeration, an impeccable taste, a sanity, and at the same time a definite individuality which, combined with first-rate virtuosity, made her performance noteworthy." From that time on, Lympany has toured the United States extensively, besides appearing in Europe and Canada.

On August 10, 1951, she married Bennett Korn, a New York radio advertising executive. They make their permanent home in New York City.

McCORMACK, JOHN, tenor. For his earlier career, see *Living Musicians,* 1940.

* * *

McCormack died in Dublin, Ireland, on September 16, 1945.

MADEIRA, JEAN, mezzo-soprano, was born Jean Browning in Centralia, Illinois on November 14, 1924. Her father—who was half English and half American Indian—worked in the coal mines; her mother was a piano teacher. Jean began taking piano lessons with her mother. When her father died in 1932, the family moved to St. Louis, where Jean studied piano for five years on a scholarship at the Leo C. Miller School of Music. During this period she won a competition entitling her to appear with the St. Louis Symphony under Golschmann in a performance of Beethoven's C Minor Concerto.

From 1941 to 1945 she attended the Juilliard School of Music as a piano student. There she met and fell in love with another piano student, Francis King Madeira, whom she married on June 17, 1947. Francis Madeira subsequently became the conductor of the Rhode Island Philharmonic and assistant professor of music at Brown University.

On the advice of Olga Samaroff, Jean Madeira turned from piano to singing in 1946. While studying voice at the Juilliard, she made numerous appearances in contralto operatic roles with the San Carlo Opera and the Chautauqua (New York) Opera. In 1947 she won the Woman of Achievement Award

JEAN MADEIRA

in St. Louis, and one year later she appeared in London in Menotti's *The Medium.*

On December 2, 1948, she made her debut at the Metropolitan Opera as the Norn in *Götterdämmerung.* In the next half dozen years she frequently appeared in principal contralto roles at the Metropolitan, including Amneris in *Aida,* Azucena in *Il Trovatore,* Ulrica in *Un Ballo in Maschera,* Dalila, and Orfeo in the Gluck opera. In 1954-1955 she appeared successfully at Covent Garden, at the Stockholm Opera, and at the Munich and Salzburg Festivals; and in the summer of 1956 she returned to the Munich and Salzburg Festivals.

Jean Madeira made her debut as a mezzo-soprano at the Vienna State Opera in the fall of 1955, when she was heard as Carmen. She was such a sensation that she received forty-five curtain calls. The following February she sang the same role at the Metropolitan Opera. "An intelligent artist who gives close thought to what she undertakes," wrote Irving Kolodin in the *Saturday Review,* "Miss Madeira had prepared herself thoroughly in the dramatic as well as musical aspects of the part, utilizing her height to advantage, also a mass of dark hair that framed her face effectively. Everything had been closely worked out to a plan and found her 'doing something' almost all the time. Mostly it was done with a suggestion of youthful suppleness not often seen."

Besides her appearances in Europe and at the Metropolitan Opera, Madeira has been heard over radio and television.

MAGANINI, QUINTO, flutist and conductor. See *Living Musicians,* 1940.

MAHLER, FRITZ, conductor. For his earlier career, see *Living Musicians,* 1940.

* * *

In 1947, Mahler was appointed principal conductor of the Erie (Pennsylvania) Philharmonic Orchestra. Since 1953 he has been the conductor of the Hartford (Connecticut) Symphony. Following World War II he has given important guest performances with the Lamoureux Orchestra and the Orchestre Symphonique of Paris, the Oslo Philharmonic, and other major orchestras in Scandinavia and Switzerland.

MAIER and PATTISON, duo-pianists. For their earlier careers, see *Living Musicians,* 1940.

* * *

Guy Maier died in Santa Monica, California, on September 23, 1956.

MAISON, RENÉ, tenor. For his earlier career, see *Living Musicians*, 1940.

* * *

Maison left the Metropolitan Opera after the 1942-1943 season. Following World War II, he appeared with leading European opera companies.

MALCUZYNSKI, WITOLD, pianist, was born in Warsaw, Poland, on August 10, 1914. His family was socially prominent in Warsaw, his father being a member of the Warsaw Stock Exchange. Intended for law, Witold attended two Polish universities. But at the same time he studied piano, and devoted all his free time either to playing music or listening to it. When he reached the determination to enter music professionally, he entered the Warsaw Conservatory, where he studied with Josef Turczynski. Upon his graduation from the Conservatory in 1936, his teacher arranged a private concert which was attended by Paderewski. The master accepted Malcuzynski as a private pupil. For about a year Malcuzynski lived with Paderewski at the latter's villa in Switzerland and worked with him daily.

In 1937 Malcuzynski entered the Chopin Competition held in Warsaw, the last such competition before World War II. He won first prize among over a hundred candidates. Another candidate was a young woman named Colette Gaveau, with whom Malcuzynski fell in love and married in 1938. They settled in Paris, where, just before the outbreak of World War II, he made his concert debut.

During the war, the Malcuzynskis escaped from Nazi-occupied France and went to South America by way of Portugal. He made an extensive tour there. He was heard by Yehudi Menuhin, who helped him enter the United States, and in 1942 he made his North American debut in New York. "All the resources of nineteenth-century piano and the superb piano effects written for it are at his command," reported Olin Downes in the New York *Times*. Appearances with several major American orchestras confirmed the good impression he made at his recital debut.

Before hostilities were terminated in Europe, Malcuzynski returned aboard a troop ship, making many appearances in England. He resumed his concert activity in Europe after the war and received particular acclaim for his interpretations of the works of Chopin.

James Abresch

WITOLD MALCUZYNSKI

When the centenary of Chopin's death was commemorated, Malcuzynski was chosen by the Kosciusko Foundation to inaugurate the Chopin celebration with a recital in Carnegie Hall in February 1949. He was also one of two recitalists selected to play in Paris on the anniversary of Chopin's death (October 17), his concert being broadcast over the French radio.

Malcuzynski maintains a rigorous concert schedule that takes him around the world. In 1949, for example, he traveled fifty thousand miles, performing on four continents; in 1953, he gave fifty concerts in South America alone. He has made over a dozen transcontinental tours of the United States.

"If there is anything that the ten fingers of Witold Malcuzynski cannot do on the keyboard, it has not yet been written," wrote Robert Bagar in the New York *World Telegram and Sun*. "For they have the command of the technical situation. They range over the keys with confidence, whether in jet-powered fortes or in the most delicate whispers. . . . The pianist molded and shaped and worked on phrases in such an ingratiating manner that the music, as it unreeled, could hardly have communicated more."

Among the many decorations he has received is the Polonia Restituta, the highest that Poland could give for cultural achievement, presented to him before the Iron Curtain descended on that country.

Malcuzynski: măl-kōō-shĭn'skē

MANNES, DAVID, violinist and conductor. For his earlier career, see *Living Musicians,* 1940.

* * *

In 1947 Mannes resigned as director of the David Mannes School of Music, and as conductor of the Metropolitan Museum of Art concerts, both in New York. Since then he has been in retirement.

MANSKI, DOROTHEE, soprano. See *Living Musicians,* 1940.

MARÉCHAL, MAURICE, cellist. See *Living Musicians,* 1940.

MARIO, QUEENA, soprano. For her earearlier career, see *Living Musicians,* 1940.

* * *

After her retirement from the opera stage, Queena Mario began writing mystery novels. Three of these had opera backgrounds: *Murder in the Opera House, Murder Meets Mephisto,* and *Death Drops Delilah.* She died in New York City on May 28, 1951.

MARKEVITCH, IGOR, conductor, was born in Kiev, Russia, on July 27, 1912. When Russia became embroiled in World War I, two years after Igor's birth, the family settled in Vevey, Switzerland. There the boy soon revealed himself to be so unusually gifted in music that Alfred Cortot began giving him piano lessons. When Markevitch was fourteen he was sent to Paris, where he studied harmony and counterpoint with Nadia Boulanger. "You have a natural feeling for harmony," Boulanger told him after he had taken only a few lessons. "As to counterpoint, there is nothing I can teach you." He was already composing, and despite his youth his works demonstrated such originality that they were performed by major musical organizations in Paris and London.

When he was seventeen he served as pianist for Diaghilev's Ballet Russe. Diaghilev commissioned him to write the music for a ballet based on Andersen's fairy tale *The Emperor's Clothes.* Unfortunately, Diaghilev died before this commission could be completed.

Markevitch's career as a conductor began after he had completed preliminary studies with Herman Scherchen. He was eighteen when he conducted his first concert, a guest performance with the Concertgebouw Orchestra of Amsterdam. The eminent Dutch critic Alois Mooser wrote: "In all my life I have only met two composers who could be said to

IGOR MARKEVITCH

possess equal ability in the art of composing and conducting, Gustav Mahler and Richard Strauss. The name of Igor Markevitch can now be added to the short list." Additional guest appearances with other important European orchestras, just before the outbreak of World War II, placed him in the vanguard of younger European conductors, particularly in the modern repertory.

In 1940 he went to Florence, Italy, to get material for a cantata he was writing about Lorenzo de Medici. While he was there, Italy entered the war, and Markevitch was compelled to remain in the city for the duration of the conflict. He found a home on the estate of the celebrated art critic Bernard Berenson.

After the liberation of Florence, in 1944, Markevitch was appointed by the Allies director of the orchestra at the May Music Festival. When the war in Europe ended, Markevitch traveled throughout Europe conducting not only symphony concerts but also opera performances at the Vienna State Opera and the San Carlo in Naples. He also made impressive appearances in the years that followed in South America and Israel, at the Exposition of Masterpieces of the Twentieth Century in Paris in 1952, and at such eminent music festivals as those in Salzburg, Vienna, Lucerne, Berlin, and Holland. In Salzburg, besides his conducting duties, he has since 1953 undertaken to direct a master class in conducting at the Mozarteum. In 1953 Markevitch settled permanently in London, and in

Markevitch: mär-kā'-vĭch

1954 he made his debut at Covent Garden with a highly acclaimed performance of Rimsky-Korsakov's *Le Coq d'Or.*

Markevitch made his American debut as guest conductor of the Boston Symphony Orchestra on March 18, 1955. He was hailed by the critics as one of the most cogent and dynamic conductors of our time, particularly for his reading of Stravinsky's *Le Sacre du Printemps.* He directed this work again when he made his New York debut, as a guest conductor of the Symphony of the Air, on January 4, 1957. "Mr. Markevitch handled its complexities as if they did not exist," wrote Howard Taubman in the New York *Times.* "This was music for which he clearly felt an affinity. Under his guidance the rites of spring were celebrated with a primitive ferocity."

In the summer of 1957, Markevitch helped inaugurate three major summer concert series in the United States: the Lewisohn Stadium Concerts on June 24; the Ravinia Festival on June 27; and the Empire State Music Festival in Ellenville, New York, on July 4. In the fall of 1957 Markevitch was assigned two important posts: conductor of the Lamoureux Orchestra in Paris and music director of the Montreal Symphony Orchestra.

MARTINELLI, GIOVANNI, tenor. For his earlier career, see *Living Musicians,* 1940.

* * *

Martinelli left the Metropolitan Opera after the 1944-1945 season, and was subsequently heard in recitals, as soloist with orchestras, and on radio and television programs. From 1953 to 1956 he was a member of the opera department of the Benedetto Marcello Conservatory in Venice, Italy. In 1956 he was appointed head of the voice department and chief consultant to the opera workshop of the Music School Settlement in New York.

MARTINI, NINO, tenor. For his earlier career, see *Living Musicians,* 1940.

* * *

Martini left the Metropolitan Opera after the 1945-1946 season. He returned to Italy to make his permanent home.

MARX, BURLE, conductor. See *Living Musicians,* 1940.

MASINI, GALLIANO, tenor. For his earlier career, see *Living Musicians,* 1940.

* * *

During and after World War II Masini's operatic appearances were concentrated in Italy.

MATZENAUER, MARGARET, dramatic soprano and contralto. For her earlier career, see *Living Musicians,* 1940.

* * *

Matzenauer has been in retirement since World War II.

MAYNOR, DOROTHY, soprano. For her earlier career, see *Living Musicians,* 1940.

* * *

In 1949, Maynor sang at President Truman's inauguration ceremonies in Washington, D.C., and made her first tour of South America. One year later she made her first tour of Europe.

MEADER, GEORGE, tenor. See *Living Musicians,* 1940.

MEISLE, KATHRYN, contralto. See *Living Musicians,* 1940.

MELCHIOR, LAURITZ, tenor. For his earlier career, see *Living Musicians,* 1940.

* * *

Melchior's twentieth anniversary at the Metropolitan Opera was celebrated on February 17, 1946, with a concert in which he appeared in several scenes from Wagner music dramas. Four years later, on February 2, 1950, he made his last appearance at the Metropolitan Opera—in *Lohengrin.* Now retired from the opera stage, he has made many appearances in night clubs, at concerts, on radio and television, and in motion pictures.

MELTON, JAMES, tenor. For his earlier career, see *Living Musicians,* 1940.

* * *

Melton left the Metropolitan Opera after the 1943-1944 season. He subsequently appeared in concerts and on numerous radio and television programs.

MENGELBERG, WILLEM, conductor. For his earlier career, see *Living Musicians,* 1940.

* * *

In 1945, immediately after V-E Day, Mengelberg was convicted of collaboration with the enemy during the Nazi occupation of Holland. The Netherlands Central Council of Honor for the Arts forbade him to conduct ever again in Holland. (The sentence was later reduced to six years.) In 1947 a gold medal once presented to him by Queen Wilhelmina was withdrawn; and in 1949 an annuity which had been granted in 1939—and which he had been receiving even after his banishment — was withdrawn. He died in exile, in Zuort, near Chur, Switzerland, on March 21, 1951.

MENGES, ISOLDE, violinist. See *Living Musicians,* 1940.

MENUHIN, YEHUDI, violinist. For his earlier career, see *Living Musicians,* 1940.

* * *

Menuhin is said to have made more appearances for the armed forces during World War II than any other musician, having given over five hundred such concerts. He was the first concert artist to perform in Paris, Brussels, Bucharest, Budapest, and Antwerp after the liberation of those cities, and the first American musician to appear in Japan and the Soviet Union since the war.

MERRILL, ROBERT, baritone, was born in Brooklyn, New York, on June 4, 1919. He attended Brooklyn public schools. His boyhood interests were divided equally between singing and baseball. His first voice teacher was his mother, Lillian Miller Merrill, herself a concert singer. He made several appearances in Brooklyn as a boy soprano. While attending New Utrecht High School, he played

ROBERT MERRILL

on the baseball team, and after that was a pitcher for a semi-professional club. He had a tryout with the Brooklyn Dodgers and was rejected; and it was only then that he definitely ruled out baseball as a career and turned to singing.

In 1936, while studying voice with Samuel Margolies, he supported himself by holding various small jobs and filling minor singing engagements, including some at summer resorts. At one of these resorts he was heard by a New York agent who arranged for a radio audition. This brought Merrill an opportunity to appear as soloist on a coast-to-coast radio program with the Spitalny orchestra. In the early part of World War II, he was engaged by the producers of Fox Movietone to sing "The Star Spangled Banner" in a nationally distributed film short. When Erno Rapee, then the conductor at Radio City Music Hall, heard Merrill he engaged him to appear at the theatre. Merrill filled an eight-week engagement there in 1943.

His opera debut took place one year later in Trenton, New Jersey, where he sang the part of Amonasro in *Aida.* In 1945 he entered the Metropolitan Auditions of the Air and won first place. This led to a successful debut at the Metropolitan Opera on December 15, 1945, in the role of the elder Germont in *La Traviata.* In the same season he was also heard as Ashton in *Lucia di Lammermoor* and Escamillo in *Carmen,* performances which, as Irving Kolodin wrote in his book on the Metropolitan Opera, "left only the question whether he would grow, artistically, to equality with his noble endowment." In the years that followed, as a leading baritone of the company, Merrill proved he could grow artistically, bringing to each of his roles not only a remarkable voice but authoritative musicianship and commanding characterizations.

In 1946 Toscanini selected Merrill to sing the elder Germont in his broadcast performance of *La Traviata* over NBC; Toscanini again chose Merrill, this time for the role of Renato, when he conducted *Un Ballo in Maschera* over NBC in 1954. In July 1946 Merrill was the only singer chosen to appear at a joint service held by both Houses of Congress in memory of President Franklin D. Roosevelt. At the service, which President Truman and other high government officials attended, Merrill sang "Eternal Father, Strong to Save," and "The Lord's Prayer." After that Merrill sang several times at birthday parties for President Truman and, in 1949, at his inauguration ceremonies.

Merrill has appeared in over twenty leading baritone roles of the Italian and French repertory. His most successful ones have been Figaro in *The Barber of Seville* (about which Cyrus Durgin said in the Boston *Morning Globe,* "He has the figure, the personal quality and the dash for Figaro, and he sings the part with rhythmic buoyance") ; the elder Germont; Amonasro; Rigoletto; Renato; Escamillo; and Rodrigo in *Don Carlo* (the last sung at the performance which inaugurated the Rudolf Bing regime at the Metropolitan Opera, and which was televised nationally).

In the spring of 1951 Merrill left for Hollywood to appear in a motion picture, *Aaron Slick from Punkin Crick.* Because this assignment conflicted with engagements at the Metropolitan Opera, and because Merrill refused to leave Hollywood at the time, he was dismissed by Rudolf Bing. But before the year was over, Merrill was restored to the company, and he has been appearing with it since. He has also appeared frequently on numerous major radio and television programs; and of his many recordings for Victor, one received the Annual Recorded Music Award in 1946.

Merrill has not lost his boyhood enthusiasm for baseball, but the sport that now engages him as an active participant is golf. He always takes a set of golf clubs when he is on a concert tour. His indoor diversions include the preparation of exotic dishes, reading anything from philosophy to detective novels, and collecting etchings and paintings.

MEYROWITZ, SELMAR, conductor. For his earlier career, see *Living Musicians,* 1940.

* * *

Just before World War II, Meyrowitz settled permanently in Paris, where he led some of the city's major orchestras. He died in Toulouse, France, in May 1941.

MILANOV, ZINKA, soprano. For her earlier career, see *Living Musicians,* 1940.

* * *

As a principal soprano of the Metropolitan Opera, she was chosen three times to appear in the opening-night performance of the season: in *Un Ballo in Maschera* in 1940; *Aida,* in 1951; and *La Forza del Destino,* in 1952. Only seven other sopranos in Metropolitan Opera history have either equaled or exceeded this record; and she is the only soprano to have appeared on two successive opening

nights. She made fourteen appearances under Toscanini and has also appeared with leading opera companies in Europe.

MILDNER, POLDI, pianist. See *Living Musicians,* 1940.

MILSTEIN, NATHAN, violinist. For his earlier career, see *Living Musicians,* 1940.

* * *

After a recital in Paris on November 2, 1956, Milstein was made Chevalier of the Legion of Honor for his achievements as "an outstanding American artist."

MISCHAKOFF, MISCHA, violinist. For his earlier career, see *Living Musicians,* 1940.

* * *

In 1951 Mischakoff was engaged as concertmaster of the Detroit Symphony Orchestra. In 1950-1951, and again in 1954, he was guest professor at the University of Colorado, and in 1953 was a visiting professor at the Royal Conservatory in Toronto.

MITCHELL, HOWARD, conductor, was born in Lyons, Nebraska, on March 11, 1911. He was one of six children, all of whom were directed by their father to music. "I started studying the piano on my sixth birthday," he told an interviewer. "I had just moved with the family to Sioux City. I didn't like the piano. My parents told me any time I got another instrument I could give it up. I was nine when a man who worked for Father gave me a tuba. That ended the piano for me. I took the tuba for two years. At eleven, I got a yen for the trumpet. I bought one and started playing at dances. In my high school days I came into contact with Arthur Poister, an organist and a fine teacher, as well as an inspiring conductor. I was first trumpet in his orchestra and band. He needed a cello, and persuaded me to take it up. I bought my first cello for thirty dollars when I was fifteen years old. Soon I was playing it in the orchestra. After six months I entered a cello contest—came out third, although I could only play in the first position."

In 1928, in a state-wide competition, he won first prize, a scholarship at the Peabody Conservatory in Baltimore. After two and a half years there, he went on to the Curtis Institute in Philadelphia, where he studied cello with Felix Salmond, also on a scholarship. While there he became first cellist of the National Symphony Orchestra in Wash-

Fabian Bachrach

HOWARD MITCHELL

ington, D.C., then being led by Hans Kindler; for the two years before his graduation from the Curtis Institute, which took place in 1935, he commuted regularly between Washington and Philadelphia.

The first time he conducted an orchestra was in the fall of 1941, when he was asked to lead some "pop" concerts of the National Symphony Orchestra at the Riverside Stadium. In 1944 Kindler appointed him assistant conductor of the orchestra, and at the same time assigned to him the children's concerts. When Kindler became ill, Mitchell was required to substitute for him at the regular performances. The first time he did so was on February 23, 1947. Frequently, at five o'clock in the afternoon Mitchell would get the scores he was required to conduct the same evening.

In February 1948 Kindler realized his health would not permit him to continue as the sole conductor of the orchestra, and Mitchell became his associate, assuming some of the concerts of the regular season. When Kindler died in 1949, Mitchell succeeded him as the permanent conductor, thus becoming one of the few conductors of a major symphony orchestra to rise from the ranks of the same organization. Under Mitchell, the activities of the orchestra were expanded to embrace a season of twenty-six weeks, instead of twenty-four, comprising one hundred concerts, instead of seventy-seven. Thirty children's concerts were now given instead of

seven, and a Junior National Symphony Orchestra of high school students was organized by him in 1951.

Mitchell conducted in Europe for the first time early in 1955, when he appeared as guest conductor of the Radiodiffusion Nationale Belge and the Royal Conservatory Orchestra, both in Brussels. He followed these performances with others in Greece and the Netherlands.

Mitchell has been honored by the National Music Council for his service to contemporary American music, the award being presented to him at the opening concert of his orchestra of the 1952-1953 season. In 1957 he received four important awards within the space of six weeks: the National Music Council Award (third time); the Catholic Music Educators Award; the Alice M. Ditson Award; and the Award of the National Association for American Composers and Conductors.

In 1930 Howard Mitchell met Alma Metcalf at the Peabody Conservatory, where they were both students at the time. They fell in love and were married in 1931. They have five children—two girls and three boys—all of them musical. His principal diversion is golf, in which he has won numerous awards in various championships in the District of Columbia. He is also fond of fishing.

MITCHELL, VIOLA, violinist. See *Living Musicians*, 1940.

MITROPOULOS, DIMITRI, conductor. For his earlier career, see *Living Musicians*, 1940.

* * *

In 1949 Mitropoulos became an American citizen, and in the same year he assumed the post of musical director of the New York Philharmonic-Symphony Society. He retained this post until the 1957-1958 season, when the pressure of other commitments compelled him to divide both the Philharmonic season and the office of principal conductor with Leonard Bernstein. While serving with the New York Philharmonic-Symphony, Mitropoulos gave distinguished performances of opera at La Scala, the May Music Festival in Florence, the Vienna State Opera, and the Metropolitan Opera. In 1956 he received the award of Orfeo d'Oro from the city of Mantua, the second conductor to be thus honored, the first having been Toscanini.

MOISEIWITSCH, BENNO, pianist. See *Living Musicians*, 1940.

MOLINARI, BERNARDINO, conductor. For his earlier career, see *Living Musicians,* 1940.

* * *

Molinari died in Rome on December 25, 1952.

MONACO, MARIO DEL. See DEL MONACO, MARIO.

MONATH, HORTENSE, pianist. For her earlier career, see *Living Musicians,* 1940.

* * *

Monath died in New York City on May 20, 1956.

MONROE, LUCY, soprano. See *Living Musicians,* 1940.

MONTEUX, PIERRE, conductor. For his earlier career, see *Living Musicians,* 1940.

* * *

Monteux resigned as musical director of the San Francisco Symphony Orchestra in 1952, giving his last concert on April 12. On November 17, 1953, he returned to the Metropolitan Opera after an absence of thirty-five years to conduct the opening night performance of the new season—a new production of *Faust.* He has since appeared as guest conductor not only at the Metropolitan Opera but also with various American orchestras. His eightieth birthday was celebrated on April 4, 1955, with an appearance as guest conductor of the Boston Symphony; the second half of the program consisted of two works written in his honor by Milhaud and Stravinsky and conducted by Charles Munch.

Monteux was made Commander of the Order of Orange Nassau by Holland in 1950, and Commander of the French Legion of Honor in 1952.

MOORE, GRACE, soprano. For her earlier career, see *Living Musicians,* 1940.

* * *

Moore died in an airplane crash in Copenhagen on January 26, 1947. Three years before her death, she completed her autobiography, *You're Only Human Once* (1944), which after her death was made into a motion picture starring Kathryn Grayson.

MORINI, ERICA, violinist. See *Living Musicians,* 1940.

MOSCONA, NICOLA, bass-baritone. For his earlier career, see *Living Musicians,* 1940.

* * *

Besides being a member of the Metropolitan Opera company since 1937, Moscona is also a principal bass-baritone of La Scala in Milan and the Teatro Reale in Rome. His appearances as guest artist with most of the world's leading orchestras include twenty-six performances under Toscanini, and nine performances under Bruno Walter. In the summer of 1949 Moscona paid a return visit to his native land, Greece, for the first time in over a decade, appearing in fourteen opera performances at the National Opera of Greece and giving a recital in an open-air stadium before an audience of 35,000. King Paul presented him with the Cross of the Royal Order of Phoenix, the highest decoration the Crown could bestow, and the first honor of its kind given to a musician; Moscona also received a a silver plaque from the National Opera, and a gold medal from the Greek Disabled Veterans. He has been an American citizen since 1945. He appeared in three opera scenes in the motion picture *The Great Caruso,* starring Mario Lanza.

MUNCH, CHARLES, conductor, was born in Strasbourg, Alsace, on September 26, 1891. The fifth of six children, he came from a musical family. His father was the founder of the St. Guillaume Choir and professor at the local Conservatory; and the world-famous organist and humanitarian Albert Schweitzer is a distant relative.

There was always music in the Munch household. The family and its friends often congregated to sing Bach cantatas or to play chamber music. As a boy, Charles' major interest was not music but locomotives. When he was six he knew the exact time the European express trains came into the Strasbourg station, and he was usually there to await their arrival.

He was given a comprehensive musical training—first at the Strasbourg Conservatory, where his principal teacher was Hans Pfitzner, and then at the Paris Conservatory, where he specialized in the violin with Lucien Capet. After World War I he studied the violin with Carl Flesch in Berlin.

Just before the outbreak of World War I, Munch began concertizing as violinist. His career was interrupted by service in the German army, into which he was conscripted because at the time Alsace belonged to Ger-

Munch: münsh

Jac-Guy

CHARLES MUNCH

many. He saw action as a sergeant gunner for four years, was gassed at Péronne, and after being wounded at Verdun was demobilized.

After the war he became professor of violin at the Strasbourg Conservatory and concertmaster of the city orchestra. In 1926 he was engaged as violinist in the Gewandhaus Orchestra in Leipzig, where he played under Bruno Walter and Wilhelm Furtwängler. He was forced to leave this job in 1929 because he refused to become a German citizen. He returned to Paris where he made his debut as conductor with the Paris Symphony Orchestra in 1933. He has explained that the reason he turned so late to conducting was that "it was much easier for me to make a living as a violinist, and I just could not afford to direct an orchestra earlier." It was his wife who made his career as a conductor possible. She was Geneviève Maury, granddaughter of one of the founders of the Nestlé chocolate firm, whom he had met when he was a student of the Paris Conservatory and whom he married in 1933. In the same year he made his debut as conductor in Paris. He made such a good impression that he was soon engaged to conduct other notable Parisian organizations, such as the Lamoureux and the Straram orchestras. In 1935, when the Paris Philharmonic Orchestra was founded by Alfred Cortot, Munch became its principal conductor; it was with this organization that his exceptional talent first became evident. In 1937 he became the principal conductor of the International Society for Contemporary Music, then being held in Paris. In 1938, and until 1946, he was the conductor of the Paris Conservatory Orchestra, in succession to Philippe Gaubert. He also made appearances with other major European orchestras.

During World War II, Munch remained in France, helping to keep up the morale of his people by performing French music for them. Whatever income he received from the occupying Nazis was turned over to the Resistance movement. He continually used whatever influence he had to protect French musicians from the Gestapo, and on several occasions even defied Gestapo orders about purging his orchestras of players condemned on racial or political grounds. He was asked to take over the direction of the Paris Opéra, but refused to do so because that meant working with avowed collaborationists.

After the war, Munch became the first French conductor to lead performances in England. After that he led numerous concerts in Europe, the Near East, and South America. His North American debut took place on December 27, 1946, when he appeared as guest conductor of the Boston Symphony Orchestra in an all-French program. Here, and in subsequent appearances with American orchestras, he proved himself to be a master of conductorial technique, a most discriminating musician, an artist of immaculate taste and judgment. "It was evident," wrote Olin Downes in the New York Times, "that we had with us a superb musician, and orchestra leader to boot."

In 1948 Munch succeeded Serge Koussevitzky as the musical director of the Boston Symphony Orchestra. He has held that post since then, and has become accepted as one of the major conductors of our generation. Temperamentally, Munch is the exact opposite of his famed predecessor. Where Koussevitzky was the martinet who treated his men with dictatorial ruthlessness, Munch is the democrat who wins them over to his way of thinking with graciousness of manner, charm, and consideration for their feelings. Koussevitzky used to put them through gruelling rehearsals in which every detail of a composition was worked over fastidiously. Munch prefers a rehearsal in which the over-all concept of a work is prepared, and in which some of the details are left to the performance itself, allowing for greater spontaneity and freshness.

In 1952 Munch took the Boston Symphony Orchestra on its first European tour, appearing in England, France, Holland, Belgium, and Germany. It was a triumph from the very first appearance. In late summer of 1956 Munch once again brought the Boston Symphony to Europe, this time to appear at the Edinburgh Festival. A few weeks later, on September 6, the Boston Symphony under Munch became the first American orchestra to play inside the Soviet Union, with a concert in Leningrad. The orchestra and conductor later appeared in Moscow and Prague.

Munch now lives in Milton, a suburb of Boston. Except for his habitual walks in the neighborhood with his Welsh terrier, he is not active physically. Most of his time is spent in his study working on new scores. He also maintains a fourteen-room apartment in Paris near the Bois de Boulogne, and there he usually spends his summers and pursues his favorite non-musical interest, Egyptology. A man of attractive appearance and winning manner, Munch was once voted by the Parisian readers of the magazine *Elle* as their second favorite for spending an evening with at dinner; the first choice went to Winston Churchill. Munch has been made Commander of the Legion of Honor, and is the author of *I Am a Conductor,* published both in French and in English, the latter edition in 1955.

MUNSEL, PATRICE, soprano, was born in Spokane, Washington, on May 14, 1925. Her father was a dentist. When Patrice was twelve she saw a performance of *Madama Butterfly* which was such a moving experience that from then on she was determined to become an opera singer. Her ability in music first revealed itself in a gift for whistling, and she received lessons from a local teacher. Vladimir Bakaleinikoff, the conductor, first recognized in Patrice a talent for singing and insisted that she study music more seriously. In her fourteenth year Patrice became a pupil of Mrs. Charlotte Lange. After two years of instruction Mrs. Lange told her pupil she had taught her all she could and that advance instruction was now required. Patrice was now sent to New York for more study and coaching with William P. Herman.

In March 1953 Patrice Munsel won the Metropolitan Auditions of the Air. S. Hurok, the impresario, signed her at once to a three-year contract for concert appearances.

On December 4, 1943, Munsel made her Metropolitan Opera debut as Philine in *Mignon.* Though Olin Downes felt that she was miscast, he wrote in the New York *Times* that "she is comely and has charm. She has flexibility and range. But the voice will have to be treated very carefully . . . before im-

PATRICE MUNSEL

posing on it burdens which, if prematurely undertaken, can bring her disaster instead of ultimate success." She was heard to far greater advantage, however, in *Rigoletto* and *The Tales of Hoffmann,* and before that first season ended it was obvious that she was a valuable addition to the Metropolitan Opera company. She was acclaimed not only for her beautiful voice, which she projected sensitively and flexibly, but also for her attractive stage appearance and personal charm. She has since then appeared at the Metropolitan Opera in principal soprano roles of the Italian and French repertory, and occasionally in the operas of Mozart. Among her successful roles have been Rosina in *The Barber of Seville,* Zerlina in *Don Giovanni,* Despina in *Così Fan Tutte,* Adele in *Die Fledermaus,* Mimi in *La Bohème,* Lucia, Juliette, and Lakmé.

In 1949-1950 Munsel made many appearances in operettas. She has also been a frequent guest on major radio and television programs; in 1946 she was voted in a national poll as the best female vocalist heard over radio. In 1952 she appeared in the title role of *Melba,* the motion-picture biography of the famous prima donna.

She made her European debut in Copenhagen in 1948. When she appeared in Sweden the same year, the critics there spoke of her as "a reincarnation of Jenny Lind."

Patrice Munsel is married to Robert Schuler, a television producer. With their daughter, Heidi Ann, they occupy a penthouse apartment in New York City overlooking the Central Park reservoir. Her domestic life has been so happy that on one occasion she has said: "I enjoy cooking a good meal even more than having an audience at my feet."

MUNZ, MIECZYSLAW, pianist. See *Living Musicians,* 1940.

MUSICAL ART QUARTET. For its earlier history, see *Living Musicians,* 1940.

* * *

This group disbanded just before World War II.

NELLI, HERVA, soprano, was born in Florence, Italy. Her father was a newspaperman who was violently opposed to the Fascist regime. When Herva was eleven, her family came to this country and settled in Pittsburgh. After learning the English language she entered the Pittsburgh Musical Institute, where she showed such talent that her parents decided to send her to Europe for further study. She herself insisted on continuing her training in this country. To finance her music lessons she worked in a glass factory while studying for three years with Mme. Frances Lewandos. She then sang with the Salmaggi Opera Company while receiving additional coaching from Nicola Palumbo.

She had made several concert appearances in New York, none of which succeeded in bringing her to the limelight, when she was

Bruno of Hollywood

HERVA NELLI

discovered and made famous by Arturo Toscanini. In 1947 Toscanini planned the broadcast of a concert performance of *Otello* and began a search for a Desdemona. Licia Albanese brought Nelli to Toscanini for an audition. After singing a few arias for the maestro, with Toscanini himself as accompanist, Nelli was accepted for the part; it is said that several hundred sopranos had been turned down before Nelli was chosen.

The broadcast of *Otello* in two installments, on December 6 and 13, 1947, brought Nelli to the attention of the entire world of music. Her remarkable performance as Desdemona was acclaimed by all the leading critics. In 1949 she appeared under Toscanini in an opera festival at La Scala, her first appearances in Europe. She made such a good impression that she was invited by La Scala to remain in Milan and appear in eight performances of *Aida.*

She made her West Coast debut, as Desdemona, on the opening night of the San Francisco Opera season in 1951-1952. Her success there brought her a contract to appear in other leading soprano roles during 1952. She also appeared at the New York City Opera, which revived *Andrea Chénier* for her. On January 23, 1954, she made her debut at the Metropolitan Opera in *Aida.*

After one of her appearances in New York, a critic of the New York *Herald Tribune* wrote: "She combines the highest arts of vocalism with a rapturously beautiful tonal palette. Intimacy there is, and detail in her singing that is unusual indeed in one who also possesses the wide sweep, the sense of drama. Here is both lyric and dramatic talent."

Herva Nelli has also toured South America in opera performances and has appeared extensively in this country in recitals and as guest artist with symphony orchestras. On several occasions she appeared under Toscanini in concert performances of operas over NBC, including a performance of *Aida,* which (like *Otello*) was recorded by Victor.

Nelli is married to Samuel Marino. They occupy an apartment in Riverdale, New York, which she herself has decorated and where she is often the hostess at elaborate dinner parties. She takes her household duties in stride, and personally prepares her dinners. Other interests include reading, motoring, and sewing.

The NEW ENGLISH SINGERS. See *Living Musicians,* 1940.

The **NEW YORK PHILHARMONIC-SYMPHONY STRING QUARTET.** For its earlier history, see *Living Musicians,* 1940.

* * *

The Quartet disbanded in 1944 when its first violinist, Mishel Piastro, resigned as concertmaster of the New York Philharmonic-Symphony Orchestra.

NEY, ELLY, pianist. For her earlier career, see *Living Musicians,* 1940.

* * *

In 1937, on her birthday, Adolf Hitler conferred on Elly Ney the honorary title of professor. Two years later she became director of the piano classes at the Salzburg Mozarteum. She has been in retirement since the end of World War II.

NIKOLAIDI, ELENA, contralto, was born in Smyrna, Turkey, on June 13, 1909. Her father was an authority on Byzantine music. She showed unusual singing ability from childhood on, and was only seven when she appeared as soloist with the church choir. Eight years later she was given a six-year scholarship for the Athens Conservatory, where she received her principal vocal training with Argyri Ghini. During her last year at the Conservatory she made her professional debut in Athens, appearing with the State Orchestra, Dimitri Mitropoulos conducting. Soon after this, she was engaged by the Athens Lyric Theatre, where she appeared in principal contralto roles of several Italian and French operas, including *Carmen,* which has since that time become one of her specialties.

The Greek government endowed her with a scholarship to study further in Vienna. Soon after arriving there she entered and won an international vocal competition entitling her to a recital appearance at the Konzerthaus. After that, she auditioned for Bruno Walter, then director of the Vienna State Opera, who engaged her for his company. She made her debut there on the opening night of the 1936-1937 season as Princess Eboli in *Don Carlo.* She became a favorite in Vienna, and remained a leading contralto of the State Opera for over a decade. In 1947 she received the honorary title of *Kammersängerin.*

In the fall of 1948 she returned for a brief visit to Athens to make a single appearance

ELENA NIKOLAIDI

as Carmen. She was such a sensation that she was compelled to make seven additional appearances in that role. After that, en route to the United States, she stopped off at London, where a successful concert led to a contract with Covent Garden.

Nikolaidi made her American debut in a recital at Town Hall, New York, on January 20, 1949. "In twenty years of music reviewing and in twice that number of years spent in listening to most of the world's best singers, I have encountered no greater voice or vocalist than Elena Nikolaidi," reported Jerome D. Bohm in the New York *Herald Tribune.* "This personable artist is gifted with a truly phenomenal expressive medium, a true contralto of enormous range. . . . Not only, however, is her voice of exceptional range and opulence, but highly individual in texture, sensuous and warm at all times, never losing quality even in the highest reaches when employed full strength, and so malleable that in the finest spun pianissimos the native beauty of her voice remains unaltered."

Her first North American tour followed. She made over seventy-five appearances in recitals and as soloist with orchestra, most of the appearances in sold-out auditoriums. Highlights of this tour included a debut on radio; a debut on Columbia Records; triumphant appearances with the New York Philharmonic-Symphony in concert performances of *Elektra*; appearances in San Francisco in which, on successive evenings, she was heard in a recital and as soloist with the San Francisco Symphony.

Her American opera debut, as Amneris in *Aida*, took place with the San Francisco Opera on September 26, 1950 (opening night of the season). "This artist," reported Alfred Frankenstein in the San Francisco *Chronicle*, "has enough vocal beauty, richness, color and radiance for an entire opera company, and musicianship as well." Her Metropolitan Opera debut followed on the opening night of the 1951-1952 season, once again as Amneris; it was no less successful. Her appearances in opera and recitals, both here and abroad, have since that time been extensive.

Nikolaidi has been honored by the King of Greece with the Golden Phoenix Cross for "cementing close cultural ties between the United States and Greece and for outstanding contributions in the fields of music and art." A special bill, signed by the President of the United States, has given her the right to remain a permanent resident of this country.

She is married to Thanos Mellos, a baritone, whom she met when they both studied at the Athens Conservatory, and whom she married just before her first visit to Vienna. Her husband has given up his own career as an opera singer to devote himself to managing that of his wife, but he engages in teaching and coaching. They have one son, Michael, with whom they occupy an old-fashioned, rambling house in New Rochelle, New York. There the family enjoys giving large dinner parties made up of specialties of the Greek cuisine.

NOBLE, THOMAS TERTIUS, organist. For his earlier career, see *Living Musicians*, 1940.

* * *

In 1947 Noble retired as organist of St. Thomas' Church in New York. He died in Rockport, Massachusetts, on May 4, 1953.

NORÉNA, EIDÉ, soprano. For her earlier career, see *Living Musicians*, 1940.

* * *

After leaving the Metropolitan Opera in 1938, Noréna returned to the Paris Opéra as a principal soprano. She has since then appeared there, and has been a guest artist in other leading European opera houses.

NORTON, EUNICE, pianist. See *Living Musicians*, 1940.

NOVAËS, GUIOMAR, pianist. For her earlier career, see *Living Musicians*, 1940.

* * *

In 1956 Novaës received the Order of Merit from the Brazilian government for her services as "an ambassadress of culture and good will to the United States."

NOVOTNA, JARMILA, soprano. For her earlier career, see *Living Musicians*, 1940.

* * *

Novotna remained with the Metropolitan Opera seven seasons, after making her debut there in 1940; for several seasons after leaving the company she made guest appearances with it. She has also appeared in non-singing dramatic roles on the stage and the screen.

ODNOPOSOFF, RICARDO, violinist, was born in Buenos Aires. Before he was able to read or write he began playing the violin on a quarter-size instrument. He was only five when he gave his first concert, in Buenos Aires. While studying in that city with a pupil of Leopold Auer, Odnoposoff continued to give a concert each year until he was twelve, when he went to Berlin for additional study with Carl Flesch. As a pupil of Flesch he received the singular honor of being allowed to appear as soloist with the Berlin Philharmonic under Kleiber, the first time that organization permitted an undergraduate artist to appear with it. In 1932 he won first prize in the International Contest in Vienna,

RICARDO ODNOPOSOFF

Odnoposoff: ôd-nô-pô'sôf

and in 1937 he once again won first prize, this time at the all-important Eugene Ysaÿe Competition in Brussels.

He had appeared extensively throughout Europe and South America, both in recitals and as soloist with orchestras, before making his North American debut. This took place at Carnegie Hall in February 1944. Noel Straus reported in the New York *Times* that he "scored a triumph and established himself as one of the outstanding violinists of the day. He took his audience by storm by his virtuosity, power, and fine performance. Odnoposoff proved to be a player in the grand manner, with a tone of extraordinary volume and richness, which he employed with a vitality and sweep which gave his work a monumental quality that was quite unusual."

Since that time, Odnoposoff has performed in all the major capitals of the music world, besides making annual extensive tours of the United States and South America. He divides his year equally between Europe and America, giving about fifty performances in each. In 1951 he made his first tour of Australia, giving forty-nine performances in eighteen weeks; in 1952 he was a soloist at the Sibelius Festival in Helsinki.

Mechanically inclined, Odnoposoff enjoys tinkering with machines and gadgets; he himself is the proud creator of several inventions which he hopes to patent as soon as they are perfected. He also has a natural gift for design, and often sketches the brochures for his promotion pieces.

OISTRAKH, DAVID, violinist, was born in Odessa, Russia, in 1908. His father, a bookkeeper, was an amateur musician who played several instruments well; his mother had been a member of the Odessa Opera chorus for thirty years. David was entered in the Odessa Conservatory when he was five. There he studied with Pyotr Stoliarsky, who remained his only teacher. In his tenth year David began giving student concerts, and at twelve performed the Beethoven Concerto in Odessa before an audience that included Prokofiev. When, in 1923, the Odessa Conservatory held a concert to honor Stoliarsky, Oistrakh was invited to play a Bach Concerto.

All formal study ended after his graduation from the Conservatory in 1926. One year later he began appearing with professional orchestras in Odessa and other Ukrainian cities. In 1927 he played the Glazunov Concerto with the Tia Symphony conducted by the composer, and a year later made his debut

DAVID OISTRAKH

in Moscow and Leningrad, once again as soloist with the Tia Symphony.

In 1930 he won first prize in a Ukrainian competition held in Kharkov. Four years later he was appointed lecturer at the Moscow Conservatory. Appointed professor of the violin there in 1939, he henceforth divided his career between teaching and concert work. In 1934 he won first prize in the All-Union music competition in Leningrad; in 1935 he made his first appearance outside the Soviet Union, performing in Turkey and winning second prize at the Wieniawski Contest in Warsaw; and in 1936 he toured Scandinavia and the Baltic countries.

His fame as a violinist can be said to have begun in 1938, when he won first prize in the celebrated Eugene Ysaÿe Contest in Brussels. When he made his debut in Paris that year, he was acclaimed as one of Europe's outstanding violin virtuosos. His status as one of the leading violinists in the Soviet Union was further solidified when, in 1942, he received the Stalin Prize.

Oistrakh gives about seventy or eighty concerts a year, both inside and out of the Soviet Union. Besides appearing as a virtuoso, he is also heard as a member of a permanent chamber-music group which gives subscription concerts in Moscow and Leningrad. His appearances outside the Soviet Union have been extensive. In 1951 he appeared at the Florence May Music Festival; in 1953 he gave highly successful concerts in Paris; in 1954 he was one of four Soviet musicians

Oistrakh: oi'-strŏk

selected to perform at the Soviet Embassy in East Berlin at a conference of Foreign Ministers; in February 1955 he became the first Soviet musician to play in Japan since World War II; and in April 1955 he made an extensive tour of Germany.

He originally intended to visit the United States in 1939 to perform at the New York World's Fair, but the outbreak of war in Europe frustrated these plans. As a result of the agreement at the summit meeting in Geneva in the summer of 1955 for an exchange of culture between the United States and the Soviet Union, negotiations were completed for him to come to the United States. The intention was for him to make his American debut in New York with the London Philharmonic Orchestra under Herbert von Karajan on November 13, 1955, but Oistrakh's sudden illness forced him to cancel this appearance. Instead, he made his debut in the United States at a recital in Carnegie Hall on November 20, with a second recital there three days later. Since his name and art had already become famous in this country through his numerous recordings, over seven thousand people stood on line to buy tickets for his American debut. All subsequent performances in New York were also completely sold out. On December 21, he appeared with the Philharmonic-Symphony under Mitropoulos in a program of three concertos, and on December 29 he presented with the New York Philharmonic-Symphony the American première of the Shostakovich Violin Concerto. In addition Oistrakh was heard in several other American cities, including Boston, Philadelphia, and Chicago. He also made American recordings for both Victor and Columbia.

"Mr. Oistrakh is more than a technician," wrote Ronald Eyer in *Musical America*. "He has a full bodied, warm, humanly inspired tone and a robustness of style. . . . He is a perfectionist, but in his perfection he has not lost soul nor the ability to communicate emotional feeling."

Howard Taubman wrote in the New York *Times*: "The most impressive thing about Mr. Oistrakh was the thoughtfulness and sensitivity of his musicianship. He is unmistakably a violinist who does not begin by thinking about how to subdue an audience through sheer brilliance."

Oistrakh's son, Igor, is also a celebrated concert violinist. Like his father, Igor studied with Stoliarsky and in 1952 won the Wieniawski Contest in Warsaw; he also received first prize in a competition in Budapest in 1949. Father and son sometimes appear in duo-violin recitals. Both share an enthusiasm for chess, driving motor cars, and Siamese cats. The Oistrakh family lives in an apartment in Moscow, and has a country villa outside the city.

OLHEIM, HELEN, contralto. See *Living Musicians,* 1940.

OLSZEWSKA, MARIA, contralto. See *Living Musicians,* 1940.

ONEGIN, SIGRID, contralto. For her earlier career, see *Living Musicians,* 1940.

* * *

Onegin died in Lugano, Switzerland, on June 17, 1943.

ORLOFF, NIKOLAI, pianist. See *Living Musicians,* 1940.

ORMANDY, EUGENE, conductor. For his earlier career, see *Living Musicians,* 1940.

* * *

Ormandy made his debut at the Metropolitan Opera on December 20, 1950, in a performance of *Die Fledermaus.* In 1949 he led the Philadelphia Orchestra on its first tour of Europe, and in 1951 and 1952 he conducted guest performances at the Sibelius Festival in Helsinki.

PADEREWSKI, IGNACE JAN, pianist. For his earlier career, see *Living Musicians,* 1940.

* * *

Paderewski returned to the United States in 1940 to plead the cause of Poland's freedom. He died in New York City on June 29, 1941. The Polish government decorated him posthumously with the Cross of Virtuti Militari, the country's highest military honor.

PANIZZA, ETTORE, conductor. For his earlier career, see *Living Musicians,* 1940.

* * *

Panizza left the Metropolitan Opera after the 1941-1942 season and subsequently became principal conductor of La Scala in Milan.

PAPI, GENNARO, conductor. For his earlier career, see *Living Musicians,* 1940.

* * *

Papi died in New York City on November 29, 1941, just as he was about to conduct a performance of *La Traviata* at the Metropolitan Opera House.

PARAY, PAUL, conductor. For his earlier career, see *Living Musicians*, 1940.

* * *

When World War II broke out, Paray was in Paris. For a while he continued his musical activities there, but after the city was occupied by the Nazis he became a leading figure in the Resistance movement. When, in 1940, the Nazis changed the name of the Colonne Orchestra because Édouard Colonne had been a Jew, Paray (who is a Catholic) resigned his post in protest. He vowed never again to conduct a concert in Paris until it was liberated. In Marseilles, then still unoccupied, he led radio concerts. When that city came under Nazi domination, Paray went on to Lyons, where once again he defied the Nazis. On May 16, a concert of German music was given in Lyons by the Philharmonic Orchestra under Clemens Krauss. The following day, in the same hall, Paray led an Orchestra in a program of French music; and at the end of his concert he asked the audience to join the orchestra in the *Marseillaise*. After that he went into voluntary exile in Monte Carlo, where he conducted opera performances.

With Paris liberated, Paray returned on October 22, 1944, to resume his former post with the Colonne Orchestra and was given a hero's welcome. In 1950 Paray received official recognition for his contribution to French music and politics by being elected a member of the Institut de France.

In 1945 Paray returned to the United States to appear as guest conductor of the Boston Symphony and the Cincinnati Symphony orchestras. Between 1949 and 1952 he served as guest conductor of the Pittsburgh Symphony Orchestra, both in Pittsburgh and on tour.

When the Detroit Symphony, which had been disbanded in 1949, was reorganized in 1951, Paray became a guest conductor for five performances. The following season he was appointed permanent conductor and musical director. In 1954 he toured the east coast with the Pittsburgh Symphony. On October 18, 1956, Detroit opened its new concert hall—the Ford Auditorium—with a concert by the Pittsburgh Symphony under Paray.

The **PASQUIER TRIO**. See *Living Musicians*, 1940.

PAULEE, MONA, mezzo-soprano, was born in Alberta, Canada, of French-Russian ancestry. When she was four years old, her family moved to the United States, settling in Portland, Oregon, where her father became a theatre manager. As a child, she was given some piano training, but a career in music was never seriously contemplated. A turning point came during her early adolescence when she entered an amateur contest, sang a popular song, and won the first prize of $10.00. From then on she was determined to be a singer. By working in a bakery wrapping bread she was able to pay for singing lessons with a local teacher. Appearances in churches, at weddings, and at various receptions led to a five-a-day booking on a small vaudeville circuit. From vaudeville she went on to light opera, and after that made occasional appearances as soloist with small orchestras and choral groups. In 1936 she was engaged by the San Francisco Opera to understudy in several leading mezzo-soprano roles and to sing minor parts.

In 1941, after three years of concentrated training, she entered the Metropolitan Auditions of the Air. Despite the fact that she had to sing at one of the preliminary auditions while suffering from bronchial pneumonia, she not only progressed to the finals, but was one of the three winners. Her debut at the Metropolitan Opera took place on November 28, 1941, as Gianetta in *L'Elisir d'Amore*. From then on, through the 1945-1946 season, she was seen in such roles as Lola in *Caval-*

MONA PAULEE

Paulee: pôl'ē

leria Rusticana, Nicklausse in *The Tales of Hoffmann,* Amneris in *Aida,* and Maddalena in *Rigoletto.*

After leaving the Metropolitan Opera she made extensive tours of the United States in recitals. She also appeared as Carmen in a Columbia Concerts Corporation production which toured the East, Middle West, and South. In 1950 she made her first tour of Central America, and in 1952 her first tour of Europe, with appearances in England, Scandinavia, and Holland. She has also been heard frequently on major radio and television programs. When Randall Thompson's opera *Solomon and Balkis* was introduced over the radio, she appeared in the principal female role of Balkis. In 1956 she was seen on Broadway in a major role in *The Most Happy Fella.*

A critic on the New York *Herald Tribune* wrote of her voice that it is "so luscious in texture that she could undoubtedly make a simple scale sound alluring. . . . She revealed her unerring stylistic assurance and superlative musicianship, and found just the right tonal colorings and applied them with perceptive sensibility."

Mona Paulee is married to Dean Holt, formerly a popular-band leader, whom she met in a San Francisco night club where they were both appearing at the time. They occupy an apartment overlooking 57th Street, near Carnegie Hall. During her travels in this country, when on tour, she and her husband prefer flying from city to city in their own private plane.

PAULY, ROSE, dramatic soprano. For her earlier career, see *Living Musicians,* 1940.

* * *

Pauly remained with the Metropolitan Opera until 1940. After World War II, she made many appearances with major European opera companies.

PEASE, JAMES, bass-baritone, was born in Bloomington, Indiana. Though he showed an unusual interest in singing from boyhood on, and revealed a native musical intelligence, he was directed not to music but to law. He attended Northwestern University, and completed his study of law at the University of Indiana. While at college, he appeared in several dramatic productions, and on one occasion filled a leading role in a musical comedy. The Dean was so impressed by him that he urged him to consider the stage as a career.

JAMES PEASE

After being admitted to the Indiana bar, Pease received a scholarship for the Academy of Vocal Arts in Philadelphia, an award which induced him to give up law for music. He remained two years at the Academy, and then made his debut with the Philadelphia Opera Company as Mephistopheles in *Faust. Newsweek* magazine, in reviewing the performance, remarked that "top honors went to James Pease." Pease continued to appear with the company for several seasons, making a good impression in such varied roles as Baron Ochs in *Der Rosenkavalier,* Arkel in *Pelléas et Mélisande,* and Colline in *La Bohème.* Deems Taylor selected him for a major role in the world première of his opera *Ramuntcho,* introduced by the company on February 10, 1942.

After guest appearances over the CBS network with the Howard Barlow orchestra, and seven engagements with the Philadelphia Orchestra under Ormandy, Pease entered the Metropolitan Auditions of the Air, which he won in 1943. The war, and his enlistment in the Army Air Corps, canceled his debut at the Metropolitan Opera. During the war Pease served as a pilot in the AAF Training Command; he was also authorized to appear at numerous rallies and on various broadcasts sponsored by the armed forces.

After his separation from the service in 1945, Pease became a member of the New York City Opera company, appearing in leading bass-baritone parts in operas by Mozart, Richard Strauss, and Wagner, as well as in the French and Italian repertory. His appearance as Baron Ochs led Virgil Thomson to write in the New York *Herald Tribune*: "I do not think I have ever seen the role played more convincingly. Force in the characterization with no horse-play, no vulgarity of any kind, made an unforgettable performance." Indicative of his versatility was the fact that he also appeared in four modern operas: Prokofiev's *The Love of Three Oranges*; Menotti's *Amelia Goes to the Ball*; Bartók's *Bluebeard's Castle*; and Alban Berg's *Wozzeck*.

Pease has appeared with most of the major American orchestras under their leading conductors. His New York debut with orchestra took place with the New York Philharmonic-Symphony on October 11, 1951, in the American première of Busoni's *Arlecchino*, given in a concert version. Since 1952 Pease has appeared frequently at the Berkshire Music Festival, where he has been seen in the American premières of Britten's *Peter Grimes* and *Albert Herring*, and in a revival of Tchaikovsky's *Pique Dame*. He has also been heard in Germany since 1952 when he joined the Hamburg State Opera in Wagnerian music dramas. He has sung in Wagner music dramas in Mainz and Vienna and, in 1954, he sang at the Bayreuth Festival.

"This versatile artist," wrote John Briggs in the New York *Post*, "sings well, which is a great deal, but many good singers can't act. As an actor, Mr. Pease has taste and talent. The timing of his comedy is superb. Every gesture is right, not too much and not too little, and shrewdly judged to bring out the maximum of laughs. Here is a performer well worth watching."

PEERCE, JAN, tenor. For his earlier career, see *Living Musicians*, 1940.

* * *

Peerce made his debut at the Metropolitan Opera on November 29, 1941, as Alfredo in *La Traviata*. "Mr. Peerce's audience," wrote Olin Downes in the New York *Times*, "was delighted and with good reason by the appealing quality of his voice and his manner of using it." Since that time, Peerce has been a principal tenor the Metropolitan, besides making appearances with other leading American and European opera companies. He has also been heard in several opera performances directed by Toscanini over NBC, including *La Traviata, La Bohème,* and *Un Ballo in*

Maschera. On June 6, 1956, Peerce began a concert tour of the Soviet Union, becoming the first major American singer to appear there since World War II.

PELLETIER, WILFRED, conductor. For his earlier career, see *Living Musicians*, 1940.

* * *

After leaving the Metropolitan Opera Pelletier founded conservatories in Montreal and Quebec, which he has since directed, and has led the Concerts Symphoniques in Montreal. Since the 1953-1954 season he has been the conductor of the Young People's concerts of the New York Philharmonic-Symphony Orchestra.

PENNARIO, LEONARD, pianist, was born in Buffalo, New York, on July 9, 1924. He went to California in his childhood and, while attending public school there began his serious study of music. He made his first public appearance as a pianist when he was seven, gave a recital at eight, and at twelve made his official professional debut by performing the Grieg Piano Concerto with the Dallas Symphony Orchestra. (He learned the Concerto in six days' time to fill this last engagement.) An appearance with the Los Angeles Philharmonic under Klemperer in 1939 added to his growing reputation as a prodigy.

In 1942 he entered the University of Southern California, where he studied piano

LEONARD PENNARIO

with Guy Maier. During that year and the following one he made important appearances as soloist with the San Francisco Symphony, Chicago Symphony, Minneapolis Symphony, and New York Philharmonic-Symphony orchestras. His career was temporarily interrupted during World War II when he served as a staff sergeant in the United States Army Air Corps in the China-Burma-India theatres, and received three bronze stars.

His career was resumed after his separation from the Air Corps. In 1947 he gave fifty-eight concerts. Since then he has toured the country annually, appearing in recitals and as soloist with most of the major symphony orchestras. "Collaboration with this young musician has been one of the happiest experiences of my life," said Dimitri Mitropoulos after Pennario had appeared as soloist with the New York Philharmonic. "I say musician because, although he possesses the technique necessary to virtuosity, he possesses what is more important, a soul."

He made his first appearances in Europe in 1951, and in 1952 returned for an even more extensive tour of Holland, France, England, and Italy, a tour which was climaxed by a concert in Paris that was sold out. One of the Parisian critics described him as "a phenomenon of the piano," while a critic of the London *New Statesman and Nation* said "nobody today plays the piano better than Pennario."

"Mr. Pennario," wrote, a critic of the New York *Times* after Pennario's recital on December 16, 1952, "has wrists and fingers second to none. . . . Not many pianists can play with the superb, transcendental virtuosity, which Leonard Pennario revealed." The critic of the New York *World Telegram and Sun* said after the same concert: "Whatever the style—lyric, dramatic or fireworks—Mr. Pennario was always there with the technical and interpretative qualifications."

Besides making appearances on important radio programs, Pennario has been heard on the sound track of a motion picture, *September Affair,* starring Joan Fontaine.

PERLEA, JONEL, conductor, was born in Ograda, Rumania, on December 13, 1900. He came from a wealthy family. At the age of seven he decided he would some day become a professional musician, and at nine he wrote his first piece of music, a waltz. After a period of study of composition with Anton Beer Wallbrunn, he went to Vienna for additional study. The city offered too many distractions to a young man of means to allow

Perlea: pâr′lā-à

Courtesy of Musical Courier

JONEL PERLEA

him to concentrate on music. He went on to Leipzig, where, at the Conservatory, he entered Max Reger's master class in composition and Otto Lohse's class in conducting.

He wrote a short orchestral work and was invited to conduct the première in Bucharest. This, his first experience with the baton, encouraged him to pursue conducting more seriously. He made his official debut as conductor with the Leipzig Opera, first leading a performance of a ballet, *Puppenfee,* and after that *Hänsel und Gretel.* A number of engagements in other parts of Germany followed. After a one-year period of service in the Rumanian army, he was appointed first principal conductor (in 1926), then general manager and music director of the Bucharest State Opera. At the same time he was engaged as director of the Bucharest Conservatory. During his eight years in these posts, Perlea extended both his experience and his reputation with appearances in guest engagements with leading symphony orchestras and opera companies in Vienna, Berlin, Warsaw, and Paris.

In August 1944 Perlea was on his way from Bucharest to Paris with his wife when they stopped off in Vienna. There they were detained by Nazi officials since they did not have the proper visas and were interned in a concentration camp. The year that followed —the first in Silesia and then in Kärnten— was an ordeal about which he prefers to remain silent. He was finally liberated by the British Army and sent to Italy for repatriation. He remained in Italy for a period, try-ing to resume his musical life there. He was finally given an opportunity to conduct a concert with the Santa Cecilia Orchestra in Rome when its own conductor was unable to give the performance. He was such a success that a second concert was scheduled for him, followed by his debut at La Scala in *Tristan und Isolde*. He then appeared frequently both in Milan and Naples. He remained a principal conductor at La Scala until 1949.

Frank St. Leger of the Metropolitan Opera heard him at La Scala and arranged for him to come to the United States to appear with the Metropolitan. But Perlea's American debut took place with the San Francisco Symphony Orchestra. A few weeks later, on December 1, he conducted *Tristan und Isolde* at the Metropolitan. "The sensitivity of his Prelude and the manner in which he supported the vocalists in the early phases of the act augured an uncommon artist," wrote Irving Kolodin. During his initial season Perlea was also heard in operas in the Italian and French repertory.

In 1955 Perlea was appointed musical director of the Connecticut Symphony Orchestra, making his debut in this post on November 9. Soon after this he was also appointed head of the orchestral department of the Manhattan School of Music.

The PEROLÉ STRING QUARTET. For its earlier history, see *Living Musicians,* 1940.

* * *

The Perolé String Quartet was disbanded soon after World War II.

PESSL, YELLA, harpsichordist. See *Living Musicians,* 1940.

PETERS, ROBERTA, soprano, was born in New York City on May 4, 1930. Her father was a shoe salesman and her mother a milliner. As a child, Roberta demonstrated an unusual aptitude for acting and mimicry, and was given numerous opportunities to appear in school productions. When her talent for singing became evident, her grandfather (who was employed at Grossinger's, a popular resort in the Catskill Mountains, where he often came into personal contact with celebrities of the theatre and music worlds) asked Jan Peerce to pass on Roberta's ability. Peerce was so impressed that he arranged for her to study with William Pierce Herman, who since that time has remained her only teacher. This was in 1943. She was taken out of school so that she might concentrate

ROBERTA PETERS

on music study. For the next seven years she was given comprehensive training not only in singing but also in acting, ballet, and languages; by the time she was nineteen she had mastered about twenty opera roles.

In 1950 she auditioned for the Metropolitan Opera, singing the Queen of the Night aria from *The Magic Flute*. She was given a contract and her debut was scheduled for January 1951 in the same opera. But on November 17, 1950, she was hurriedly called to Rudolf Bing's office to be informed that Nadine Conner, who was scheduled to sing the part of Zerlina in *Don Giovanni* that night, was ill and that she would be used as a last-minute substitute. Thus her Metropolitan Opera debut was an unscheduled one. She went through the performance with such ease and aplomb, both vocally and histrionically, that she was immediately hailed as one of the most important new sopranos engaged by the Metropolitan Opera in several years. In subsequent performances—particularly as Rosina in *The Barber of Seville*, Sophie in *Der Rosenkavalier*, Despina in *Così Fan Tutte*, Olympia in *The Tales of Hoffmann*, Gilda in *Rigoletto*, and Susanna in *The Marriage of Figaro*—her reputation was firmly established. On two occasions, besides her debut, she was required at the last moment to substitute for indisposed sopranos: in 1951, when she replaced Genevieve Warner as Gilda, and in 1954 when she took Nadine Conner's place as Susanna in *The Marriage of Figaro*. In 1951 she appeared at Covent

Garden during the Festival of Britain in a gala performance of *The Bohemian Girl* under Sir Thomas Beecham.

In the New York *Herald Tribune*, Francis D. Perkins has praised Roberta Peters for her "assurance, vivacity, visual and vocal dramatic persuasiveness," and has described her singing as "fluent . . . well phrased and expressive."

In April 1955 she married Bertram Fields, owner of a chain of hotels. This was her second marriage. Her first, in 1952, to Robert Merrill, the baritone of the Metropolitan Opera, ended in divorce.

PETRI, EGON, pianist. For his earlier career, see *Living Musicians,* 1940.

* * *

From 1940 to 1946 Petri was pianist-in-residence at Cornell University in Ithaca, New York. Since 1947 he has held a similar post at Mills College in Oakland, California.

PIASTRO, MISHEL, violinist. For his earlier career, see *Living Musicians,* 1940.

* * *

Piastro resigned as concertmaster of the New York Philharmonic-Symphony Orchestra in 1943, and subsequently became the conductor of the Longines Symphonette radio program.

PIATIGORSKY, GREGOR, cellist. For his earlier career, see *Living Musicians,* 1940.

* * *

Since World War II, Piatigorsky has served as head of the cello department of the Curtis Institute and as director of chamber music of the Berkshire Music Center at Tanglewood, in Lenox, Massachusetts. He has also established scholarships for composition and cello in several conservatories in Paris and America. In 1957 he received the Gold Medal of the Royal Philharmonic Society, London.

PICCAVER, ALFRED, tenor. See *Living Musicians,* 1940.

PINZA, EZIO, bass. For his earlier career, see *Living Musicians,* 1940.

* * *

Pinza left the Metropolitan Opera in 1949 and entered the Broadway musical theatre to score a personal triumph in the Rodgers and Hammerstein musical play *South Pacific.* After that he appeared in several motion pic-tures, in another Broadway musical, *Fanny,* and on many important radio and television programs. After suffering a heart attack in the summer of 1956 he announced that his singing career was over. He died in Stamford, Connecticut, on May 9, 1957.

PITZINGER, GERTRUDE, contralto. See *Living Musicians,* 1940.

PLOTNIKOFF, EUGENE, conductor. For his earlier career, see *Living Musicians,* 1940.

* * *

Plotnikoff died in New York City on September 28, 1951.

POLACCO, GIORGIO, conductor. See *Living Musicians,* 1940.

PONS, LILY, soprano. For her earlier career, see *Living Musicians,* 1940.

* * *

The twenty-fifth anniversary of Pons' debut at the Metropolitan Opera was celebrated on January 3, 1956, with a gala evening in which she appeared in scenes from two of her most successful operas, and was the recipient of numerous gifts and honors.

PONSELLE, CARMELA, mezzo-soprano. See *Living Musicians,* 1940.

PONSELLE, ROSA, soprano. For her earlier career, see *Living Musicians,* 1940.

* * *

In 1954 Ponselle emerged briefly from a seventeen-year period of retirement to make a few recordings.

POUISHNOFF, LEFF, pianist. See *Living Musicians,* 1940.

PRIHODA, VASA, violinist. For his earlier career, see *Living Musicians,* 1940.

* * *

In 1942 the report was circulated that Prihoda had committed suicide in Prague, and his obituary was published in American and English music journals. But this report proved false. After the war, he concertized in London, Paris, and the Near East.

PRIMROSE, WILLIAM, violist. For his earlier career, see *Living Musicians,* 1940.

* * *

Primrose remained first violist of the NBC Symphony Orchestra five years, resigning in

1942 to devote himself to concert appearances. He has been heard in the principal music centers of America and Europe, and at many leading music festivals, including the Pablo Casals Festival in Prades, France. In 1955 he was appointed a member of the faculty of the Juilliard School of Music.

The **PRO-ARTE QUARTET.** See *Living Musicians,* 1940.

PRÜWER, JULIUS, conductor. For his earlier career, see *Living Musicians,* 1940.

* * *

Prüwer settled in New York City in 1940, devoting himself to teaching. He died there on July 8, 1943.

RABIN, MICHAEL, violinist, was born in New York City on May 2, 1936. Both parents were professional musicians. His father is a member of the violin section of the New York Philharmonic-Symphony, and his mother a concert pianist who gave up her own career to devote herself to her family. Michael demonstrated that he was a born musician in early childhood. At three he disclosed he had perfect pitch by identifying the tones of an automobile horn. He began piano lessons with his mother when he was five. While visiting a friend of the family who had a violin collection, he came upon a miniature violin which he seized upon so eagerly that the friend lent it to him. His father gave him only a few basic lessons before he began playing. For a while, he continued studying both the violin and the piano, but in his eighth year his preference for the former instrument led him to concentrate on it. His father placed him with Ivan Galamian, who has remained his only teacher.

Before making his debut, Rabin was heard and praised by such eminent musicians as Dimitri Mitropoulos and George Szell. Mitropoulos said, "Michael Rabin is the violin genius of tomorrow," and Szell remarked, "Michael Rabin is the greatest violin talent that has come to my attention during the past two or three decades."

Rabin's debut took place in Carnegie Hall in the fall of 1950. He was well received. His first appearance with the New York Philharmonic-Symphony (his father playing in the violin section) took place on November 29, 1951, when he performed Paganini's D major Concerto. In the New York *Times,* Olin Downes spoke of Rabin's "astonishing mastery of his instrument." And he added:

Rabin: rä′bin

MICHAEL RABIN

"Mr. Rabin appears to have simply everything. He is so completely the master of every technical problem, that a passage of superlative difficulty is merely an excitement and a stimulus for him—an additional incentive to make music." Francis D. Perkins wrote in the New York *Herald Tribune:* "The youthful violinist has little, if anything, further to learn."

During that same season Rabin not only appeared five times with the New York Philharmonic and four times at Carnegie Hall, but was also soloist with the New York Philharmonic-Symphony when under Mitropoulos it made a precedent-shattering appearance at the Roxy Theatre for two weeks. The following season Rabin made his first tour of Australia and New Zealand. Since then he has made annual tours of the country, appearing with major orchestras and in recitals, besides concertizing abroad. He also played for the sound track of the motion picture *Rhapsody,* starring Elizabeth Taylor.

RABINOF, BENNO, violinist. See *Living Musicians,* 1940.

RACHMANINOFF, SERGE, pianist and conductor. For his earlier career, see *Living Musicians,* 1940.

* * *

Rachmaninoff died in Beverly Hills, California, on March 28, 1943.

RAPEE, ERNO, conductor. For his earlier career, see *Living Musicians,* 1940.

* * *

Rapee died in New York City on June 26, 1945.

RASCHER, SIGURD, saxophonist. See *Living Musicians,* 1940.

RASELY, GEORGE, tenor. See *Living Musicians,* 1940.

REGGIANI, HILDE, soprano. See *Living Musicians,* 1940.

REINER, FRITZ, conductor. For his earlier career, see *Living Musicians,* 1940.

* * *

Reiner left the Pittsburgh Symphony in 1948 to become one of the principal conductors of the Metropolitan Opera, making his debut there in *Salome* on February 4, 1949. In 1953 Reiner resigned from the Metropolitan Opera and assumed the post of musical director of the Chicago Symphony Orchestra. In 1955, soon after the opening of the new building of the Vienna State Opera on the Ringstrasse, he was invited there to give several guest performances.

REISENBERG, NADIA, pianist. See *Living Musicians,* 1940.

RENARDY, OSSY, violinist. For his earlier career, see *Living Musicians,* 1940.

* * *

During World War II, while serving in the United States Army, Renardy gave over four hundred concerts for the armed forces.

RESNIK, REGINA, mezzo-soprano, was born in the Bronx, New York City, on August 30, 1922. Her father was a leather manufacturer. Regina attended elementary schools in the Bronx, was graduated from James Monroe High School in 1938, and received her Bachelor of Arts degree from Hunter College in 1942. While going to high school she started to take voice lessons from Rosalie Miller, who has remained her only teacher. On October 27, 1942, she made her concert debut at the Brooklyn Academy of Music, in Brooklyn, New York. That same fall, she was engaged as an understudy for the New Opera Company (directed by Fritz Busch), which was giving performances on Broadway. When the principal soprano sched-

REGINA RESNIK

uled to sing Lady Macbeth in Verdi's *Macbeth* fell ill suddenly, Regina Resnik was called to substitute for her. It was on this occasion, on December 5, 1942, that she made her debut. The performance was so good that the Opera Nacional of Mexico City engaged her in 1943, and there she sang under Erich Kleiber's direction such soprano roles as Leonore in *Fidelio* and Micaela in *Carmen.*

In April 1944 she won first prize in the Metropolitan Auditions of the Air. In May of the same year, she appeared with the New York City Opera in soprano roles, scoring successes as Santuzza in *Cavalleria Rusticana* and Frasquita in *Carmen.* She was scheduled to make her debut at the Metropolitan Opera on December 9 of the same year. But a few days earlier, Zinka Milanov, scheduled to appear as Leonore in *Il Trovatore,* became ill. No replacement could be found, and the Metropolitan Opera called Resnik even though she had never appeared in that role and had not seen the score in over two years. She was given only one rehearsal, but her debut on December 6 proved successful. The critic of the New York *Herald Tribune* described her performance as "astonishingly satisfying" and said she had "excellent natural equipment, good training, and sound musical instincts."

For a decade Regina Resnik continued to appear in soprano roles at the Metropolitan Opera. During this period she was also heard at the San Francisco Opera, the Central City Festival in Colorado, and in July 1953 at the Bayreuth Festival, where she sang the role of Sieglinde in *Die Walküre.* Besides appearing in the traditional Italian, French and German repertory, Resnik was also heard in the world première of Bernard Rogers' *The Warrior,* the American première of Benjamin Britten's *The Rape of Lucretia,* and the Metropolitan Opera première of Britten's *Peter Grimes.*

In 1955 Regina Resnik began assuming mezzo-soprano roles. She made her debut in this new range at the Cincinnati Zoo Opera in July, when she appeared as Amneris in *Aida.* Her second debut at the Metropolitan Opera, this time as a mezzo-soprano, took place on February 15, 1956, when she appeared as Marina in *Boris Godunov.* "Miss Resnik," wrote Harriet Johnson in the New York *Post,* "has made the change successfully, and has improved her personality stage-wise along with the transformation. She looked the part of the noble, lovely Marina and sang with beauty of tone, with a vibrant dark quality in the lower voice, and with dramatic impressiveness." Afterwards she sang at the Metropolitan such important mezzo roles as Ortrud in *Lohengrin* and Giulietta in the *Tales of Hoffmann.*

On July 16, 1946, Regina Resnik married Harry W. Davis, a New York attorney. They have one child, a son.

RETHBERG, ELISABETH, soprano. For her earlier career, see *Living Musicians,* 1940.

* * *

Rethberg made her last appearance at the Metropolitan Opera in *Aida* on March 6, 1942, and for a period after that was heard in recitals and in performances of oratorios.

RHENÉ-BATON, conductor. See *Living Musicians,* 1940.

RICCI, RUGGIERO, violinist. See *Living Musicians,* 1940.

RINGWALL, RUDOLPH, conductor. For his earlier career, see *Living Musicians,* 1940.

* * *

In 1956 Ringwall retired as associate conductor of the Cleveland Orchestra, terminating an association with that organization which had begun forty years earlier.

ROBESON, PAUL, baritone. For his earlier career, see *Living Musicians,* 1940.

* * *

Robeson's open espousal of the Soviet Union has made him *persona non grata* in American musical circles since the end of World War II. Denied a passport by the State Department because of his refusal to sign an affidavit that he was not a Communist, he has been unable to travel abroad. His public appearances in this country have been mostly in conjunction with left-wing political rallies and meetings.

RODZINSKI, ARTUR, conductor. For his earlier career, see *Living Musicians,* 1940.

* * *

In 1943 Rodzinski left the Cleveland Orchestra to become musical director of the New York Philharmonic-Symphony Orchestra. He held this post four years, and from 1947 to 1948 held a similar position with the Chicago Symphony. Since leaving Chicago, he has established his permanent home in Florence, Italy, and has confined his activities as a conductor to guest appearances in Europe.

ROESGEN-CHAMPION, MARGUE-RITE, harpsichordist and pianist. See *Living Musicians,* 1940.

ROSE, LEONARD, violoncellist, was born in Washington, D.C. on July 26, 1918. When he was a child, his family moved to Florida, where he was raised and educated. In his tenth year he began studying the cello with Walter Grossman; three years later he won a Florida State Contest in the cello division. He made several appearances in Florida before coming to New York in his fifteenth year to continue studies with his cousin, Frank Miller, solo cellist of the NBC Symphony Orchestra. In 1934 he was awarded a scholarship for the Curtis Institute of Music where for four years he was a pupil of Felix Salmond.

His studies completed, Rose joined the cello section of the NBC Symphony Orchestra, conducted by Toscanini, in 1938. He stayed there only one season, receiving an appointment as solo cellist of the Cleveland Orchestra. During the four years he held the latter post, he made fourteen appearances as guest artist with the orchestra. In October 1943 he was engaged as first cellist of the New York Philharmonic-Symphony, and the following season he made his first appearance as soloist with that orchestra. He occupied the first desk until 1951 and made his last American appearance with the New York Philharmonic on April 5, 1951, performing Bloch's *Schelomo* and Saint-Saëns' Concerto in A minor. "It was in the nature of a public

LEONARD ROSE

farewell," reported Howard Taubman in the New York *Times*. "The truth, of course, is that Mr. Rose has been a virtuoso of the cello for some time, but his playing has always been a blend of technical musicianship and a simple, innate modesty. He may have to step out a little more in the months ahead, but it is hard to believe that his essential musical personality will change much."

Rose's concluding appearance with the New York Philharmonic, as a member of the orchestra, was at the Edinburgh Festival in September 1951. After that he launched his career as a virtuoso. His first tour, during 1951-1952, included appearances with many major orchestras as well as numerous recitals. During 1952-1953 he made thirteen appearances with eleven leading orchestras. Subsequent appearances not only in this country but in the principal music centers of the world placed him in the front rank of living cellists. Louis Biancolli wrote in the New York *World Telegram and Sun* after one of Rose's New York recitals: "My guess is that Leonard Rose is the best cellist since Pablo Casals." And Bruno Walter, under whose baton Rose has frequently played, has said: "Leonard Rose's profound musicianship, technical perfection, his emotional warmth and the rare beauty of his tone have been a source of pure joy for me in all the years of our musical association. The cause of the cello's musical literature can be in no better hands than his."

ROSEN, MAX, violinist. For his earlier career, see *Living Musicians,* 1940.

* * *

After World War II, Rosen retired from the concert stage and devoted himself to teaching. He died in New York City on December 16, 1956.

ROSENSTOCK, JOSEPH, conductor. was born in Cracow, Poland, on January 27, 1895. He was a child prodigy, making appearances as a pianist when he was eleven. His musical education took place at the Vienna Conservatory, and later he studied composition privately with Franz Schreker. His training completed, he joined the faculty of the Berlin Academy. Fritz Busch persuaded him to abandon teaching for conducting, and engaged him as his assistant with the Stuttgart Opera. Four weeks after this appointment, Rosenstock led a performance of *The Bartered Bride* without a single rehearsal and without consulting a score. In 1920 he was engaged as principal conductor of the Darmstadt Opera, and five years later he was elevated to the post of musical director. From 1925 to 1927 he was principal conductor of the Wiesbaden Opera.

In 1929, when Artur Bodanzky resigned from the Metropolitan Opera as principal German conductor, Rosenstock was engaged to replace him. Rosenstock's American debut took place on October 30, 1929, in a performance of *Die Meistersinger.* He remained only a single season, and Bodanzky resumed his old post. Back in Europe, Rosenstock filled the post of music director of the Mannheim Opera from 1930 to 1933.

With the rise of Hitler, Rosenstock lost both his Mannheim post and all his personal possessions. He fled to Japan, where for the next five years he led the Nippon Philharmonic Orchestra. When Japan became involved in World War II, his life once again became precarious. He was exiled to a primitive mountain village where he suffered indescribable hardships until the war's end, when he was liberated by American troops. At the request of General Willoughby he reorganized the Nippon Philharmonic and resumed concerts with that organization.

He came to the United States in 1946 to settle permanently in this country. In 1948 he became a conductor of the New York City Opera. "Rosenstock revealed himself not only as an excellent musician and leader," wrote Olin Downes in the New York *Times* following a performance of *The Marriage of Figaro* on October 14, "but as a really sensitive artist, one who understood the traditions of

JOSEPH ROSENSTOCK

the opera and the essence of the score." In the fall of 1951, Rosenstock replaced Lázlo Halász as the company's artistic director. His initial season in this post was made memorable by the first repertory production in the United States of *Wozzeck*. In addition to his appearances with the New York City Opera, Rosenstock was for several seasons director of the Aspen Music Festival in Aspen, Colorado, and also appeared as guest conductor of symphony orchestras in Europe; occasionally he appears in the dual role of solo pianist and conductor.

On December 16, 1955, Rosenstock resigned as musical director of the New York City Opera but remained as a conductor. In 1956-1957 he undertook an extensive tour of Japan, conducting over fifty programs in the concert hall and over radio and television. On this occasion he received the 1956 Cultural Award of the Japan Broadcasting Company, the first time this honor was accorded a foreigner.

Rosenstock occupies an apartment in the Washington Square section of New York, surrounding himself with a precious collection of paintings and *objets d'art*, many of them acquired in the Orient. He is a soccer fan, and sometimes becomes an active participant by indulging in scrimmages.

ROSENTHAL, MORITZ, pianist. For his earlier career, see *Living Musicians,* 1940.

* * *

Rosenthal died in New York City on September 3, 1946.

ROSING, VLADIMIR, tenor. For his earlier career, see *Living Musicians,* 1940.

* * *

After World War II Rosing joined the New York City Opera Company as stage director and consultant.

ROSS, HUGH, choral conductor. See *Living Musicians,* 1940.

ROSS, LANNY, tenor. See *Living Musicians,* 1940.

ROSSI-LEMENI, NICOLA, bass, was born in Constantinople in November 1922. His father was Italian, a colonel in the Italian army; his mother was Russian. Before embarking on a musical career, he studied law in Italy with the intention of entering diplomatic service. With the entry of Italy into World War II, his studies were interrupted. He was inducted into the Italian army and often sang for the troops; it was then that he decided to abandon diplomacy for music. After the war he studied singing intensively; he made his concert debut in Verona and a highly successful opera debut at La Scala in Milan. After additional appearances not only at La Scala but also in other major Italian opera houses, and in Latin America, he made his North American debut at the San Francisco opera on October 2, 1951, as Boris Godunov. Alfred Frankenstein described the singer in the San Francisco *Chronicle* as "a new star . . . [whose] talents are immense. The adjective 'king-sized' has been done to death in contemporary journalism, but you don't know what it really means until you have seen this man, his overwhelming physique and his imperial bearing." In the San Francisco *News,* Cecil Smith proclaimed Rossi-Lemeni as "the finest Boris Godunov since Feodor Chaliapin."

On November 16, 1953, Rossi-Lemeni made his debut at the Metropolitan Opera as Mephistopheles in *Faust.* "From the moment of his first appearance," wrote Ronald Eyer in *Musical America,* "there was no doubt that a personality of impressive dimensions occupied the stage. At all times in command of himself and of the situation, he set forth his own detailed conception of the roguish devil with vigor, with style, and with a sure touch for the theatrical effective pose and gesture. . . . Mr. Rossi-Lemeni is a singing actor of great potentialities whose future development should repay careful attention."

Rossi-Lemeni remained at the Metropolitan Opera only a single season. He has since

Rossi-Lemeni: rōs'sē lĕ-mä'nē

NICOLA ROSSI-LEMENI

appeared regularly at La Scala, where he is a principal bass, and where on December 8, 1956, Handel's *Julius Caesar* was revived for him, at his own request. He has also made appearances in other leading European opera houses, at leading European music festivals, and in South America.

ROSTROPOVICH, MSTISLAV, cellist, was born in 1927 in Azerbaijan, U.S.S.R., in the city of Baku, on the shores of the Caspian sea. Both parents were musicians. His father was a professional cellist, and his mother an excellent pianist. When, in 1931, his father was engaged by the Gnessin Institute as a teacher of the cello, the family settled in Moscow. There, when he was only five, Mstislav taught himself to play the piano and was soon participating in chamber-music performances at home. When he was about eight, his father started teaching him the cello, and at eleven he started composition.

From 1934 to 1941 he attended the Preparatory Seven-Years School for talented musical children and received a comprehensive academic and musical education. In 1943 he entered the Moscow Conservatory, where he specialized in the study of the cello with Semeon Kozolupoff. While a Conservatory student, Rostropovich often appeared in concerts of sonata music with the pianist Svyatoslav Richter, and in performances of chamber music with the violinist Leonide Kogan, and

the celebrated pianist Emil Gilels. His study at the Conservatory was interrupted during World War II, when his family was evacuated to the Urals. But his training was continued as soon as the war in Europe ended and it was completed in 1948, after he had won the all-Union contest for cellists in the Soviet Union and the first prize in cello playing at the International Youth Festival in Prague.

His studies over, Rostropovich became a professor of cello at the Moscow Conservatory (a post he still retains) and began his career as a virtuoso. He was only twenty-four when, in 1951, he was acclaimed for his performance in Moscow of all six Bach solo cello suites. That same year he was also heard outside the Soviet Union for the first time, when, with eight other Soviet artists, he performed at the Florence May Festival in Italy. Howard Taubman, who heard him at this time, reported in the New York *Times*: "Rostropovich . . . was also first class. His tone was big, clean and accurate, and his musicianship was searching." After that, he gave performances in London, Paris and other music centers of the western world, besides making extensive tours of the Soviet Union.

When, after the summit meeting in Geneva during the summer of 1955, an exchange of culture between the United States and the Soviet Union was agreed upon, the Soviet embassy telephoned Frederick C. Schang of Columbia Artists suggesting that Rostropovich tour the United States. Once the necessary clearance was obtained from the American State Department, Rostropovich arrived in the United States in April 1956. His debut took place at a recital in Carnegie Hall on April 4. "Mr. Rostropovich," reported Jay S. Harrison in the New York *Herald Tribune*, "is first a musician, then a technician. Digital wonders are not his prime concern—he is no dazzler, no hypnotist, no demon of the bow. Nor does he try to be. . . . The meretricious is clearly not his way. He is sober, serious, intense, and devoted." A few weeks later he appeared as soloist with the New York Philharmonic-Symphony in the American première of Prokofiev's Second Cello Concerto. "Once again," wrote Howard Taubman in the New York *Times*, "his wares encompassed brilliance of technique, a singing tone, and best of all searching musicianship."

Apart from music, Rostropovich's principal interest is in mechanics and engineering. He

Rostropovich: rôs-trô-pô'vĭch

MSTISLAV ROSTROPOVICH

subscribes to all the Russian technical periodicals, and one of his prize possessions is a model of a French express train presented to him soon after his first appearances in Paris.

ROTH STRING QUARTET. For its earlier history, see *Living Musicians,* 1940.

* * *

In 1946 the Quartet became associated with the University of California in Los Angeles, and in 1957 it made its first tour of Europe since World War II. Besides Feri Roth, who remains its first violinist, the Quartet now includes Cesare Pascarella, violoncello; Laurent Halleux, viola; and Thomas Marrocco, second violin.

ROTHIER, LEON, bass. For his earlier career, see *Living Musicians,* 1940.

* * *

Rothier's last appearance at the Metropolitan Opera was in *Manon* on February 25, 1939. After that he devoted himself to teaching, coaching and, in 1944, to appearances in a non-musical Broadway play, *A Bell for Adano.* In 1949 his fiftieth anniversary as a singer was celebrated with a New York recital. He died in New York City on December 6, 1951.

RUBINSTEIN, ARTUR, pianist. See *Living Musicians,* 1940.

RUBINSTEIN, BERYL, pianist. For his earlier career, see *Living Musicians,* 1940.

* * *

Beryl Rubinstein died in Cleveland, Ohio, on December 29, 1952.

RUDOLF, MAX, conductor, was born in Frankfurt, Germany, on June 15, 1902. After graduation from the local high school he attended both the University of Frankfurt and Hoch's Conservatory. In 1922 Rudolf was appointed conductor at the Municipal Theatre in Freiburg. One season later he was engaged by the Hesse Opera in Darmstadt, and in 1925 he was elevated to the post of principal conductor. From 1929 to 1935 he was conductor of the German Opera in Prague. During this period he also appeared several times as guest conductor of the Berlin Philharmonic. Between 1935 and 1940 he conducted in Gothenburg, Sweden, serving as principal conductor of the Gothenburg Orchestral Society, besides directing choral and radio concerts.

In 1940 he came to the United States, settling here permanently, and becoming a citizen in 1946. Soon after his arrival he joined the faculty of the School of Music of the Central YMCA College in Chicago. In 1944 he made his first American appearance as an opera conductor with the New Opera Company in New York City.

Rudolf made his debut at the Metropolitan Opera on January 13, 1946, in a benefit concert. Two months later, on March 2, he made his first opera appearance there when he led a performance of *Der Rosenkavalier.* Since that time he has been one of the company's principal conductors, distinguishing himself particularly in the Wagner and Mozart repertory. In 1947 he directed the world première of Bernard Rogers' *The Warrior* and the first recording made by the Metropolitan Opera for Columbia Records, *Hänsel und Gretel.* In 1950 he was elevated to the position of artistic administrator.

Besides appearing with the Metropolitan Opera, Rudolf has conducted opera performances with the Cincinnati Summer Opera, at the Lewisohn Stadium in New York, and at Robin Hood Dell in Philadelphia. He has also appeared as guest conductor of many American symphony orchestras, making his debut in this capacity with the New York

MAX RUDOLF

Philharmonic-Symphony Orchestra in the fall of 1955.

Rudolf has served as guest instructor at the Juilliard School of Music and is the author of *The Grammar of Conducting* (1949).

RUHLMANN, FRANÇOIS, conductor. For his earlier career, see *Living Musicians,* 1940.

* * *

Ruhlmann died in Paris on June 6, 1948.

SABATA, VICTOR DE, conductor. For his earlier career, see *Living Musicians,* 1940.

* * *

De Sabata returned to the United States to appear as guest conductor of the Pittsburgh Symphony on November 12, 1948. Indicative of his importance as a conductor was the fact that two New York newspapers sent their critics to attend his first concert, described as his second American debut. In 1949 De Sabata inaugurated the season of the Chicago Symphony, and in 1950 he appeared as guest conductor of the New York Philharmonic-Symphony. During this period he also scored major successes not only in Italy but also at the Salzburg Festival and with the principal orchestras of Europe.

SACK, ERNA, soprano. See *Living Musicians,* 1940.

SALMOND, FELIX, cellist. For his earlier career, see *Living Musicians,* 1940.

* * *

Salmond died in New York City on February 19, 1952.

SALZEDO, CARLOS, harpist. See *Living Musicians,* 1940.

SAMINSKY, LAZARE, choral conductor. See *Living Musicians,* 1940.

SAMMONS, ALBERT, violinist. For his earlier career, see *Living Musicians,* 1940.

* * *

Sammons died in London on August 24, 1957.

SANDOR, GYORGY, pianist, was born in Budapest, Hungary, on September 21, 1912. His mother was an excellent amateur musician who gave each of her five children musical training; musicales, in which all the children participated, were frequent events in the Sandor household. Gyorgy attended the Madach High School. Of all the children he showed the greatest natural aptitude for music, and he entered the Academy of Music in Budapest in 1927 for a comprehensive musical course. There, during the next six years, his teachers included Béla Bartók and Zoltan Kodály. In 1933 Sandor was graduated with diplomas in piano and composition; two years earlier he had had a successful debut as a concert pianist in Budapest.

Until 1938 he concertized in all the principal cities of continental Europe and Scandinavia. In February 1939 he made his American debut at Carnegie Hall, and was well received. Appearances throughout the country that year were followed by extensive tours of the Americas.

In 1942 Sandor enlisted in the United States Army. He served in the Signal Corps, Intelligence Service, and Special Services until 1944, when he was discharged. During this period he was made an American citizen. Returning to concert work, he gave a successful concert at Carnegie Hall which was followed by a tour not only of the United States but also of South America. In South America he was referred to as "the pianist who came back to life" because before his arrival the rumor had spread that he had died. Since that time he has concertized in the capitals of the world. On February 8, 1946, he attracted international attention when he performed the world

Sandor: shăn'dôr

Columbia Records

GYORGY SANDOR

première of Béla Bartók's Third Piano Concerto with the Philadelphia Orchestra under Ormandy. "Mr. Sandor's reading was tense and dynamic and thoughtful," reported Louis Biancolli in the New York *World Telegram and Sun,* when Sandor repeated his performance in New York. "You felt a special fervor, too—the special pleading of a friend and countryman."

Besides giving concerts, Sandor has lectured on musical interpretation and piano technique at the University of Mexico City and the University of Bogotá. He is a sports enthusiast, his favorites in this field being skating, skiing, swimming, and tennis.

SANROMÁ, JESÚS MARÍA, pianist. For his earlier career, see *Living Musicians,* 1940.

* * *

Sanromá made his first extensive tour of Central and South America in the summer of 1945.

SARGENT, SIR MALCOM, conductor. For his earlier career, see *Living Musicians,* 1940.

* * *

In 1947 Sargent was knighted. In 1950 he was appointed principal conductor of the BBC Symphony Orchestra.

SAYÃO, BIDU, soprano. For her earlier career, see *Living Musicians,* 1940.

* * *

Sayão left the Metropolitan Opera in 1951 and was subsequently heard in opera houses in Europe and South America.

SCHERCHEN, HERMANN, conductor. For his earlier career, see *Living Musicians,* 1940.

* * *

Scherchen became known to American music lovers after World War II through his extensive recordings for Westminster. After the war, he established master classes in conducting in Venice, Italy.

SCHERMAN, THOMAS KIELTY, conductor, was born in New York City on February 12, 1917. His father founded and has since become chairman of the board of the Book-of-the-Month Club; his mother, Bernardine Kielty, is an author, columnist, and editor. After attending the Horace Mann and Lincoln schools in New York, Scherman attended Columbia University, where he majored in mathematics and from which he was graduated in 1937. Simultaneous with his academic education he received a thorough musical training, principally at the Mannes School of Music, where his teachers included Frank Sheridan and Isabella Vengerova (piano), Hans Weisse (composition and theory), and Carl Bamberger (conducting). After that he studied piano and conducting at the Juilliard School of Music and took graduate courses in music at Columbia University.

His first activity in music took place during his undergraduate days at Columbia when he served as accompanist for the Columbia University Glee Club. In 1939 he assisted Otto Klemperer as conductor of a chamber orchestra performing a series of concerts at the New School for Social Research.

Before Pearl Harbor, Scherman entered the army as a private and during the war rose to the rank of captain in the Signal Corps. After his discharge, in 1946, he originated a radio program over the Mutual Network called "Let's Go to the Opera," which presented excerpts from the great operas in English. During this period he also conducted several performances over radio station WQXR, and in the summer of 1947 served as assistant conductor of the Opera Nacional in Mexico City.

In the fall of 1947 Thomas Scherman organized the Little Orchestra Society, which made its bow in Town Hall, New York, on

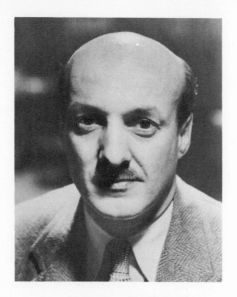

THOMAS SCHERMAN

October 20. The aim of this organization was to present unusual programs made up of premières, revivals of neglected masterworks, and important new works which failed to get a hearing with larger orchestras. Olin Downes reported in the New York *Times* that the Little Orchestra Society was "a freshening force in the musical life of the city," and Virgil Thomson wrote in the New York *Herald Tribune* that the orchestra has "taken a place in our musical life that no other society has filled in many years."

The orchestra and conductor have remained faithful to their original ideal of invigorating the musical scene with novel and at times exciting program-making, which even includes the presentation of neglected operas in concert form. While doing this, Scherman has forged new trails for the American concert stage. He inaugurated the European tradition of allowing audiences to attend the final rehearsal; he instituted adventurous children's concerts, at some of which new children's operas were introduced; he initiated Saturday morning sessions at his studio where composers could present their new works. In 1954, through the agency of the Book-of-the-Month Club, he helped organize a new recording venture: the Music Appreciation Records, on which a musical masterwork, presented in a complete performance, was coupled with an analysis of the work, often by Scherman himself.

Scherman has made several tours with his orchestra and has produced his children's concerts in several Eastern cities besides New York. For his contribution to music he was honored with a Medal of Excellence from Columbia University in 1952, and again in 1956 on the occasion of the tenth anniversary of the founding of the Little Orchestra Society; in May 1954 he received a citation from the National Association of American Composers and Conductors. In 1954 and 1955 Scherman was a guest conductor at the Lewisohn Stadium in New York and on June 5, 1957 he appeared as a conductor of the Berlin Philharmonic Orchestra in a German-American Music Festival presented by that orchestra in Berlin.

Scherman resides in a studio apartment near Carnegie Hall. Though music dominates his life, he finds time to do extensive reading, participate in an occasional game of bridge or tennis, and to indulge in his favorite diversion of cooking.

SCHIØTZ, AKSEL, tenor, was born in Roskilde, Denmark, on September 1, 1906. He received a comprehensive academic education, being graduated in 1930 from the University of Copenhagen where he specialized in languages. For the next eight years he was a schoolmaster in various Danish schools, teaching languages, music, and Scripture.

Singing had always been an avocation, and music a passion. In 1939 he decided to abandon teaching and turn to music as a profession. After a short period of voice study in Stockholm with John Forsell, Schiøtz made his opera debut with the Copenhagen Royal Opera in 1939 as Ferrando in *Così Fan Tutte*; in the same year he also made his concert debut with a song recital in Copenhagen.

During the next few years, he appeared in opera and oratorio performances in Denmark and sang in numerous recitals, making a profound impression not only because of his innate musicianship but also because of the wide range of his musical versatility, which covered virtually every style and school.

After the Nazis invaded Denmark, Schiøtz refused to sing any German *Lieder* in public, as the Nazis asked him to do, since he realized his performances would be utilized as pro-German propaganda. Instead he concentrated mostly on Danish music, and was able to present a rich library of Danish folk and art songs, much of it hitherto unknown. While continuing his career, he also became engaged in the Resistance movement in Denmark. For his political activity during World War II, he was made a knight in 1947 by the late King Christian X.

After the war, he gave song recitals over the Danish radio which were heard by an

Schiøtz: shüts

Courtesy of Musical Courier

AKSEL SCHIØTZ

executive of an English recording firm, who contracted with him to make records. These disks—of music ranging from Monteverdi to the moderns, from oratorio to song—made the name of Schiøtz known throughout the world of music. In 1946 Schiøtz made his successful debut in England when he appeared with the Glyndebourne Opera in Britten's *The Rape of Lucretia.*

Towards the end of 1946 Schiøtz began revealing startling physical symptoms which the doctors soon diagnosed as a brain tumor. The operation that followed was successful, but it brought about a paralysis of the right half of his face and affected his vocal cords. Nevertheless, Schiøtz refused to concede that his career was over. He began to study singing anew, as if he were a novice. His return to the concert stage was made in Copenhagen in September 1948 and was so successful that he was required to give a second concert ten days later.

In the fall of the same year he toured the United States, making his American debut in New York on October 20, 1948. The critics remarked sadly that his recent serious illness had seriously affected the quality and volume of his singing; but they were unanimous in praising the consummate artistry and musical penetration with which each number was rendered. In 1949 Schiøtz made appearances at the Edinburgh Festival, and in the same year the students of the University of Copenhagen

elected him "Artist of Honor." Since the early 1950's, Schiøtz' appearances on the concert stage have been infrequent.

SCHIPA, TITO, tenor. For his earlier career, see *Living Musicians,* 1940.

* * *

Schipa returned to the Metropolitan Opera for the season of 1940-1941, and in 1947 he made a concert tour of the United States. In 1955 he was appointed by the Italian government a representative to the opera festival held in the principal cities of Belgium.

SCHIPPERS, THOMAS, conductor, was born in Kalamazoo, Michigan, on March 9, 1930. He attended the Kalamazoo High School, and received his musical training at the Curtis Institute in Philadelphia from 1944 to 1945, Yale University in 1946, and the Juilliard School of Music during the summers of 1945 and 1946. He was only seventeen when he was chosen by Eugene Ormandy as one of five finalists in a conductors' competition to direct a concert of the Philadelphia Orchestra at the Academy of Music in Philadelphia.

Two years later, he made a more official debut when Gian-Carlo Menotti selected him to conduct his opera *The Consul,* which opened on Broadway on March 15, 1950. He subsequently also conducted this opera in Paris and London. Upon returning from Europe he was appointed resident conductor of the New York City Opera, making his debut there on April 9, 1952, in a performance of Menotti's *Amahl and the Night Visitors.* During the next three years he conducted not only operas from the standard repertory but also such novelties as Ravel's *L'Heure Espagnole* and the world première of Aaron Copland's *The Tender Land.* "The measure of a conductor is his performance in unfamiliar music," wrote John Briggs in the New York *Times* after one of Schippers' appearances at the New York City opera. "By this standard, Mr. Schippers' performance was very fine, indeed."

While conducting at the New York City Opera, Schippers filled several engagements as guest conductor of American symphony orchestras, including the Philadelphia Orchestra, the NBC Symphony, and the Boston Symphony at Tanglewood. On December 27, 1954, he led the première of Menotti's *The Saint of Bleecker Street* in New York, conducting the opera during its entire New York run. After that, in May 1955, he made a

Schippers: shĭp′ẽrz

THOMAS SCHIPPERS

notable debut at La Scala in Milan with the same work.

On March 26, 1955, Schippers made his debut with the New York Philharmonic-Symphony Orchestra; Olin Downes described him in the New York *Times* as "a conductor of very exceptional gifts and an unusual approach to his task. Mr. Schippers is admirably precise in his beat, clear as a bell in his musical conceptions, and of sensitive taste, interprets without exaggeration or overemphasis or any of the tricks of the trade of a modern conductor who intends at any cost to impress, if not startle, an audience. He is as economical of gesture and movement as he is in complete control of the orchestra and of himself. . . . He seeks balance, beauty and proportion in his readings, and this with a highly becoming seriousness and modesty of demeanor."

During the late spring and summer of 1955, Schippers was heard in Europe—with the Scarlatti Orchestra in Paris and at the festivals in Aix-en-Provence and Bordeaux. Towards the end of the same year, on December 24, he made his debut at the Metropolitan Opera in a revival of *Don Pasquale*. "Mr. Schippers," wrote Howard Taubman in the *New York Times*, "knows how to keep his forces together. . . . He keeps things moving but he is wise enough to give the singers a certain flexibility. . . . The Metropolitan cooperated to make Mr. Schippers' debut a happy occasion by giving him an ex-

cellent and neatly blended cast." This was the third time in the history of the Metropolitan Opera that an American-born musician was engaged for its staff of conductors (the others were Nahan Franko and Max Bendix).

SCHMITZ, ÉMILE ROBERT, pianist. For his earlier career, see *Living Musicians*, 1940.

* * *

In the period between the two world wars, Schmitz taught piano in the United States at the Golden Gate College in San Francisco and the McCune School of Music in Salt Lake City. He died in Paris on September 6, 1949.

SCHNABEL, ARTUR, pianist. For his earlier career, see *Living Musicians*, 1940.

* * *

Schnabel died in Axenstein, Switzerland, on August 15, 1951.

SCHNEEVOIGT, GEORG, conductor. For his earlier career, see *Living Musicians*, 1940.

* * *

Schneevoigt died in Malmö, Sweden, on November 28, 1947.

SCHOLZ, HEINZ and ROBERT, duo-pianists. See *Living Musicians*, 1940.

SCHORR, FRIEDRICH, baritone. For his earlier career, see *Living Musicians*, 1940.

* * *

Schorr's last appearance at the Metropolitan Opera took place on March 2, 1943 as the Wanderer in *Siegfried*. Following his retirement from the opera stage he joined the faculty of the Hartt School of Music in Hartford, Connecticut. In 1950 he was appointed adviser on German operas at the New York City Opera. He died in Farmington, Connecticut, on August 14, 1953.

SCHUMANN, ELISABETH, soprano. For her earlier career, see *Living Musicians*, 1940.

* * *

Schumann became an American citizen in 1944. She died in New York City on April 23, 1952.

SCHURICHT, CARL, conductor, was born in Danzig, Germany, on July 3, 1880. His father was a builder of pipe organs, and his mother was an excellent pianist and singer.

Schuricht: shoo′rĭкt

As a child, Schuricht attended the Berlin Hochschule für Musik, where his teachers included E. Rudorff and Engelbert Humperdinck and where he received a scholarship in composition. He subsequently attended Max Reger's master class in composition.

His studies completed, he served his apprenticeship as conductor with various opera houses in Zwickau, Dortmund, and Weimar, among other cities. In 1909 he became conductor of the Rülscher Gesangverein in Frankfort-on-the-Main. Two years later he was appointed conductor in Wiesbaden, where, in 1922, he was elevated to the post of general music director; he filled this assignment until 1944. Meanwhile he made many guest appearances in Europe. In 1933 he served as conductor of the Berlin Philharmonic Choir and gave impressive performances with the Concertgebouw Orchestra of Amsterdam. He became such a favorite in Holland in the succeeding years that in 1938 he received from Queen Wilhelmina the Order of Orange-Nassau.

In 1944 he became involved in difficulties with the Nazi officials and had to flee from Germany and settle in Switzerland. Since then he has held no permanent post with any opera company, nor has he been the permanent conductor of any orchestra. But he has appeared extensively in guest performances throughout Europe.

When the Vienna Philharmonic Orchestra made its first tour of the United States in 1956, Schuricht was one of its two conductors. This, however, was not his American debut. He appeared in a single concert in St. Louis in 1927, a visit that was suddenly curtailed when he became ill.

His second American debut took place with the Vienna Philharmonic in Washington, D.C., on November 4, 1956. Three days later he appeared with the Vienna Philharmonic in Carnegie Hall, New York. "There was courtliness in his manner as he came out for the first time," reported Howard Taubman in the New York *Times*. "Once he started the program, Herr Schuricht was all artist. There were no mannerisms in his wide, dependable beat. His musicianship was to be noted at once in the phrasing of Mozart's D major Symphony." During this tour Schuricht conducted eleven concerts.

"When I was young" Schuricht told an interviewer, "I concentrated on the moderns— Stravinsky, Bartók, Hindemith, and the others. I still like them. But more and more I am in demand as an interpreter of classical and romantic music. In France I am considered

Courtesy of Musical Courier

CARL SCHURICHT

a Schumann specialist. In Denmark they call me a Brahms specialist. In Holland I am considered a Bruckner specialist." But, he added, he is essentially an exponent of "an old tradition." "I have nothing against what music is now," he declares, "but feel it is important to pass on a sense of tradition from age to youth."

Away from music, Schuricht's hobby is toy soldiers. He has a large collection, mostly Louis XV soldiers, and there is nothing that brings him more relaxation.

SCHUSTER, JOSEPH, cellist. For his earlier career, see *Living Musicians,* 1940.

* * *

Schuster resigned as first cellist of the New York Philharmonic-Symphony in 1943 to devote himself to a concert career. Since then he has appeared throughout the world of music in recitals and as soloist with major orchestras.

SCHWARZKOPF, ELISABETH, soprano, was born in Jarotschin, near Posnan, Poland, on December 9, 1915. She attended the Berlin Hochschule für Musik where she won numerous prizes. There a vocal teacher insisted on training her as a contralto. After two and a half years of this kind of training, while continuing her regular curriculum, she studied privately with Dr. Egenolf, who succeeded in undoing all of the damage perpetrated by the first teacher. Now prepared as

Schwartzkopf: shvärts′kôpf

ELISABETH SCHWARZKOPF

a soprano—and after a period of study in Leicester, England, on a League of Nations scholarship—she was engaged by the Charlottenburg Opera in Berlin, making her debut on Easter Day, 1938, as the first Flower Maiden in *Parsifal*. Before her first season with that company ended, she was appearing four times a week in about twenty different minor roles. She supplemented her meager salary by singing over the radio and performing for experiments in tape recording.

She was given her first important roles at Charlottenburg in 1941—Oscar in *Un Ballo in Maschera*, Musetta in *La Bohème*, Lauretta in *Gianni Schicchi*, and Zerbinetta in Richard Strauss' *Ariadne auf Naxos*. Her performance in the last-named role made such an impression on Maria Ivogün, the celebrated concert and opera singer, that she took on Schwarzkopf as a private pupil.

One of Ivogün's achievements was to train Schwarzkopf as a singer of *Lieder*. Schwarzkopf's first song recital took place in Vienna in November 1942 and was so successful that Karl Boehm, principal conductor of the Vienna State Opera, invited her to appear with his company as Zerbinetta, and as Blöndchen in *The Abduction from the Seraglio*. These appearances led to her engagement as principal soprano of the company. A serious illness made it impossible for her to fill this engagement. Between 1943 and 1944 she was in temporary retirement, from which she emerged late in 1944 to make successful appearances at the Vienna State Opera as Blöndchen, Musetta, Rosina in *The Barber of Seville,* and Gilda in *Rigoletto.*

When the Vienna State Opera was closed down because the theatre was wrecked by bombs during World War II, Schwarzkopf entered a second period of retirement. She returned to concert activity only after the war was over—with a triumphant appearance in Vienna in January 1946, an occasion upon which Herbert von Karajan described her as "potentially the best singer we have." She also returned to the Vienna State Opera, which resumed performances at the Theatre-an-der-Wien, and within a few months' time appeared in a large variety of major roles in the French, Italian, and German repertories. In 1947 and again in 1948 she gave triumphant performances at the Salzburg Festival.

Her European fame developed rapidly with immense successes at Covent Garden, beginning with 1947, at Bayreuth in 1951, and at the Lucerne and Florence festivals. In Venice, in 1951, she appeared in the world première of Stravinsky's *The Rake's Progress,* and early in 1952 she made a sensational debut at La Scala in *Der Rosenkavalier.* In 1953, when she returned to La Scala, she was seen in the world première of Carl Orff's *Trionfi.*

Schwarzkopf made her American debut with a recital at Town Hall on October 25, 1953. Since she had already become known to American music lovers through her recordings, the house was sold out. As a critic on *Musical America* wrote after a later recital: "Her singing displayed the exquisite finish, technical mastery, and interpretative felicity that had marked her debut." In October 1954, she returned to the United States for an extended three-month tour. And in October 1955 she made her American opera debut with the San Francisco Opera as the Marschallin in *Der Rosenkavalier.* Mildred Norton reported that this debut presented "a poised and vibrant new personality with a vocal radiance and a personal grace." In that same month, Schwarzkopf received from Toscanini the Orfeo prize, instituted that year in Mantua, Italy for distinguished musicians.

Schwarzkopf is married to Walter Legge, a recording executive in London and the founder of the London Philharmonia Orchestra. Her hobbies include skiing, mountain climbing, and cooking.

SCHWEITZER, ALBERT, organist. For his earlier career, see *Living Musicians*, 1940.

* * *

Schweitzer won the Nobel Peace Prize in 1954. One year later he was honored at Buckingham Palace in London by Queen Elizabeth II with the insignia of an honorary member of the Order of Merit. (The latter distinction has come to only one other non-Briton —Dwight D. Eisenhower.) Schweitzer's film biography was released in the United States in 1957.

SCHWIEGER, HANS, conductor, was born in Cologne, Germany, in 1906. He received an intensive academic education in local schools and at the universities of Cologne and Bonn. His musical training was equally comprehensive, culminating at the Cologne Academy of Music, where he studied composition with Walter Braunfels and conducting with Hermann Abendroth.

After leaving the Academy of Music in 1927, he was appointed assistant conductor to Erich Kleiber at the Berlin State Opera, where he served a three-year apprenticeship. In 1930 he was recommended by the Director of the Prussian State Theatre for the post of principal conductor of the Cassel State Theatre. One year later he became conductor in Augsburg, where, under his direction, the famous Augsburg Festival plays, "Am Roten Tor," were inaugurated.

In 1932 he went on to Mayence to become general music director of that city, conductor of its opera and symphony performances, and director of its Academy of Music. Four years later he assumed the post of general music director in Danzig, serving as the representative of the state in all matters relating to music. His most important European assignment came in 1936 when he was selected to succeed Leo Blech as principal conductor of the Berlin State Opera. He never filled this job, however. The seething political situation in Nazi Germany led him to leave his native land. He arranged for a concert tour in Japan and from there made his way to the United States, where he established permanent residence and in 1945 became a citizen.

His first major assignment in this country was as artistic director of the Columbia Music Festival in Columbia, South Carolina, in 1939. There, during the next two years, he not only led the festival concerts but also organized a children's chorus and a series of chamber-music concerts, and conducted various choral

HANS SCHWIEGER

groups. In 1944 he was appointed to the conducting staff at the New York City Center of Music and Drama; in 1945 he founded and became musical director of the Fort Wayne Philharmonic. Three years after that, he assumed the post he still holds, that of music director of the Kansas City Philharmonic.

When Schwieger appeared as guest conductor of the Chicago Symphony Orchestra at Grant Park, in the summer of 1945, Felix Borowski wrote in the *Sun*: "At Grant Park last evening the symphony orchestra presented . . . a new conductor—and a richly gifted one. . . . His players were alert and responsive to a beat that was firm and incisive. . . . Only an imaginative interpreter could have worked the minor miracle which Mr. Schwieger accomplished. . . . Mr. Schwieger did honor to it by letting the music speak for itself and yet coloring it with a large dignity and unbroken line which . . . a masterpiece deserves."

On October 2, 1956, Schwieger made his debut with the San Francisco Opera in a performance of *Così Fan Tutte*. In a report to the New York *Times*, Howard Taubman wrote: "Mr. Schwieger knows his Mozart and approached him with delicacy and refinement."

Early in 1956, Schwieger announced that he would henceforth divide his year between Kansas City and Nuremberg, Germany. Six months each year he devotes himself to directing two of Nuremberg's opera houses and the Nuremberg Civic Orchestra.

Schwieger: shvē'gĕr

SCOTT, NORMAN, bass-baritone, was born in New York City on November 30, 1918. He received his academic education in New York city public schools and at the City College of New York. He had a pleasant voice but the idea of becoming a professional singer did not occur to him for a long time. "I used to sing a bit in college," he recalls, "and several times my father spoke about me to his friend, Armand Tokatyan, famous tenor of the Metropolitan Opera. Finally, at Christmas time in 1939, we received a card from Mr. Tokatyan asking to have me brought around. He then introduced me to his friend, the voice teacher William Herman. They asked me to sing something, and I sang 'Drink to Me Only with Thine Eyes' in a crooning falsetto voice. I thought that tenor was the only kind of voice worth having for a man singer."

William Herman accepted Scott as a pupil and became his only teacher. One of the first things Herman did was to train Scott's voice as a bass-baritone. "I was so disappointed," continues Scott, "that I doubted if I was any longer interested in studying voice. It took me several months to get used to the idea. Gradually, I began to discover the enormous repertory for bass and baritone, and the great range of emotions which the low voice can express."

During World War II, Scott served as a line officer in the Navy. For two years he participated in numerous combat landings in the South Pacific. He received the Presiden-tial citation awarded his ship for its successful operations.

Scott's first experiences in opera came after the war with the Juilliard Opera Workshop and with the American Theatre Wing. In 1948 he was called to audition for Toscanini, who was looking for a basso in forthcoming performances of Beethoven's Ninth Symphony and Verdi's *Requiem*. After he had sung several excerpts from both works, with the Maestro at the piano, Toscanini said to him simply: "You will do." Scott appeared under Toscanini in Beethoven's Ninth Symphony in what was the Maestro's debut on television, and after that in the *Requiem* in a Carnegie Hall performance. On the latter occasion, Olin Downes praised Scott's "fine bass and authoritative delivery," in the New York *Times* and added that Scott used his voice "with the most exceptional understanding and interpretative vigor." Scott subsequently appeared under Toscanini in radio performances of *Aida* and *Falstaff*.

From 1949 to 1951 Scott was a member of the New York City Opera Company where, besides appearing in the regular repertory, he was also seen in the world première of Tamkin's *The Dybbuk*. In the fall of 1951 he made his debut at the Metropolitan Opera in *Rigoletto*. He has since then appeared there in principal baritone and bass roles in the French and Italian repertory, and in 1953 he appeared in the American première of Stravinsky's *The Rake's Progress*. He has also been heard in guest performances with other leading opera companies in America, on the concert stage, and as soloist with leading orchestras. In 1952 he appeared as soloist with the New York Philharmonic-Symphony in the American première of Milhaud's *Christophe Colomb*.

SEEFRIED, IRMGARD, soprano, was born in Köngetried, Swabia, Germany, on October 9, 1919. Her father, a high school teacher, gave her lessons in singing and piano when she was only five. Three years later she made her first public appearance, as a soloist with a choral group appearing in Bad Wörishofen. Four years later, she made her opera debut in the part of Gretel in *Hänsel und Gretel*.

The death of her father imposed economic hardship on the family. To support herself while studying music, Seefried made appearances at weddings and parties. For four years she attended the Augsburg Conservatory, where she received vocal training from Professor Albert Mayer. Still uncertain about

NORMAN SCOTT

Seefried: zā'frēd

becoming a professional musician, she attended the University of Munich for a year and a half with the intention of studying medicine. During this period she also attended the State Academy of Music, from which she was graduated with a teacher's license in 1939.

A successful audition with Herbert von Karajan, then music director of the Aachen Stadttheater, encouraged her to specialize in music. She was engaged by that company for minor roles, and made her debut there in 1939 in the part of the offstage priestess in *Aida*. In three years' time she was assigned such major parts as Agathe in *Der Freischütz*, Marie in *The Bartered Bride*, Pamina in *The Magic Flute*, and Susanna in *The Marriage of Figaro*.

On May 2, 1943, she made her debut at the Vienna State Opera, as Eva in *Die Meistersinger*—the youngest singer ever engaged by that company for leading roles. She continued appearing there until 1945, when the opera house was demolished by bombs from an air attack. During this period she was selected by Richard Strauss to appear as the Composer in *Ariadne auf Naxos* in a performance celebrating his eightieth birthday.

The year of 1946 was significant for Seefried. She married Wolfgang Schneiderhan, concertmaster of the Vienna Philharmonic Orchestra (and subsequently founder and first violinist of the Schneiderhan String Quartet, one of the most distinguished chamber-music groups in Central Europe). In that same year she also made her first appearance in France.

One year later she became associated for the first time with the Salzburg Festival, where, from that time on, she was to be a major attraction. Appearances followed in opera, recitals, oratorios, concerts with orchestras in most of the leading cities of Europe, and at other major festivals, such as those in Edinburgh, Glyndebourne, Florence, and Wiesbaden. She also returned to the Vienna State Opera when after World War II that company resumed performances at the Theatre-an-der-Wien, and she appeared with the organization during its tours of Europe. She was given the highest honor that the Austrian government could confer on a musician—the title of *Kammersängerin*.

Even before she made her American debut, Seefried was known to American music lovers through her many remarkable recordings. She was, then, no stranger when she made her first American appearance. This took place on October 19, 1951, when she was heard as

IRMGARD SEEFRIED

soloist with the Cincinnati Symphony Orchestra. Two months later she gave her first New York recital. On that occasion, Olin Downes described her voice in the New York *Times* as "of decided natural beauty.... The tones ... were well matched in quality throughout the range. They were clear, bright, and free. She used them like a real musician, keeping them true to pitch and treating the vocal line with care. She had a wide dynamic range at her disposal and with her keen intelligence knew how to reserve the full power of the voice for concluding numbers."

She made several tours of the United States before making her debut at the Metropolitan Opera, on November 20, 1953. On this occasion she was making her three hundredth appearance in the role of Susanna in *The Marriage of Figaro*. Mr. Downes now wrote: "The shining light of this performance was Miss Seefried, whose beautiful voice and brilliancy and authority of style won her instant recognition for her vocal achievement. She was a finished and delightful artist throughout in every note that she made."

Seefried has been the recipient of several major honors. Among these are the Lilli Lehmann Award of the Mozart Association of Salzburg, and the Mozart Medal presented by the City of Vienna in conjunction with the Mozart Association of Austria.

SEGALL, BERNARDO, pianist. See *Living Musicians*, 1940.

SEGOVIA, ANDRÉS, guitarist. See *Living Musicians,* 1940.

SEIDEL, TOSCHA, violinist. For his earlier career, see *Living Musicians,* 1940.

* * *

During World War II Seidel served in the Navy. Since the war he has lived in Hollywood and has worked in the music divisions of several leading motion-picture studios.

SERAFIN, TULLIO, conductor. For his earlier career, see *Living Musicians,* 1940.

* * *

After leaving the Metropolitan Opera in 1934, Serafin became musical director of the Teatro Reale in Rome, and after that, until 1947, of La Scala in Milan. He returned to the United States in 1952 to give several performances with the New York City Opera.

SERKIN, RUDOLF, pianist. See *Living Musicians,* 1940.

SEVITZKY, FABIEN, conductor. For his earlier career, see *Living Musicians,* 1940.

* * *

Sevitzky resigned as music director of the Indianapolis Symphony Orchestra after the 1954-1955 season. In 1956 he filled guest appointments with orchestras in Havana, Mexico, Central and South America, and early in 1957 in Western Europe, Greece, and Yugoslavia.

SHAVITCH, VLADIMIR, conductor. For his earlier career, see *Living Musicians,* 1940.

* * *

Shavitch died in Palm Beach, Florida, on December 26, 1947.

SHAW, ROBERT, conductor, was born in Red Bluff, California, on April 30, 1916. The son of a minister, he was directed to the church. An early love for choral music was instilled in him by his mother, a choir singer, who often had her children perform hymns and folk songs to entertain the neighbors. In 1934 Shaw attended Pomona College, in Claremont, California, after he had become an assistant minister. At college he became the conductor of the glee club and demonstrated such ability that his group became one of the finest in the West. Pomona College was selected by Warner Brothers as the setting for a film entitled *Varsity Show,* starring

ROBERT SHAW

Fred Waring. When Waring heard Shaw's glee club he invited the young man to appear in a minor role in the picture. In 1938 he brought Shaw to New York and engaged him to train the chorus affiliated with his orchestra. While holding this post with the Waring orchestra for seven years, Shaw also directed choral groups for several Broadway stage productions and radio programs.

Meanwhile, in 1941, Shaw organized a choral group of his own, the Collegiate Chorale, made up of 125 amateur singers from the Marble Collegiate Church in New York. Each singer contributed $10.00 a year to defray the expenses of the organization and all deficits after that were defrayed by Shaw himself. The first appearance of this group was with the National Orchestral Association in Carnegie Hall early in 1942. After a succeeding concert in Town Hall, New York, the group toured the country and appeared with major orchestras and under such distinguished conductors as Stokowski, Koussevitzky, and Toscanini. In 1943, as a result of his work with his group, Shaw received a citation from the National Association of American Composers and Conductors as the "year's most important American-born conductor."

In 1944 Shaw became choral director of the RCA Victor Chorale and received a Guggenheim Fellowship to study the theory and techniques of instrumental and choral conducting. In 1945 he served several months in the Navy. After the war he became head of the choral department of the Juilliard School of Music and the Berkshire Music Center in Lenox, Massachusetts.

In 1948 he founded a new chorus, this time made up of forty-two professional singers. It was named the Robert Shaw Chorale. From 1948 to 1956, except for a two-year period between 1949 and 1951 (when Shaw went into temporary retirement to study conducting in America and Europe), Shaw led this organization in distinguished choral concerts. The chorus has also performed with most of the major American orchestras. What Rudolph Elie wrote in the Boston *Herald* is characteristic of critical reaction everywhere to the Shaw Chorale: "The tonal quality was ravishingly beautiful at all dynamic levels, the balance nearly incredible, the attack miraculous, the enunciation and stylistic approach to the languages superb. . . . In fine we have here an organization of advanced vocal soloists combining their voices and interpretative capacities under the direction of a superb choral conductor to produce music of the utmost authenticity and seriousness of style, yet capable also of making contact in the more popular styles without losing artistic standing." As the leader of this Chorale, Shaw has been recognized as one of the foremost choral conductors of our day. Virgil Thomson once wrote: "I do not know his equal in the choral field today," while Toscanini is reputed to have said that Shaw was "the choral maestro I have been looking for."

Robert Shaw has also appeared as guest conductor of several symphony orchestras, including the NBC, the New York Philharmonic-Symphony, the Boston Symphony, and the Philadelphia Orchestra. For several seasons he has led summer orchestral concerts in San Diego, California. In October 1956, Shaw was appointed associate conductor of the Cleveland Orchestra (in succession to Rudolph Ringwall), where his duties included assisting George Szell and conducting several symphony concerts, the Cleveland Orchestra Chorus, and the children's concerts. He made his debut in this new post on December 13, 1956, in a performance of the *Missa Solemnis.* Because of the demands made upon him by this new appointment, Shaw was compelled to relinquish the leadership of the Robert Shaw Chorale.

Robert Shaw is married to Maxine Farley, formerly a department store executive in New York. His favorite hobbies are woodwork and swimming.

SHERIDAN, FRANK, pianist. See *Living Musicians,* 1940.

SHURE, LEONARD, pianist. See *Living Musicians,* 1940.

SIEPI, CESARE, bass, was born in Milan, Italy, on February 10, 1923. Planning to become a schoolteacher, he attended Milan schools for an academic training. Though he always loved music, studied voice with Chiesa, and sang publicly in his fifteenth year, he had no professional aspirations until he was eighteen. At that time some of his friends urged him to enter a national competition in Florence. Though he knew only two arias, he entered and won first prize. An opera impresario from a town near Venice engaged him for his company. Siepi made his opera debut in Schio, near Venice, in the role of Sparafucile in *Rigoletto,* and was so well received that from this time on he gave serious consideration to undertaking a career in opera.

The war brought his career to a temporary halt. When Nazi troops occupied Italy, Siepi escaped to Switzerland, where he remained during the war years. After the war, Siepi was engaged to appear at La Scala, in Milan, in *Nabucco,* on the occasion of the reopening of that theatre. He continued appearing at La Scala in major bass roles not only in the Italian repertory but also in several Wagnerian music dramas; he was also heard in a gala presentation of Boïto's *Mefistofele* which Toscanini directed in one of his rare appearances at La Scala after World War II. Besides performing at La Scala, Siepi was successfully received at the festivals in Salzburg and Edinburgh, and in concert and opera performances in England, Scandinavia, Switzerland, and Spain.

Siepi made his debut at the Metropolitan Opera as a last-minute replacement for Boris Christoff, the Bulgarian bass, who could not appear because he had not been cleared by the United States Department of State. Rudolf Bing engaged Siepi by transatlantic telephone. Siepi's first American appearance opened the 1950-1951 season, and the opera was *Don Carlo.* His fine delineation of the role of Philip II and his beautiful voice drew unanimous praises from the New York music critics. In subsequent appearances at the Metropolitan—particularly in such roles as Don Basilio in *The Barber of Seville,* Mephistopheles in *Faust,* Boris Godunov, and Don Giovanni—Siepi proved to be one of the best singing-actors on the contemporary stage. As Olin Downes wrote after Siepi's perform-

Siepi: syä′pē

CESARE SIEPI

ance in *La Forza del Destino* on the opening night of the 1951-1952 season: "Another of the great singers . . . was Cesare Siepi, the Padre Guardino. Who has a nobler tone, a finer command of a wholly exceptional voice?"

On January 27, 1951, Siepi made his American concert debut by appearing in a performance of Verdi's *Requiem* performed at Carnegie Hall by the NBC Symphony under Toscanini. This time Mr. Downes said of him: "Mr. Siepi had everything that the basso part requires, the noble sonorous tone, the finished technique, and beyond all that, the great spirit." This performance was recorded by RCA Victor, as was another performance of Verdi's *Requiem* in which he participated and which was conducted by Victor de Sabata.

Besides his appearances at the Metropolitan Opera, Siepi has been heard in this country with the San Francisco Opera, in recitals, as soloist with major orchestras, and on many major radio and television programs. He has also been starred in a motion-picture adaptation of *Don Giovanni* filmed by a British company in Salzburg.

SILOTI, ALEXANDER, pianist. For his earlier career, see *Living Musicians*, 1940.

* * *

Siloti died in New York City on December 8, 1945.

SINGER, JACQUES, conductor, was born in Przemsyi, Poland, in 1912. His father conducted symphony orchestras and choruses.

Jacques received violin training at an early age. When he was seven, he gave concerts in Poland. Two years later, the family settled in the United States, and in 1925 Singer made his American debut with a recital in Town Hall, New York. A scholarship now brought him to the Curtis Institute of Music, where he studied with Carl Flesch. Later music study took place with Leopold Auer, and at the Juilliard Graduate School with Paul Kochanski and Rubin Goldmark.

When he was eighteen, he was engaged as violinist by the Philadelphia Orchestra and during the next few years he played under many outstanding conductors. Leopold Stokowski, the orchestra's music director, became interested in him and in 1935 asked him to conduct a contemporary work at one of the rehearsals.

When, in 1937, the citizens of Dallas, Texas, organized a symphony orchestra and sought a conductor, Stokowski recommended Singer, saying: "He is one of the greatest conductorial talents I know." His debut in Dallas took place on February 1, 1938, and was editorially described by the Dallas *Morning News* as "a spectacular triumph." Singer remained with the Dallas Orchestra five years and was responsible for lifting it to a place of importance among America's symphonic organizations.

During the early part of World War II, Singer was offered a commission in Special Services, but he turned it down to enter the army as a combat private. He saw active service in New Guinea, Bataan, and Corregidor, receiving three battle stars. While in uniform he conducted army band concerts, including the first concert given in Corregidor after its recapture by American forces.

Following his separation from the army, Singer conducted in 1946 a series of summer concerts in New Orleans — twenty-eight in eight weeks—which broke attendance records there. A few months later he made a guest appearance with the Vancouver (British Columbia) Symphony Orchestra which was so sensational that he was offered the post of permanent conductor and music director. Under his leadership this orchestra expanded its activities from a ten-week season to one of twenty-five weeks, and included in its performances numerous broadcasts (twenty-five of them sponsored by an oil company), as well as concerts of choral music (with an organization Singer founded for this purpose) and festivals of Canadian music.

In 1952 Singer went to New York, where he conducted the orchestra for the Broadway

JACQUES SINGER

performances of Shakespeare's *Anthony and Cleopatra* and Bernard Shaw's *Caesar and Cleopatra* starring Laurence Olivier and Vivien Leigh. In the spring of 1953 he appeared as guest conductor in Israel, conducting the Israel Philharmonic, the Jerusalem Radio Orchestra, and the Haifa Symphony. During this visit, he directed the Haifa Symphony in the first symphony concert ever given in Nazareth. "The warm ovations," the mayor of Haifa wrote him, "crowned by the prolonged standing ovation you were given had no parallel in Haifa, or in Israel, for that matter, since Arturo Toscanini's appearance in the country many years ago."

In 1954 Singer was appointed musical director of the Corpus Christi (Texas) Symphony Orchestra, making his debut on October 18. John Rosenfeld, reviewing this concert in the Corpus Christi *Times* said: "Each number of the program was a living thing, eloquence in transmission. . . . Singer is an artist to his finger tips."

Besides appearing in Corpus Christi, Singer gave successful guest performances in Mexico City and Guatemala in 1955, and in Guatemala and with the Indianapolis Symphony Orchestra in 1956.

SINGHER, MARTIAL, baritone, was born in Oloron, in the Sainte-Marie section of the Pyrenees, France, on August 14, 1904. Directed to a teaching career by his father, a civil engineer, Martial received his academic education in local schools, at the University

of Toulouse and at the St. Cloud Normal School in Paris. Though he had been singing from childhood on, when he had appeared as a choirboy in Bayonne, he entertained no thought of becoming a professional singer until his twentieth year. He began singing publicly in 1924, and in 1927 was heard by Édouard Herriot, Minister of Public Instruction, who encouraged him to study singing seriously. Singher now entered the Paris Conservatory, where he remained three years; he studied with André Gresse, Pierre Chereau, and Maurice Fauré, and received numerous awards.

Upon leaving the Conservatory, Singher was offered an engagement with the Paris Opéra. But, feeling he was not yet ready, he turned down this offer to devote himself to some additional training with various teachers, including Juliette Fourestier.

His opera debut took place in Amsterdam on November 14, 1930, when he appeared as Orestes in Gluck's *Iphigénie en Tauride*. He will never forget that debut because of an amusing episode. "I was in my dressing room during intermission," he told an interviewer, "wearing shorts and one sandal, when an usher came in and said something in Dutch. I didn't understand a word, but I thought, 'Ah, they told me I would be paid at intermission.' I put a towel around my shoulders and went hopping off on one sandal. Where he took me was not to the cashier's but the royal box. Princess Juliana was there, and some other people. They were all in magnificent evening dress. The Princess did not seem to mind. She came to hear me afterwards, in London."

A month later he made his first appearance at the Paris Opéra, this time as Athanaël in *Thaïs*. For a while he was assigned only minor parts. But the following May he was called in as a last-minute replacement for Vanni Marcoux, leading baritone of the Paris Opéra, in a performance of *Otello* starring Lauritz Melchior. "There were eleven curtain calls after the second act," recalls Singher, "only I was too bruised to enjoy them, for Mr. Melchior hurled me boldly into the footlights during our passionate dialogue. He was not used to so light an Iago. . . . After that performance I was given a new contract as a leading baritone." Singher has since remained the leading baritone of the company.

During the next few years, Singher's career was rich in achievement. In 1932 he appeared for the first time in a Wagnerian role when he played the part of Telramund opposite Marjorie Lawrence's Ortrud (her Paris debut) in *Lohengrin*. This was followed by his appear-

MARTIAL SINGHER

ance in all the four baritone roles of *The Tales of Hoffmann* in Amsterdam; his creation for Paris of the role of Orestes in Richard Strauss' *Elektra*; and his appearance in such interesting world premières and revivals as Georges Witkowski's *La Princesse Lointaine,* Reynaldo Hahn's *The Merchant of Venice,* Darius Milhaud's *Maximilien,* and Rameau's *Castor et Pollux.*

In 1936 he made the first of several annual appearances at the Teatro Colón in Buenos Aires, featured in the German as well as the French repertory. Subsequently he made successful appearances at Covent Garden, Glyndebourne, and the Florence May Music Festival.

In 1940 Singher married Eta Busch, the daughter of Fritz Busch. The Singhers were preparing to leave for South America in June 1940 when the Ministry of Fine Arts announced that no artists would be allowed to leave France. During the war years Singher continued to appear at the Paris Opéra.

In November 1941 Singher was finally given a four-month permit to visit South America. That winter he came to the United States, appeared with the Metropolitan Auditions of the Air, and was offered a contract. But because of difficulties with the American immigration officials, Singher's Metropolitan Opera debut did not take place that year, but on December 10, 1943, when he appeared as Dapertutto in *The Tales of Hoffmann.* He gave, wrote Virgil Thomson in the New York *Herald Tribune,* "a stage performance of incomparable elegance and did a piece of singing that for perfection of vocal style has not

been equaled since Kirsten Flagstad went away." Singher made another favorable impression the following January when he was heard in the tenor role of Pelléas in *Pelléas et Mélisande.* "Singher," wrote Olin Downes in the New York *Times,* "was the glory of the evening. Vocally impeccable and dramatically superb, he animated the opera personally and gave it the authority of his perfect French declamation." In a later performance of *Pelléas,* Martial Singher also performed the baritone role of Golaud; no other singer has ever appeared in both these roles.

Singher celebrated the twenty-fifth anniversary of his opera debut, to the day, by appearing on the opening night of the Metropolitan Opera season, on November 14, 1955, in the four baritone roles in *The Tales of Hoffmann.*

Away from music, Singher's interests are many and varied. He likes reading, dancing, spending social evenings with friends, and all kinds of ball games.

SLENCZYNSKI (SLENCZYNSKA), RUTH, pianist. For her earlier career, see *Living Musicians,* 1940.

* * *

Slencyzinska suspended her concert activity for a decade beginning with 1940. During this period she was graduated from the University of California, and then served as professor of music at the College of Our Lady of Mercy in Burlingame, California. She returned to the concert stage at the Carmen Bach Festival in California in 1951. Since then her appearances throughout the country have been extensive. She wrote her autobiography, *Forbidden Childhood,* in collaboration with Louis Biancolli (1957).

SLEZAK, LEO, tenor. For his earlier career, see *Living Musicians,* 1940.

* * *

Leo Slezak died in Egern, Bavaria, on June 1, 1946.

SLONIMSKY, NICOLAS, conductor. For his earlier career, see *Living Musicians,* 1940.

* * *

In 1956 joined the faculty of the Peabody Conservatory in Baltimore.

SMALLENS, ALEXANDER, conductor. For his earlier career, see *Living Musicians,* 1940.

* * *

Between 1952 and 1955 Smallens was the principal conductor of the *Porgy and Bess* company which toured with the Gershwin opera in Europe, the Near East, South America, Mexico, and the Soviet Union and countries behind the Iron Curtain.

SMETERLIN, JAN, pianist. See *Living Musicians,* 1940.

The SOCIETY OF ANCIENT INSTRU-MENTS. For its earlier history, see *Living Musicians,* 1940.

* * *

The founder and director of the Society of Ancient Instruments, Henri Casadesus, died in Paris on May 31, 1947.

SOKOLOFF, NIKOLAI, conductor. See *Living Musicians,* 1940.

SOLOMON, pianist. See *Living Musicians,* 1940.

SOLOMON, IZLER, conductor, was born in St. Paul, Minnesota on January 11, 1910. When he was nine years old his family moved to Kansas City, where he began to study the violin. He showed such talent that a local organization subsidized his musical education. He went East and divided his time between New York and Philadelphia, studying music and playing the violin in orchestras. In 1928 he was appointed to the department of music at Michigan State College in East Lansing. There he continued his music study with Michael Press, concert violinist who was director of the College's music department.

Solomon's first experience as a conductor came in East Lansing with an orchestra which he helped found and of which he was concertmaster. One day, just before a concert, the orchestra's conductor died, and Solomon substituted for him. He remained the conductor of the orchestra.

When the Music Project of the Federal Works Administration was organized, Solomon was appointed music director for the State of Michigan. He created such a well-rounded and progressive program of musical activity that in 1935 Guy Maier, regional director, invited him to Chicago to become principal conductor of the Illinois Symphony Orchestra, a WPA organization. It was during his six years as conductor of this orchestra that Solomon first attracted attention, particularly with his cogent readings of contemporary works, some of them new to Chicago. Nikolai Sokoloff, national director of music

IZLER SOLOMON

for WPA, considered Solomon's orchestra the best in the country under the auspices of his program.

In 1939 Solomon became director of the Women's Symphony Orchestra. After that he appeared frequently over the radio and as guest conductor of major American orchestras, including the NBC Symphony, the Philadelphia Orchestra, the Chicago Symphony, and the Buffalo Philharmonic. In 1941 he was appointed conductor of the then newly organized Columbus (Ohio) Philharmonic, which in a few years' time he helped to develop from a semi-professional group giving only three concerts a season into a full-sized symphonic organization with ten subscription concerts a season, eleven "pop" concerts, five children's concerts, and performances on tour. He stayed in this post nine years.

In 1951, with Serge Koussevitzky and Leonard Bernstein, he conducted the Israel Philharmonic Orchestra during its tour of the United States and Canada. In 1956 Solomon was named permanent conductor of the Indianapolis Symphony Orchestra. In the same year he was also engaged as director of the Aspen Festival in Colorado.

SOLTI, GEORG, conductor, was born in Budapest, Hungary, on October 21, 1912. His musical training took place at the Budapest High School for Music. When he was fourteen he heard an orchestral concert led by Erich Kleiber. From that day on, his all-consuming ambition was to become a conduc-

Solti: shōl'tē

GEORG SOLTI

tor. He was graduated from the High School for Music in 1930 with diplomas in conducting, piano, and composition.

In 1937 Solti made his conducting debut at the Budapest Opera with *The Marriage of Figaro.* "That was quite some night," Solti recalls. "All my friends and relatives left at intermission on hearing the news that Hitler had marched into Austria. They were sure he would continue his march right into Budapest. So dampened were the spirits of everybody in the opera house that nobody was much concerned about my debut, and after the performance there was no celebration."

Solti remained conductor at the Budapest Opera until 1938, when he left Hungary and settled in Switzerland, where he spent the war years. "Those were hard times," he says. "I had to start piano again, and in 1942 won the first prize in the Geneva competition and gave concerts. Ansermet gave me my first chance to conduct again, with the Swiss Radio Orchestra in 1944. Then, after the war, when they were looking for a non-Nazi conductor for Munich, I was invited there by the American authorities. No food, no light, no facilities—but great musical enthusiasm."

Solti remained six years in Munich, serving as director-general of music of the city. In this office he led distinguished performances with the Munich Opera, as well as symphony concerts. He left Munich in 1952 to assume the post he still occupies, that of director-general of music of Frankfurt-on-the-Main. There he is the musical director of the Frankfurt Opera and conductor of the Museum concerts. While holding this office, he has often appeared as guest conductor with other leading European orchestras and opera companies, and at such major European festivals as those in Salzburg and Edinburgh.

Georg Solti made his American debut on September 25, 1953, with the San Francisco Opera in *Elektra.* "His direction was always musically sensitive and finely controlled," reported *Musical America.* The following January he was equally impressive when he made his American debut as symphony conductor in guest appearances with the San Francisco Symphony.

Solti's New York debut took place on March 14, 1957, with the New York Philharmonic-Symphony. It was, as Howard Taubman wrote in the New York *Times,* "an impressive affair. . . . Mr. Solti left no doubt that he has the gift of leadership and a mature musical point of view."

SOMIGLI, FRANCA, soprano. See *Living Musicians,* 1940.

SPALDING, ALBERT, violinist. For his earlier career, see *Living Musicians,* 1940.

* * *

Spalding made his last concert appearance, in New York City on May 26, 1950, and afterwards went into retirement to devote himself to "writing, teaching, and composing." Before that he had completed an autobiography, *Rise to Follow* (1946). He died in New York City on May 26, 1953.

SPEAKS, MARGARET, soprano. See *Living Musicians,* 1940.

SPIVAKOVSKY, TOSSY, violinist, was born in Odessa, Russia, on February 4, 1910. Exceptionally precocious in music, he was given his first violin lessons in childhood and made his concert debut in Berlin when he was only ten. An intensive musical training followed at the Berlin Hochschule für Musik, where his principal violin teachers were Arrigo Serrato and Willy Hess. In 1928 Spivakovsky was engaged as concertmaster of the Berlin Philharmonic Orchestra, one of the youngest musicians ever to hold this significant post. He resigned in 1933 to concertize through Europe, and from 1933 to 1941 he made many tours of Australia and New Zealand. He became particularly identified with the musical life of Australia not only through

Spivakovsky: spē-và-kôv′skē

TOSSY SPIVAKOVSKY

his many concerts, but also through his appearances over the radio and his teaching engagements.

Spivakovsky came to the United States in 1941 and made his American debut in Carnegie Hall. While his brilliant technique was admired, his success in this country did not begin until a year later, when he was engaged as concertmaster of the Cleveland Orchestra. On November 23, 1942, he appeared as soloist with that orchestra in a performance of the Tchaikovsky Concerto which was broadcast throughout the country. He attracted national attention a few months later when, with the same orchestra, he gave the American première of Béla Bartók's Violin Concerto. When Spivakovsky later repeated his performance in San Francisco with the San Francisco Symphony, Alfred Frankenstein wrote in the *Chronicle*: "At intermission there were only two questions that people asked each other: was this the best since the sensational debut of Heifetz thirty years ago, or was this just the best, period? You can answer either question in the affirmative as far as this department is concerned. One can say without hesitancy that he probably possesses the most colossal technique of any violin soloist now before the public."

In 1945 Spivakovsky resigned as concertmaster of the Cleveland Orchestra to concentrate on concert appearances. His tours of this country—both in recitals and as soloist with all the major orchestras—have since confirmed the early impression that he is one of the foremost living violinists. Virgil Thomson has written in the New York *Herald Tribune* that "he is a sensationally effective violinist. . . . The gypsy style is his meat; there he is forceful, varied, brilliant and explosive. His classical violin playing has a certain grandeur." And Irving Kolodin said in the *Sun*: "Spivakovsky plays with virtuoso assurance, plenty of vitality, and above all, a brilliant command of the resources of his instrument."

STASSEVITCH, PAUL, violinist and pianist. See *Living Musicians,* 1940.

STEBER, ELEANOR, soprano, was born in Wheeling, West Virginia, on July 17, 1916. Her father was a bank clerk. Her mother, an amateur soprano who frequently appeared at civic and charity functions, gave Eleanor her first vocal lessons. When it became apparent that the girl had unusual talent, she was sent for further study to the New England Conservatory in Boston. A scholarship —and the income she received by singing in churches and over the radio, and by playing the piano in a dancing school—enabled her to continue her studies there until her graduation in 1938. Her principal vocal teacher was William L. Whitney, whom Steber acknowledges to be one of the most significant influences in her career. Another of Whitney's students at the time was a young man named Edwin Bilby, with whom Steber fell in love and whom she married.

Whitney prepared Steber for the opera stage. She made several appearances in Boston with the Federal Music Project between 1935 and 1939, her first opera appearance being in an English-language production of *The Flying Dutchman*, in which she was heard as Senta. In 1939 she went to New York to receive some additional coaching from Paul Althouse. One year later she was a winner in the Metropolitan Auditions of the Air.

Her Metropolitan Opera debut took place on December 7, 1940, in the role of Sophie in *Der Rosenkavalier*. "Steber's security and vocal finish," wrote Irving Kolodin, "marked her as an American soprano in a hundred." When the same opera opened the Metropolitan Opera season nine years later, Steber appeared as the Marschallin.

Since her Metropolitan Opera debut, Steber has appeared in over twenty-five leading roles in the French, Italian, and German repertory. In the New York *Herald Tribune*, Virgil Thomson described her Desdemona in *Otello* as "perfect from every point of view. . . . She

Steber: stē'bĕr

ELEANOR STEBER

moved the heart and she sang very beautifully, indeed." She has been equally distinguished in the Mozart and Wagner repertory. In 1945 she made her debut at the San Francisco Opera, and in 1946 at the Central City Opera Festival in Colorado. Subsequently she was acclaimed in major European music festivals—at Edinburgh, Florence, Glyndebourne, and Bayreuth. In 1957 she made a world tour under the auspices of the United States Government and the American National Theatre and Academy. She has also been heard frequently in this country in recitals and over radio and television.

"The timbre of her voice," wrote Alfred Frankenstein in the San Francisco *Chronicle,* "is of the most moving and ethereal sweetness and purity, but warm despite its delicacy. Her style of interpretation is altogether of a piece with her style of vocal production. It is simple, dignified, exquisite in its subtly achieved phrasing and magnificently just, both to letter and the spirit of the music in hand."

STEFANO, GIUSEPPE. See DI STEFANO, GIUSEPPE

STEINBERG, WILLIAM (HANS WILHELM STEINBERG), conductor. For his earlier career, see *Living Musicians,* 1940.

* * *

In the fall of 1941, Steinberg made his debut with the San Francisco Opera in *Fal-*

staff. He appeared there again during the next few seasons. In 1945 he was engaged as musical director of the Buffalo Philharmonic Orchestra, and seven years after that he assumed a similar post with the Pittsburgh Symphony. He visited New York with the Pittsburgh Symphony on November 16, 1956, on which occasion Howard Taubman wrote in the New York *Times*: "Under William Steinberg's leadership, this orchestra has developed into one of the most satisfying in the country, not far behind the country's best." Steinberg made his debut as conductor for motion pictures when he recorded the score for *Song of Love,* the cinema biography of Robert Schumann.

STERN, ISAAC, violinist. For his earlier career, see *Living Musicians,* 1940.

* * *

Stern made an extensive tour of Australia and New Zealand in the summer of 1947, giving 125 concerts in ten months, and in the summer of 1950 he appeared at the first Pablo Casals festival in Prades, France. In the spring of 1956 he toured the Soviet Union, becoming the first concert artist from the United States to perform in the Soviet Union in ten years, and the first American artist ever to appear on Soviet television. Stern played for the sound track of the motion picture *Humoresque,* and appeared in *Tonight We Sing.*

STEVENS, RISË, contralto. For her earlier career, see *Living Musicians,* 1940.

* * *

Stevens made her first appearances in Paris in 1949, and in 1954 she made her debut in Italy, creating the leading female role in Virgilio Montari's *La Figlia del Diavolo* at La Scala in Milan. She has appeared in several motion pictures including *The Chocolate Soldier* and the Academy Award winner, *Going My Way.*

STEWART, REGINALD, conductor. For his earlier career, see *Living Musicians,* 1940.

* * *

In 1941, Stewart was appointed musical director of the Baltimore Symphony Orchestra and head of the Peabody Conservatory in that city. He resigned his post with the Baltimore Symphony in 1952.

STIEDRY, FRITZ, conductor. For his earlier career, see *Living Musicians,* 1940.

* * *

Stiedry made his debut at the Metropolitan Opera on November 15, 1946, with *Siegfried,* and has since then been one of the company's principal conductors.

STIGNANI, EBE, mezzo-soprano, was born in Naples, Italy, on July 10, 1907, the only child of a salesman. Revealing a remarkable bent for music from childhood on, she was encouraged by her parents to pursue her study. In her tenth year she entered the Naples Conservatory, where for several years she specialized in piano. At fifteen, while singing in the Conservatory chorus, she was discovered by Augustino Roche, the choral director, who encouraged her to specialize in vocal study.

She was graduated from the Conservatory in 1925. During the graduation ceremonies she sang several numbers which were heard by the director of the San Carlo Opera Company in Naples. He gave her a contract. Her debut with that company as Amneris in *Aida* proved so successful that in the next four months she was asked to appear in over fifty performances.

During the same year in which she made her debut she auditioned for Toscanini, then musical director of La Scala. The maestro engaged her for his company, and she made her debut there as Princess Eboli in *Don Carlo,* Toscanini conducting. Stignani remained a principal soprano of the company for the next three years, frequently appearing under Toscanini. When, in 1928, Toscanini resigned from La Scala, Stignani also withdrew and made extensive appearances throughout Europe and South America.

Her American debut took place with the San Francisco Opera Company in 1938. She was so well received that she was given a contract for the following season. The outbreak of World War II in Europe prevented her from returning, and she did not again appear with the San Francisco Opera until 1948. Her appearances in San Francisco that year were followed by an extensive twenty-thousand-mile tour of the United States, culminating with a New York recital on December 13, 1948. On that occasion, Virgil Thomson wrote in the New York *Herald Tribune* that "there is no questioning the perfection of her style. . . . The poise of her voice through-

Courtesy of Musical Courier

EBE STIGNANI

out is impeccable; no flaw is evident in the schooling of her instrument for execution."

Stignani married Alfredo Sciti, an engineer, in 1940. With their son they maintain their home on a farm in Imola, near Bologna, Italy.

STOCK, FREDERICK, conductor. For his earlier career, see *Living Musicians,* 1940.

* * *

Stock died in Chicago, Illinois, on October 20, 1942.

STOESSEL, ALBERT, conductor. For his earlier career, see *Living Musicians,* 1940.

* * *

Stoessel died in New York City on May 12, 1943.

STOKOWSKI, LEOPOLD, conductor. For his earlier career, see *Living Musicians,* 1940.

* * *

Stokowski was the conductor of the New York City Symphony from 1944 to 1945, and at the Hollywood Bowl from 1945 to 1947. In 1955 he was appointed principal conductor of the Houston Symphony Orchestra. He collaborated with Walt Disney on, and conducted the music for, the animated motion picture *Fantasia.*

Stignani: stĕ-nyä′nē

STRAUSS, RICHARD, conductor. For his earlier career, see *Living Musicians,* 1940.

* * *

During World War II Strauss lived mostly in Switzerland. After the war, in 1947, he visited London and conducted a concert of his own works during a Strauss festival. His eighty-fifth birthday was celebrated throughout the world of music in 1949, a few months before his death in Garmisch-Partenkirchen, Bavaria, on September 8, 1949.

STUECKGOLD, GRETE, soprano. See *Living Musicians,* 1940.

SUKOENIG, SIDNEY, pianist. See *Living Musicians,* 1940.

SULLIVAN, BRIAN, tenor, was born Harry Joseph Sullivan in Oakland, California. When he made his first important appearances on the Broadway stage he was advised by Equity, the actors' union, to change his name since another member was called Joseph Sullivan. Sullivan, the singer, then decided to assume the name Brian, which he had just chosen for his yet unborn first son. Brian Jr. was born on the same day that his father made his bow on the stage with his assumed name.

Sullivan attended the public schools in Los Angeles. His talent for singing did not become evident until his junior year at the Manual Arts High School when he appeared

BRIAN SULLIVAN

in a student presentation of *The Pirates of Penzance.* His performance encouraged him to consider singing as a career. For the next five years, Sullivan studied voice with Lillian Backstrand Wilson, while holding part-time jobs. In his twenty-first year he appeared as Count Almaviva in the American Music Theatre's production of *The Barber of Seville* in Pasadena. He did so well that an impresario came to him backstage to inquire if he would sing the role in Italian in a performance starring John Charles Thomas.

For a while he continued appearing in various musical productions, and one winter toured with the *Ice Follies.* During World War II he served for two years in the infantry. After the war, Emil Cooper engaged him to appear as Florestan in *Fidelio* at the Central City Festival in Colorado, where he sang twelve times in twenty-four days.

His next engagement was in New York, where he signed a contract to appear as Gaylord Ravenal in a revival of *Show Boat.* When he accepted this engagement he did not know that the run of the show was nearing an end; had he known, he would not have taken the assignment. As it was, his excellent performance was the stepping stone in 1947 for a major role in Kurt Weill's *Street Scene.* *Street Scene* was a turning point in Sullivan's career, for it was in this production that he was heard by the directors of the Metropolitan Opera, who engaged him for the company. His debut at the Metropolitan Opera took place in Britten's *Peter Grimes* on February 23, 1948. Since then he has sung leading tenor roles in the Wagner repertory and in several important operas presented by the Metropolitan in English translations, including Gluck's *Alceste* (in which Flagstad made her last Metropolitan appearances) and *La Bohème* (which in 1953 was telecast on a national hookup). Among other operas in which he has scored major successes were Richard Strauss' *Arabella, Boris Godunov, The Magic Flute* and *Così Fan Tutte.*

Sullivan lives in Manhasset, Long Island, with his wife and three children. His favorite pastime is cabinet-making.

SVANHOLM, SET, tenor, was born in Västerås, Sweden, on September 2, 1904. His father, a minister in the local Lutheran church, taught him to play the organ. As a boy, Svanholm sometimes played at the regular services. After graduating from high school and completing his one-year term of military service, he served as organist in Tillberga. Then, after making preparations for a teaching career, he assumed his first teaching job

Svanholm: svän'hôlm

in 1924 in the nearby village of Saeby, where he remained two years.

He then decided to get a comprehensive musical training. To finance his musical education, he gave several organ recitals, then in 1927 entered the Stockholm Conservatory, where he studied piano, composition, and counterpoint for two years. From 1930 to 1931 he studied voice with John Forsell. At that time Forsell had four pupils. Two of them were Joel Berglund and Jussi Bjoerling, each to become famous as opera singers; the third was a young soprano named Nina Hogstedt (daughter of the President of the Cameral Court in Stockholm), who in 1934 gave up her own career to become Svanholm's wife.

After completing his studies, Svanholm held various musical jobs: He directed and sang in oratorio performances; he directed services at the St. James Church; he taught oratorio singing at the Stockholm Conservatory. While holding these various posts he embarked upon a career in opera, making his debut as a baritone in the role of Silvio in *Pagliacci* at the Stockholm Opera in 1930. For the next half dozen years or so he continued appearing in baritone roles. Then, convinced by his wife that he was a tenor, he retrained his voice, learned a new repertory, and returned to opera in 1936 in his new voice as Radames. Bruno Walter heard that performance and engaged him for the Vienna State Opera, where Svanholm made his debut as Siegmund in *Die Walküre*. Svanholm's success in Vienna, particularly in the Wagner repertory, marked the beginning of his international fame. He soon appeared in Graz, Munich, and Prague, and at the world-famous festivals in Salzburg and Bayreuth.

He was scheduled to appear in America during the 1940-1941 season but the war interfered. During the war years he was heard with the Stockholm Opera. In 1946 he was appointed singer to the Swedish Court. In the summer of that same year he made successful appearances in Rio de Janeiro. On September 17, 1946, he made his American debut with the San Francisco Opera as Lohengrin. A few weeks later, on October 5, he was heard with the Chicago Opera as Tristan. And on November 15 he made his debut at the Metropolitan Opera in the title role of *Siegfried*.

Svanholm has since then appeared in leading tenor roles at the Metropolitan Opera and in the other major opera houses of America and Europe. Though his greatest successes have come in Wagnerian roles, he has also

SET SVANHOLM

distinguished himself as Otello, Radames in *Aida,* and Florestan in *Fidelio,* and also in such modern operas as *Peter Grimes.*

On July 1, 1956, Svanholm was appointed director of the Royal Opera in Stockholm. (He was the second Metropolitan Opera singer to assume this position; Joel Berglund held the post between 1942 and 1949.)

The Svanholms, who have six children, maintain their permanent home in Stockholm. His principal diversions are found in sports —mostly in swimming, tennis, bicycling, and skiing.

SWARTHOUT, GLADYS, mezzo-soprano. For her earlier career, see *Living Musicians,* 1940.

* * *

Swarthout left the Metropolitan Opera after the 1944-1945 season, and since then has appeared in concerts, over radio and television, and in motion pictures.

SZANTHO, ENID, contralto. See *Living Musicians,* 1940.

SZELL, GEORGE, conductor. For his earlier career, see *Living Musicians,* 1940.

* * *

Szell made his debut at the Metropolitan Opera on December 9, 1942, with *Salome.* After four years at the Metropolitan, where he gave distinguished performances of the German repertory, he was appointed music director of the Cleveland Orchestra. Still holding his post in Cleveland, he returned to the Metropolitan Opera during the 1953-1954 season for a few guest appearances, but soon became involved in difficulties with the management over artistic procedures and resigned in January 1954, requesting that he be released from further performances. In 1957 it was announced that beginning with the 1957-1958 season Szell would join Eduard van Beinum as a principal conductor of the Concertgebouw Orchestra in Amsterdam. This new appointment does not interfere with his duties in Cleveland.

SZENKAR, EUGEN, conductor. For his earlier career, see *Living Musicians,* 1940.

* * *

Szenkar settled in Rio de Janeiro in 1939 and founded the Brazilian Symphony Orchestra. After World War II he made many guest appearances with orchestras in England, Austria, Israel, and Egypt. In 1952 he was engaged as principal conductor of the Düsseldorf Opera and Düsseldorf Symphony in Germany.

SZIGETI, JOSEPH, violinist. For his earlier career, see *Living Musicians,* 1940.

* * *

Szigeti appeared in the motion picture *Hollywood Canteen* and wrote an autobiography, *With Strings Attached* (1947).

TAGLIAFERO, MAGDA, pianist. See *Living Musicians,* 1940.

TAGLIAVINI, FERRUCCIO, tenor, was born in Reggio Emilia, a province in north Italy, on August 15, 1913. His father was the overseer of an estate. As a child, Ferruccio sang in the church choir, and in his boyhood was acclaimed for his performance of several opera arias at an elementary school concert. Despite his gift for singing he refused to take vocal lessons; his ambition was to become an electrical engineer. (He did study violin for a while.) A maneuver by his father led to a scholarship for the Parma Conservatory. The father dared the boy to sing in a Conservatory competition and, on that dare, the boy appeared and won a scholarship, even though he had never had a lesson. For a while he placated his father by studying with Italo Branucci at the Conservatory, but his ambition to be an electrical engineer soon brought him back home.

Tagliavini: tä-lyä-vē'nē

FERRUCCIO TAGLIAVINI

After a period of military service, he won first prize in a singing contest at the Florence May Musical Festival in 1938. This, apparently, convinced him that his future lay with music. He received seven months of training with Amadeo Bassi, and on October 28, 1939, made his opera debut at the Teatro Communale in Florence as Rodolfo in *La Bohème.* Before long he was invited to appear in many other leading Italian opera houses, including La Scala in Milan, the Teatro Reale in Rome, and the San Carlo in Naples. It was not long before he was regarded throughout Italy as a leading tenor.

He first became known to Americans through the troops stationed in Italy who spoke enthusiastically of his singing after his appearances in American army camps. They further came to know him in this country through his numerous recordings.

In 1946 Tagliavini toured South America and Mexico. His road stretched north, and on October 2 he made a sensational North American debut with the Chicago Opera as Rodolfo. A few months later, on January 10, 1947, he made his Metropolitan Opera debut, once again as Rodolfo. Howard Taubman wrote in the New York *Times* that "the old house had more excitement than it has known in weeks. . . . When the tenor took a solo curtain call at the end of the third act, you would have thought that a new Caruso had been discovered." Mr. Taubman went on to say: "Mr. Tagliavini is the real thing so far as a lyric voice is concerned. His voice is well placed, well schooled and under fine control. He can sing with resounding sonority, and he can spin out a pianissimo of rare texture. . . . He sings with intelligence."

Tagliavini gained further popularity with the American public through his many appearances in concerts, over radio and television, and in motion pictures made in Europe. His most successful films have been *The Barber of Seville, The King's Jester* (based on *Rigoletto*), and *Voglio Vivere Così*.

He is married to the prima donna Pia Tassinari. They met in 1940 when both appeared in a performance of *L'Amico Fritz* at the Palermo Opera. Since their marriage in 1941 they have often appeared together in opera performances. They were first seen together in this country when Tassinari made her Metropolitan Opera debut in the title role in *Tosca* on December 26, 1947.

TAJO, ITALO, bass, was born in Pinerolo, near Turin, Italy, on April 25, 1915. His father was an engineer who traveled extensively with his wife and children. Four of the five Tajo children were born in countries other than Italy. The fifth was given the name Italo because he was the only one born in the native land of his parents.

Italo showed an unusual gift for music early in life. As a boy he sang in the church choir of his native city. The choir director suggested that he study singing seriously, but his father objected since he planned making his son a doctor. When Italo was seventeen, his father relented. The boy began studying voice with Nilde Stinche-Bertozzi.

He made his official opera debut in 1935 at the Teatro Regio in Turin, where he appeared in the Nibelungen cycle of Wagner under Fritz Busch. The conductor was so impressed by Tajo that he brought him that season to England to appear at Glyndebourne and make some recordings with that company. At Glyndebourne, Tajo was acclaimed as an outstanding interpreter of Mozart's basso roles. His success led to his engagement at the Edinburgh Festival the following season.

During World War II Tajo served as a grenadier guard in Rome, a post which allowed him time to study new operatic roles. After the war he appeared in Italy's foremost opera houses, including La Scala, acclaimed in a great variety of roles besides those in the Wagner and Mozart repertory; among the operas in which he scored his greatest successes were *Boris Godunov, L'Amore dei Tre*

Courtesy of Musical Courier

ITALO TAJO

Re, Don Pasquale, Boïto's *Mefistofele, L'Elisir d'Amore, Der Rosenkavalier,* and *Faust.* In nine years' time he appeared in over eighty different roles, including those in rarely heard operas by Pizzetti, Wolf-Ferrari, and Giordano.

He first became known to American audiences both through his recordings and his numerous motion pictures filmed in Europe. The latter included *The Barber of Seville, L'Elisir d'Amore, Lucia di Lammermoor,* and *Faust.* His American debut took place with the Chicago Opera on September 30, 1946, as Ramfis in *Aida.* He subsequently appeared with the San Francisco Opera.

TALICH, VACLAV, conductor. For his earlier career, see *Living Musicians,* 1940.

* * *

In 1941 Talich resigned as principal conductor of the Czech Philharmonic to devote himself to the direction of the National Theatre in Prague. He left the latter post in 1945 following internal strife in the opera house, but returned two years after that. In 1948 the new political regime in his country compelled him to withdraw again. In 1949 he became conductor of a chamber-music ensemble in Bratislava.

TALLEY, MARION, soprano. See *Living Musicians,* 1940.

Tajo: tä'yō

TAS, HELEN TESCHNER, violinist. See *Living Musicians,* 1940.

TAUBER, RICHARD, tenor. For his earlier career, see *Living Musicians,* 1940.

* * *

On September 5, 1945, Tauber made his American debut on the Broadway stage in Franz Lehar's *Yours Is My Heart Alone.* He died in London on January 8, 1948.

TEBALDI, RENATA, soprano, was born in Pesaro, Italy, on January 2, 1922. Her father was a professional cellist who played in orchestras of theatres and small opera houses. Renata's parents raised her to be a musician — originally a concert pianist. At thirteen she began studying piano with a cousin and made such progress that she was soon enrolled in the Pesaro Conservatory. Not until she was seventeen was the discovery made that she had a remarkable voice; at that time vocal study supplemented that of the piano.

When she began to suffer pains of the shoulder and back from too much application to the piano, she decided to concentrate on singing. A period of vocal study followed at the Parma Conservatory, and afterwards she became a pupil of Carmen Melis; later study of operatic roles took place with Giuseppe Pais. After the outbreak of World War II, she had to study by herself, mostly in air-raid shelters.

RENATA TEBALDI

Tebaldi: tĕ-bàl′dē

In May 1944 she made her opera debut in Rovigo in Boïto's *Mefistofele.* She sang in this opera three times. In December 1945 she appeared in *Otello.* The difficulty of travel during the war arrested the development of her career at this time. "When it was possible to make a journey I traveled in box-cars," she now recalls. "Once they found out I was a singer they gave me special treatment by allowing me to sit on the bags in the mail car."

In 1946, on his first return visit to Italy in many years, Toscanini asked to have young singers audition for him, since he wanted to select some to appear with him at concerts at La Scala in Milan. Tebaldi told an interviewer what happened: "The man who was calling out the names from a long list probably knew nothing about me for he called out *Signore* Tebaldi. I sang 'La mamma morta' from *Andrea Chénier,* and then the maestro let me sing the whole last act of *Otello.* Toscanini said, 'Brava, brava,' and told his son Walter to take my name and address. I was chosen." She was one of six soloists to appear with Toscanini, and the only one new to La Scala audiences. She sang excerpts from Rossini's *Mosè* and was given an ovation.

This appearance with Toscanini in Milan was the beginning of her successful career. Before long she appeared not only at La Scala in opera performances, but also in other major Italian opera houses, and she was soon conceded to be the most important new soprano to emerge in Italy since the war. After that her success was repeated in Paris, London, Rio de Janeiro, Buenos Aires, Portugal, and Spain. Some European critics did not hesitate to call her "the greatest soprano in the world," and opera audiences throughout Europe went into a frenzy over her performances.

First known in this country through records, which provided evidence that she had not been overestimated, Renata Tebaldi made a sensational American debut at the San Francisco Opera on September 26, 1950 in the title role of *Aida,* one of her most brilliant roles. Some of the San Francisco critics spoke of her appearances in the city as the most sensational operatic event taking place there in over a quarter of a century.

Her debut at the Metropolitan Opera took place on January 31, 1955, as Desdemona in *Otello.* Olin Downes spoke of her in the New York *Times* "as an artist of exceptional quality, intelligence, and sincerity." When Tebaldi was heard in *La Bohème* on February 10, Mr. Downes called her interpretation of Mimi "a revelation." "We have heard no Mimi who moved us so much by the sincerity and the gripping emotion that she gave the part." Tebaldi was scheduled to sing her most famous role, Aida, the same season, but illness delayed that performance until the following fall, on November 19, 1955. "Her Aida," wrote Howard Taubman in the New York *Times*, "was worth waiting for. . . . The Italian soprano has a mind and personality, and leaves her own impress on whatever role she undertakes. . . . When her turn comes to sing, Miss Tebaldi does so with sovereign musicianship. Her voice has remarkable range; it can swell into a gorgeous fortissimo and it can be refined to an ethereal pianissimo. She has a way of giving individual character to a phrase, with a color or delicate regard . . . that intensifies the emotional impact."

Tebaldi, who has mastered over thirty principal soprano roles, has herself described her voice as "somewhere between a lyric and dramatic soprano. . . . You might say it's a lyric with more power or dramatic with less power." Her voice was dubbed in on the sound track of the motion picture *Aida*, released in this country; her singing was also heard in a film adaptation of *Lohengrin* made in Italy and entitled *Colonne Sonore*.

TELMÁNYI, EMIL, violinist. For his earlier career, see *Living Musicians*, 1940.

* * *

In 1940 Telmányi was appointed professor of the violin at the Conservatory of Aarhus, and one year later he became a member of its board of governors. In 1949 he instructed the violin maker Arne Hjorth to construct for him a violin bow combining the advantages of the modern bow with those of the bow used in Bach's time. Since then he has demonstrated its use in performances of Bach's violin music.

TELVA, MARION, contralto. See *Living Musicians*, 1940.

TEMPLETON, ALEC, pianist. See *Living Musicians*, 1940.

TENTONI, ROSA, soprano. See *Living Musicians*, 1940.

TERTIS, LIONEL, violist. For his earlier career, see *Living Musicians*, 1940.

* * *

Soon after World War II Tertis retired from the concert stage and devoted himself to experiments in the design and improvement of the viola.

TEYTE, MAGGIE, soprano, was born Margaret Tate, in Wolverhampton, England, on April 17, 1888. Her parents, both of whom were musical, encouraged her to study voice seriously. She attended the Royal College of Music in London and then spent four years in Paris studying privately with Jean de Reszke and Reynaldo Hahn. In her seventeenth year she appeared in a Mozart festival in Paris as Zerlina in a concert performance of *Don Giovanni* starring Lilli Lehmann and Édouard de Reszke. Soon after this she appeared in a joint concert with Paderewski in Monte Carlo, and made her opera debut there as Zerlina.

Engaged by the Opéra-Comique in Paris for minor roles, she was suddenly selected by the management to take over the role of Mélisande which Mary Garden had created there in *Pelléas et Mélisande*. She spent nine months studying the part with Debussy himself, and then in 1908 scored such a major success that she was engaged to appear sixteen times the following season in the same opera. After repeating her performance of the role at Covent Garden and in the English provinces—and after creating the role of Suzanne in Wolf-Ferrari's *The Secret of Suzanne* in Munich — Maggie Teyte came to America to make her debut in Philadelphia, on November 4, 1911, as Cherubino in *The Marriage of Figaro*. A few months later she appeared there in the American première of Massenet's *Cendrillon*. In 1922 she joined the Chicago Opera Company, where she stayed three seasons, and for two seasons after that she appeared with the Boston Opera.

Immediately after World War I, she toured both America and Europe extensively in song recitals, achieving recognition as an outstanding interpreter of French art songs, particularly the songs of Debussy. In 1921 her marriage to W. S. Cottingham led to her semi-retirement. But a decade later, following her divorce, she returned to the concert stage, appearing frequently in joint concerts with Alfred Cortot, and over the BBC. In 1938 and 1939 she returned to the United States, hoping to resume here her concert career, interrupted in 1920, but found that she had been forgotten; she was unable to interest either concert managers or radio executives in sponsoring her comeback. But after she made some recordings of French songs in Europe, widely circulated in this country after 1942, her reputation was reestablished with many discriminating music lovers.

During the war years she toured Great Britain, singing for the armed forces in camps

Teyte: tāt

Courtesy of Musical Courier

MAGGIE TEYTE

and hospitals. For her services to French music during the war she was decorated with the Croix de Lorraine in 1945. After the war she returned to the United States for a five-month tour, her first performance being a radio program on August 20, 1945. The following November 1, she gave her first New York recital in over two decades; the concert hall was sold out weeks before the concert. "Miss Teyte is fifty-six years young both vocally and artistically," reported Harriett Johnson in the New York *Post*. "She enkindles the music she sings with heartiness and warmth. . . . She is an intensely interesting artist of richly mature and remarkable talent."

On March 25, 1948, Maggie Teyte returned to the American opera stage, appearing in a few guest performances with the New York City Opera in the role that first made her famous—Mélisande. Olin Downes described this performance in the New York *Times* as an "interesting phenomenon." He added: "Its eloquence, its revelation of character and emotion came with song. For Miss Teyte is not only authoritative mistress of every measure from standpoint of musicianship and style but she colors her tones with the text and accomplishes everything that dramatic interpretation suggests by means of vocal device."

THEBOM, BLANCHE, mezzo-soprano, was born in Monessen, Pennsylvania, of Swedish ancestry, on September 19, 1919. When she was a girl her family moved to Canton,

Ohio, where her father was employed at the Republic Steel Mills. In Canton she attended the public schools, sang in the church choir, and appeared in a school production of *Martha*.

Her ambition was to become a schoolteacher, but serious financial reverses in the family forced her to seek out a shorter route by which to earn a living. After attending business school, she found employment as a secretary in a realty office. During this period, she continued filling occasional engagements as a singer in church choirs and at weddings.

In 1938 she went with her parents on a trip to Sweden. Aboard the *Kungsholm*, en route to Europe, she was invited to appear at the ship's concert. The audience included Kosti Vehanen, the accompanist of Marian Anderson. He was so impressed by Thebom that he urged her to study singing seriously and prepare for a professional career in music. Back in this country, she was financially aided by her employer, Alvin Gibbs. In 1939 her vocal study began in earnest. During the next few years she worked with several teachers—including Edyth Walker and Lothar Wallerstein—and received training not only in singing and the operatic repertory but also in dramatics, languages, and dancing.

In 1940 she auditioned for S. Hurok, the impresario, who signed her to a contract. In October 1940 she made her concert debut with a recital in Sheboygan, Wisconsin. One month later she appeared as soloist with the Philadelphia Orchestra under Ormandy in Brahms' *Alto Rhapsody*. For more than a year after that she toured the country in recitals, mostly in small cities, and occasionally appeared as a soloist with a major orchestra. On January 12, 1944, she made her New York concert debut in Town Hall. Noel Straus wrote in the New York *Times*: "The richly gifted artist disclosed the finest natural voice of any new singer heard so far this season."

In the summer of 1944 she was engaged to appear and sing in several sequences in the motion picture *When Irish Eyes are Smiling*. That winter, on November 28, 1944, she made her debut with the Metropolitan Opera, during its visit to Philadelphia, as Brangäne in *Tristan und Isolde*. On December 14, she appeared for the first time in New York with the Metropolitan Opera company as Fricka in *Die Walküre*. She scored, as Noel Straus reported, "an immediate success. Her gifts as vocalist were matched only by her histrionic ability in a deeply impressive portrayal, projected with the poise of a veteran artist of the lyric stage."

Thebom: thē'bŏm

BLANCHE THEBOM

Blanche Thebom has since been a mainstay of the Metropolitan Opera company in the Wagnerian repertory, but she has also been heard in many mezzo-soprano roles in Italian and French operas. In 1955 she created for America the role of Adelaide in Strauss' *Arabella*. She has also been heard with the San Francisco Opera, and other major companies in this country and abroad. In the summer of 1947 she appeared at the Golden Jubilee celebration of the Stockholm Opera. When she returned to the Stockholm Opera in 1956 it was to make her debut as a soprano, and she was heard as Elisabeth in *Tannhäuser*. During this visit she received the Order of Vasa from Queen Louisa, the first foreign woman to be so honored.

Thebom is the founder and sole contributor to the Blanche Thebom Scholarship Fund, which she started in 1948.

THIBAUD, JACQUES, violinist. For his earlier career, see *Living Musicians,* 1940.

* * *

Thibaud returned to the United States in 1947 after an absence of fifteen years, making his first reappearance on January 2 as soloist with the New York Philharmonic-Symphony under Stokowski. On September 1, 1953, while en route from Paris to French Indo-China to entertain French troops there, he was killed in an airplane crash when his plane crashed into Mt. Cemet in the French Alps.

THIBAULT, CONRAD, baritone. For his earlier career, see *Living Musicians,* 1940.

* * *

Since World War II, Thibault has combined appearances on the concert stage with many appearances on radio and television.

THILL, GEORGES, tenor. For his earlier career, see *Living Musicians,* 1940.

* * *

Thill was starred with Grace Moore in a motion-picture adaptation of *Louise* filmed in France.

THOMAS, JOHN CHARLES, baritone. For his earlier career, see *Living Musicians,* 1940.

* * *

In 1940 Thomas appeared in the motion picture *Kingdom Come*. He left the Metropolitan Opera after the 1942-1943 season, and in 1951 was appointed executive director of the Santa Barbara Music Academy in California.

THORBORG, KERSTIN, contralto. For her earlier career, see *Living Musicians,* 1940.

* * *

In 1944 Thorborg was appointed singer to the Swedish Court. She left the Metropolitan Opera after the 1945-1946 season and confined her appearances to the Royal Opera in Stockholm and other European opera companies.

TIBBETT, LAWRENCE, baritone. For his earlier career, see *Living Musicians,* 1940.

* * *

Tibbett's twenty-fifth season with the Metropolitan Opera was celebrated on January 21, 1949, during a performance of *Peter Grimes*. He left the Metropolitan Opera soon after that and made appearances in concerts and on radio and television. In 1956 he replaced Ezio Pinza in the Broadway musical *Fanny*.

TINAYRE, YVES, tenor. See *Living Musicians,* 1940.

TOKATYAN, ARMAND, tenor. For his earlier career, see *Living Musicians,* 1940.

* * *

Tokatyan left the Metropolitan Opera after the 1945-1946 season and subsequently appeared only in European opera houses.

TOSCANINI, ARTURO, conductor. For his earlier career, see *Living Musicians,* 1940.

* * *

After an absence of fifteen years, Toscanini returned to Italy in 1946 to conduct ten concerts at La Scala in Milan, between May 11 and June 26. In 1950 he made an extensive tour of the United States with the NBC Symphony. He made his last appearance as conductor on April 4, 1954, with the NBC Symphony, after which he went into retirement. In November 1955 he received the Insignia of the Grand Cross of the Order of the Lion of Finland, the highest honor that Finland can confer on a non-citizen. In the same year the city of Mantua· presented him with the award of Orfeo d'Oro for services to music.

On New Year's day, 1957, Toscanini suffered a stroke from which he never recovered. He died quietly in his sleep on January 16, 1957, in his eighty-ninth year. A Requiem Mass was performed at St. Patrick's Cathedral in New York on January 19. On February 18, Toscanini was buried in Milan as 250,000 mourners stood bareheaded in the rain to pay him their last respects.

TOTENBERG, ROMAN, violinist. For his earlier career, see *Living Musicians,* 1940.

* * *

In 1947 Totenberg was appointed head of the violin department of the Santa Barbara Music Academy in California.

TOUREL, JENNIE, mezzo-soprano, was born in Montreal, Canada, on June 22, 1910, the daughter of a Russian businessman. When she was one year old, her family moved to Paris, where she received her education. She was six when she was given her first musical instruction, on the flute, and two years later she was taught piano. Though she detested practicing, she became such an accomplished pianist by the time she was sixteen that a concert career was planned for her. Meanwhile, she often delighted relatives and friends with her singing and was encouraged to train her voice seriously. For two years, beginning in 1926, she studied with Anna El-Tour.

A member of the Opéra-Comique company heard her sing at a party in 1933 and arranged for her to audition for the directors. They engaged her that year. During the next seven years she sang principal mezzo-soprano roles, including two of her favorites, Carmen and Mignon.

Tourel: tōō-rĕl'

She paid her first visit to the United States in 1937, making her debut at the Metropolitan Opera during its spring season, on May 15, as Mignon. Though well received, she made no more appearances at the Metropolitan at this time, but continued to perform at the Opéra-Comique.

Three days after the Nazi troops entered Paris, she fled from the city and went to Lisbon. Her intention was to leave for the United States at once, but this trip was delayed by a prolonged illness. She finally arrived in this country in January 1941. An effort to get an engagement with the Metropolitan Opera failed because at this time the company was comparatively small and the roles she could sing had already been committed to others. She did find an opening with the Montreal Opera and later the same year with the New Opera Company and the New York City Opera.

Fame in the United States came on October 7, 1942, when she made the first of three appearances with the New York Philharmonic-Symphony under Toscanini in Berlioz' *Roméo et Juliette.* "She is a singer in the great tradition," wrote Virgil Thomson in the New York *Herald Tribune.* "Her voice is beautiful, her diction clear, her vocalism impeccable and her musicianship tops." Within the next few years she was heard with the Boston Symphony under Koussevitzky and with the NBC Symphony under Stokowski in the American première of Prokofiev's *Alexander Nevsky.* After her highly successful concert

JENNIE TOUREL

debut at Town Hall, in 1943, Thomson wrote again: "Miss Tourel's conquest . . . was . . . without any local parallel since Kirsten Flagstad's debut at the Metropolitan Opera."

Tourel returned to the Metropolitan Opera stage early in 1944 to appear triumphantly not only as Carmen and Mignon, but also as Adalgisa in *Norma* and Rosina in *The Barber of Seville*. Her first appearance there as Rosina on March 14, 1945, was a historic event, for this was the first time that the role was sung at the Metropolitan by a mezzo-soprano, as Rossini had intended. Oscar Thompson wrote in the New York *Sun*: "Last night, Jennie Tourel restored the vivacious feminine role to its original voice and the notes of the Rosina part were sung as they were written. Miss Tourel sang them very well—better, in fact, than the sopranos who have appeared in the part in recent memory."

Tourel is also a highly successful concert artist. Capable of singing in seven languages, and with a remarkable vocal range that extends from low G to high C, she is one of the most versatile artists on the present-day concert stage. Besides distinguishing herself in the traditional operatic and concert repertory, she has also been acclaimed for her performances of contemporary works. Among the last are Leonard Bernstein's *Jeremiah Symphony*, the new version of Hindemith's *Das Marienleben*, and Stravinsky's *The Rake's Progress*, in all three of which she appeared in the world premières.

Her first European tour took place in 1947 and was launched with a performance in London which inspired the critic of the London *Times* to call her "the greatest new singer to be heard here since the war." In 1949 she made her first tour of Israel, singing seventeen concerts in twenty-one days. Since then she has not only been heard in opera houses and on the concert stages of America, Europe, and South America, but has also been featured at such major European festivals as those in Holland, Edinburgh, Venice, and Prades.

TOYE, GEOFFREY, conductor. For his earlier career, see *Living Musicians*, 1940.

* * *

Toye died in London on June 11, 1942.

The TRAPP FAMILY CHOIR. For its earlier history, see *Living Musicians*, 1940.

* * *

In 1950 the Trapp Family Singers made a four-month tour of Central and South Amer-

ica, and an additional four-month tour of Europe. They then made a triumphal return to their native city of Salzburg, in Austria, with three appearances at the Festival. In 1951 their activities included a tour of the Pacific Islands, and in 1953 tours of Israel and South Africa. Their conductor, Franz Wasner, was elevated to the rank of Monsignor by Pope Pius XII.

Maria Augusta Trapp became an American citizen in 1948 and settled in Stowe, Vermont. She is the author of *The Story of the Trapp Family Singers* (1949).

TRAUBEL, HELEN, soprano. For her earlier career, see *Living Musicians*, 1940.

* * *

Traubel left the Metropolitan Opera after the 1951-1952 season following a dispute with the management over her right to appear in night clubs. After that she was heard not only in night clubs but also in recitals, on radio and television, and in motion pictures. In 1955 she was starred in a Rodgers and Hammerstein musical on Broadway, *Pipe Dream*.

The TRIO OF NEW YORK. For its earlier history, see *Living Musicians*, 1940.

* * *

The Trio of New York disbanded soon after World War II. Two of its members are now dead (see Carl Friedberg and Felix Salmond).

TUCKER, RICHARD, tenor, was born Reuben Ticker in Brooklyn, New York, on August 28, 1916. He was one of five children, the son of a furrier who occasionally sang as a cantor in local synagogues. "Even as a kid," he told an interviewer, "I always knew that the Metropolitan Opera would be my goal." He was always singing; at the age of six he was a member of a local choir. In Brooklyn elementary schools and at New Utrecht High School he distinguished himself both in sports and in singing. His academic schooling ended after his graduation from high school. Now sixteen years old, he worked first as a runner on Wall Street, and then in the textile industry, before starting a little dyeing business of his own. "It was a toss-up between business and singing," he recalls, "so I finally settled on both. That meant holding down a job and studying voice at night for years. It wasn't easy. And I kept going after athletics at the same time—baseball, football, and handball."

RICHARD TUCKER

He began his vocal studies with serious intent when he was seventeen. After some of these preliminary studies were over, he embarked upon a career as a cantor in synagogues, finally holding a lucrative post with the Brooklyn Jewish Center on Eastern Parkway in Brooklyn. (Even as a successful opera singer, and while filling engagements with the world's foremost opera houses, he regularly officiates at services during important Jewish holidays either in leading synagogues or at the Concord Hotel, a resort in the Catskill Mountains.)

He never forgot his operatic ambitions. Encouraged by a friend, Sara Perelmuth —whom he was to marry on February 11, 1936—he went to study singing with Paul Althouse. (Sara Perelmuth, incidentally, was the sister of another tenor destined to reach the heights in opera—Jan Peerce.) For a while Tucker sang in operettas with the Chicago Theatre of the Air, and in 1939 made his concert debut at Town Hall, New York. Then in 1944 he had a successful audition at the Metropolitan Opera. He made his debut there on January 25, 1945, as Enzo in La Gioconda. "He sang," reported a critic of the New York Times, "with warmth and expressiveness, and his acting was natural and easy." From then on he assumed leading tenor roles, mostly in the Italian and French repertory. In 1949 a critic of the New York Times described him as "among the finest tenors at large," and Louis Biancolli wrote in the New York World Telegram that his was

"the only voice I've heard in years that reminds me of the Enrico Caruso I know on records." On November 14, 1955, Tucker helped open a new season for the Metropolitan Opera in The Tales of Hoffmann.

The year of 1949 was eventful. Toscanini selected him to sing Radames in Aida with the NBC Symphony over the NBC network. Tucker also made his debut in Italy in the Verona Arena, where he appeared in Rigoletto and La Gioconda, and where he received one of the warmest demonstrations ever given an American singer; he was the first American tenor to appear in Italy since the end of the war. A few years later, in the spring of 1955, he made his debut at La Scala, after a standing invitation of six years which he had been previously unable to accept. As a member of La Scala, Tucker made history by being the first American ever asked to make an official La Scala recording; thus he became the first tenor to record with both La Scala and the Metropolitan Opera.

Tucker resides in Great Neck, Long Island, with his wife and three sons. In 1952 he received a citation from the National Father's Day Committee for "outstanding public service in the field of father-child relationships." He is still a devotee of sports, often joining his sons in games of punchball, basketball, handball, softball baseball, or golf. Other interests include the writing of comic verses, photography, and gardening. Since each of his sons plays a musical instrument, musical soirées in the Tucker household are frequent events.

TURECK, ROSALYN, pianist. See *Living Musicians*, 1940.

TURNER, CLARAMAE, contralto, the daughter of a California engineer, was born in Eureka, California. As a girl, she often traveled with her father to different parts of the country. Though she had no musical instruction, she delighted in hearing and learning the folk music of the various regions she visited. When she was seventeen she was given a guitar as a gift, and soon after this received her first fee as a singer—three dollars for an appearance at a social function of the Native Daughters of the Golden West in Eureka. From then on she was determined to become a professional singer. As a high school student she started studying voice with Maude Homan Riley. She signed up for a post-graduate course at the same high school because a delegation from that school had been invited to appear at the Golden Gate

Exposition. At this Exposition, Turner won first prize in all the classifications in which she was entered.

Turner then went to San Francisco for additional study with Nino Comel, Giacomo Spadoni, and Kurt Herbert Adler. During this period she joined the chorus of the San Francisco Opera and made numerous appearances over the local radio stations. Her concert debut took place in a San Francisco church in 1942.

In 1945 she decided to leave the Opera chorus and go to New York to advance her career. Before leaving California, however, she was offered a position with the Bush Street Music Hall in the Gilbert and Sullivan repertory. In her first season with this company she made about 250 appearances; she also appeared three times a week on a radio program broadcast over a national network. During one of her performances with the Bush Street Music Hall company she was heard by Gaetano Merola, director of the San Francisco Opera, who engaged her for contralto roles in the French and Italian repertory.

After a season with the San Francisco Opera, she went to New York, where she auditioned both for the Metropolitan Opera and for the composer Gian-Carlo Menotti. Menotti selected her to create the title role of his opera *The Medium*, on May 8, 1946. The Metropolitan Opera audition was equally successful. Turner had to forgo her appearances in *The Medium* to make her Metropolitan Opera debut as Amneris in *Aida* on December 4, 1946. For the next four years she made successful appearances at the Metropolitan Opera not only in the French and Italian repertory, but also in Richard Strauss' *Salome,* Johann Strauss' *Fledermaus,* and *Hänsel und Gretel.* Since then she has been heard with major opera companies in the United States, Canada, and Latin America. She has appeared in seventy-five different contralto roles. On one occasion, at the San Francisco Opera, she achieved the unique feat of appearing in one evening in all the three operas of Puccini's group of one-act operas, which includes *Il Tabarro, Suor Angelica,* and *Gianni Schicchi.* She made her screen debut in 1955 in the motion-picture adaptation of the Rodgers and Hammerstein musical play *Carousel.*

She is married to an engineer, Frank Hoffman, and maintains her home in Forest Hills, New York. To keep in trim for her many

CLARAMAE TURNER

appearances in opera and concerts she follows a Spartan regime during the music season, restricting herself to the simplest diet, rising and going to bed early each day, and taking vigorous exercises during the day.

UPPMAN, THEODOR, baritone, was born in California, where he received his early academic and musical training. As a high school student he worked on the maintenance crew of a golf course in Stanford to earn money to go east for musical training. He finally received a scholarship for the Curtis Institute. Later additional study of music and drama took place in Stanford, California, where he appeared in several musical productions.

In 1943 he entered the army in a tank-destroyer battalion, being among the first troops to storm the Normandy beachhead on D-Day. A month later he was assigned to the first all-GI entertainment unit, formed to appear before troops in France and Germany; he also gave several recitals for French Relief.

After the war he returned to California, where he appeared in a performance of *The Magic Flute.* This led to an appearance with Maggie Teyte in a concert performance of *Pelléas et Mélisande* by the San Francisco Symphony under Monteux. A year later Teyte asked Uppman to appear with her in a performance of the opera by the New York City Opera Company on March 25, 1948. Meanwhile, in 1947, two important awards—

THEODOR UPPMAN

the Atwater Kent Auditions award and the Gainsborough Foundation award—set the stage for an extensive concert tour throughout California and the Pacific Coast and guest appearances with the San Francisco Opera. During this period he also sang for the sound track of several motion pictures, including *Mourning Becomes Electra*, and appeared for the first time over a radio network. Between 1949 and 1951 he was heard at various American festivals and as soloist with several major American orchestras.

He made his New York concert debut in 1951, and soon after that appeared in a supporting role in a Broadway play, *Courtin' Time*, which was a box-office failure. Since it was necessary for him to support his family, he returned to California and for a while worked in a factory. Then David Webster, manager of Covent Garden, engaged him to create the role of Billy Budd, in Britten's opera of the same name. This performance, at Covent Garden on December 1, 1951, marked Uppman's debut in London. The London *Times* said his characterization was "a most convincing materialization of Melville's half-drawn character, and his great monologue in the form of a broadside ballad was sung with a noble strength and tenderness." He returned to London in 1952 once again to appear as Billy Budd, and during the late spring of that year he was heard in the Britten opera in Paris during the festival weeks.

In 1952 and 1953 Uppman toured the United States with the Gershwin Concert Orchestra; he also made many appearances on radio and television. In the summer of 1952, and again in 1953, he was heard at the Colorado Central City Opera in *Faust* and Richard Strauss' *Ariadne auf Naxos*. In 1952 he appeared over NBC-TV in the American première of *Billy Budd*.

On November 27, 1953, Uppman made his debut at the Metropolitan Opera as Pelléas, Monteux conducting. "Real emotion brought Mr. Uppman's Pelléas to life in a complete and wonderful way," reported Virgil Thomson in the New York *Herald Tribune*. He sang, continued Mr. Thomson, "with a warmth of feeling and a spontaneity of expression all unusual these days; and his appearance was so charming, his grace so unaffected that one believed him at every moment." As a result of Uppman's success in this role, Monteux invited him to appear under his direction in the Debussy opera performed the following spring at the Opéra-Comique.

Uppman has since been a leading baritone of the Metropolitan Opera, has made numerous appearances with symphony orchestras and on radio and television, and appeared in a motion picture, *Androcles and the Lion*, based on the play by Bernard Shaw.

URBANEK, CAROLYN, soprano. See *Living Musicians*, 1940.

VAN BEINUM, EDUARD. See BEINUM, EDUARD VAN.

VAN GORDON, CYRENA, contralto. See *Living Musicians*, 1940.

VAN HOOGSTRATEN, WILLEM, conductor. See *Living Musicians*, 1940.

VARNAY, ASTRID, dramatic soprano, was born in Stockholm, Sweden, on April 25, 1918. Both parents were professional musicians: Her mother, Maria Yavor, was a well-known coloratura soprano, while her father, Alexander Varnay, was an impresario who established the first opera company in Oslo. Astrid was only four when she began attending rehearsals and performances of opera—in Buenos Aires. "I think that during that period I must have memorized subconsciously most of the soprano roles of the standard repertory." She was five years old when her family came to the United States and finally established a permanent residence in Jersey City, New Jersey. There she attended the

Varnay: vär'nī

public schools and for eight years studied piano at the New Jersey Musical College. A few appearances as soprano in school productions at the William L. Dickinson High School first fired her with the ambition of becoming a singer.

During her senior year in high school, the family moved to New York City. To support herself while continuing her music studies she found various jobs—first as a stenographer, and after that as a clerk in a bookstore near Carnegie Hall.

In 1938 she applied for an audition with the principal Wagnerian coach at the Metropolitan Opera, Herman Weigert, who was to become her teacher and later her husband. On February 23 she sang for Weigert, who immediately offered to coach her. Afterwards Weigert brought her to George Szell, then one of the opera company's leading conductors. Szell, in turn, had her sing for Edward Johnson, who engaged her for the spring season of 1941. In 1941 Weigert continued to coach Varnay in the Wagnerian dramas in preparation for her debut.

Varnay's debut at the Metropolitan Opera came about unexpectedly. A few hours before a scheduled Saturday afternoon performance of *Die Walküre,* Lotte Lehmann, the Sieglinde, became indisposed. Varnay was hurriedly recruited to substitute for her, even though she had had no rehearsals, and had never before appeared on an operatic stage. Since this performance—on December 6, 1941 —was broadcast, her debut was heard throughout the country. "Miss Varnay," reported Noel Straus in the New York *Times,* "made an instantaneous success. . . . "The exceedingly comely . . . soprano acted with a skill and grace only possible to those with an inborn talent for the theatre. . . . In fact, Sieglinde in Miss Varnay's hands was one of the most satisfying and convincing portrayals the season has brought."

Six days later, Varnay again appeared on the stage of the Metropolitan, and once again as a last-minute replacement—this time for Helen Traubel, scheduled to sing Brünnhilde in *Die Walküre.* One New York critic said: "As Sieglinde she did the improbable, and as Brünnhilde the impossible" *Time* magazine remarked: "Astrid Varnay can just about pick up Brünnhilde's helmet where Flagstad had put it down."

These impressive performances brought her a permanent place in the Wagnerian repertory at the Metropolitan Opera. Since then she has been the only soprano to have per-

ASTRID VARNAY

formed all eleven soprano roles and all three major contralto roles of the Wagnerian repertory at a major opera house.

Her importance as a Wagnerian soprano was extended in 1947 when she appeared in the first complete *Ring* cycle to be performed at the Teatro Colón in Buenos Aires. She received world recognition in 1951 when she became the first American singer to perform Brünnhilde at the Bayreuth Festival. Her debut at the Wagnerian shrine was so triumphant that the seventy-five-year tradition of forbidding curtain calls was broken to allow her to acknowledge the enthusiastic response of the audience. Since then she has participated frequently at the Bayreuth Festivals. She helped open the 1953 season there in *Lohengrin,* and then made ten appearances in four weeks. In the summer of 1956 Bayreuth presented her with a special and newly instituted award given to an artist appearing at Bayreuth for five consecutive seasons; Varnay received this honor after her forty-ninth performance.

The year of 1951 was particularly significant for Varnay. Besides her first Bayreuth appearances, she also made her European debut by appearing as Lady Macbeth in Verdi's *Macbeth* at the Florence May Music Festival; she was invited by the United States Department of State to sing at the Allied Festival of the Arts in Berlin, her debut in that city; she made highly successful appearances as soloist under Wilhelm Furtwängler at the Lucerne Festival; she appeared seven times at Covent Garden during the Festival of Britain; and she was seen with the San Francisco Opera in *Fidelio,* an opera which was revived for her.

While essentially a Wagnerian soprano, and one of the foremost on any stage, Varnay has been successful in other roles as well. In 1942 she appeared in the world première of an American opera — Menotti's *The Island God* at the Metropolitan. She has been seen in several of the world's leading opera houses in the Italian repertory. Of her interpretation of Italian roles, the critic of the San Francisco *Chronicle* wrote: "Here at last is the Italian dramatic soprano of whom American opera has been sorely in need for a very long time—one of the most silken voices in opera, matched by impeccable musicianship." One of her triumphs came in the role of Elektra, in the Richard Strauss opera, which the Metropolitan Opera revived for her during the 1951-1952 season. She has been acclaimed in other operas by Strauss, notably as Salome in Covent Garden and the Munich Opera, and as the Marschallin in *Der Rosenkavalier* at the Metropolitan Opera.

Varnay became an American citizen in 1943. The following year she and Herman Weigert were married. He died in New York City in 1955.

VILLABELLA, MIGUEL, tenor. See *Living Musicians,* 1940.

VINAY, RAMÓN, tenor, was born in Chillan, Chile, in 1912. His father earned his living making equipment for horses; his mother, who died when Ramón was only five, loved singing and instilled in him an early love for music. Vinay's father, who was of French birth, fought for his native land during World War I. Then, deciding to stay in France permanently, he called his three sons to join him there. From 1920 to 1926, Ramón Vinay lived in Digne, where he studied electrical engineering. When he was fifteen his father sent him to Mexico to continue his studies there; he supported himself during this period by working in a cloth factory.

He began to study singing in Mexico and appeared in a French club there. In 1934 he joined a traveling opera company, making his debut with that organization in Mexico in the principal baritone role of *Il Trovatore.*

His income from singing was so meager that he finally decided to give up music and open a box factory. This became a thriving business employing seventy-five workers. But his singing teacher prevailed upon him to re-

RAMÓN VINAY

turn to the stage. He did so in 1939, making appearances with a small opera company and over a local radio station. He was heard by a Broadway producer, Lee Shubert, who brought him that year to New York to appear in a successful revue, *Streets of Paris.* When that show closed, Vinay returned to Mexico and until 1943 continued appearing in minor opera houses in baritone roles. His last performance as a baritone took place in 1944 in Mexico City in a presentation of *Aida* with a cast including Zinka Milanov, Bruna Castagna, and Frederick Jagel.

Shortly after this, while managing his own opera company, Vinay was forced to sing the opening tenor aria in *Cavalleria Rusticana* when the scheduled singer became temporarily indisposed. This single experience led him to try tenor roles. After a year of training, he made his second debut—this time as a tenor— with the National Opera Company in Mexico in the title role of Verdi's *Otello.* This was in June 1944. In 1945 he made his North American opera debut with the New York City Opera as Don José in *Carmen.* For a season he sang principal tenor roles with that company and gave such a fine account of himself that he was offered a contract by the Metropolitan Opera. His debut there took place on February 22, 1946, as Don José. "He has," wrote Robert Bagar in the New York *World Telegram,* "a powerful voice, a good stage presence, and a good deal of innate temperament." On December 9, 1946, Vinay scored a personal triumph at the Metropolitan Opera when, on ten hours' notice, he substituted for

Vinay: vē-nĭ'

Torsten Ralf in the title role of *Otello*. Otello in the Verdi opera has since been one of his greatest roles. He has sung it over 270 times in twenty-four leading opera houses of the world. He was acclaimed in the role at the Salzburg Festival and in the Toscanini performance with the NBC Symphony which was broadcast over the NBC network and recorded by Victor.

Besides appearing as a principal tenor at the Metropolitan Opera—and not only in the French and Italian repertory but often in Wagnerian music dramas — Vinay has been heard in all the leading opera houses of Europe and South America and at most of the world's leading festivals, including those at Bayreuth, Salzburg, Holland, Florence, and Bilbao.

Vinay is married to Mobley Lushanya, a Chickasaw Indian, who has had a career in opera as a soprano. They maintain two homes, a New York apartment, and a château in southern France. Vinay is an omnivorous reader of history, biography, and travel books; enjoys tinkering with gadgets; and is an enthusiastic physical culturist.

VIÑES, RICARDO, pianist. For his earlier career, see *Living Musicians,* 1940.

* * *

Viñes died in Barcelona, Spain, on April 29, 1943.

VIOLIN, MISCHA, violinist. See *Living Musicians,* 1940.

VIROVAI, ROBERT, violinist. See *Living Musicians,* 1940.

VOGEL, ADOLF, bass-baritone. See *Living Musicians,* 1940.

VRONSKY and BABIN, duo-pianists. See *Living Musicians,* 1940.

WALLENSTEIN, ALFRED, conductor. For his earlier career, see *Living Musicians,* 1940.

* * *

In 1947 Wallenstein received the Alice M. Ditson Award for his contribution to American music. He resigned as musical director of the Los Angeles Philharmonic after the 1955-1956 season and devoted himself to guest appearances with that and other orchestras.

WALTER, BRUNO, conductor. For his earlier career, see *Living Musicians,* 1940

* * *

After the termination of World War II, Walter resumed his appearances with the foremost European orchestras and opera companies. Upon his return to the Vienna State Opera he was given a hero's welcome. On his eightieth birthday, the Vienna Municipal Council presented him with the Honorary Ring of the City of Vienna for his services to music. At this time, too, he announced that he would terminate a thirty-four-year association with the New York Philharmonic-Symphony at the conclusion of the 1956-1957 season. He wrote an autobiography, *Theme and Variations* (1946).

WARFIELD, WILLIAM, baritone, was born in West Helena, Arkansas. His father was a Baptist minister who had educated himself and whose aim was to educate his five sons. The family moved to Rochester, New York, when William was three years old. There the father assumed the post of pastor at the Mount Vernon Baptist Church, where William received his first musical experiences by singing in the choir. At the same time he took piano lessons.

In high school, his teacher, Elsa Miller, recognized his singing ability, gave him some lessons, and then entered him in a competition sponsored by the Music Educators National Conference in St. Louis. He won first prize, which brought him a scholarship for the East-

WILLIAM WARFIELD

man School of Music. After several years there, he was graduated in 1942.

Immediately after his graduation, Warfield entered the army and because of his talent for languages was assigned to the Military Intelligence Center at Camp Ritchie, Maryland.

After being separated from the army, Warfield returned to the Eastman School for some graduate study. It was interrupted when he received an offer to tour with the road company of the Broadway revue *Call Me Mister*. After a year of these performances, he enrolled in the American Theatre Wing's Professional Training Program for music study with Yves Tinayre and Otto Herz.

After playing minor roles in several Broadway productions, including Blitzstein's opera *Regina*, Warfield made his concert debut in Town Hall in March 1950. His versatility was proved by his exacting program, which ranged from the music of the thirteenth century to contemporary American songs. Jerome D. Bohm said in the New York *Herald Tribune*: "Warfield proved a truly extraordinary singer, endowed with a phenomenal voice which he projected with complete artistry throughout a long, highly exacting program."

This debut was the beginning of Warfield's successful career as a concert singer. In less than five years he gave nearly three hundred concerts in the United States, Europe, and Australia, besides appearing as soloist with many major symphony orchestras and oratorio societies and at several important festivals. His Australian tour in 1950 was the first occasion on which the Australian government invited an artist who had not yet achieved international fame. His appearances at the Lewisohn Stadium in New York, in the summer of 1954, also broke precedent: this was the first time a singer had appeared there in three different performances in a single season.

Warfield has also distinguished himself in motion pictures and on the stage. On the screen he was seen in a new adaptation of Kern's *Show Boat*, produced by MGM and released in 1952; he was also featured in a screen musical version of *Huckleberry Finn* starring Danny Kaye and Gene Kelly. In 1952 he was selected to perform the role of Porgy in the successful revival of Gershwin's *Porgy and Bess* that toured America, Europe, and the Near East with sensational results. The New York *Times* reported on September 18, 1952, that "the individual performance of William Warfield as Porgy was hailed in a manner that Berlin reserves only for its greatest classical opera stars." A few weeks later *Newsweek* noted that Warfield "was lionized" in Vienna.

One of the sopranos who appeared in the principal female role of Bess was Leontyne Price. Warfield and Price were married in New York City on the day before they left this country with the opera company for its first tour of Europe. In January 1952 the Mayor of Rochester proclaimed a William Warfield Day, during which the singer received a scroll designating him "Rochester's Musical Ambassador to the World."

In 1956, with the cooperation of the American National Theatre Academy's International Exchange, Warfield made an extensive tour of Europe, the Near East, and Africa. Many of his concerts marked the first appearance of a major concert artist in such out-of-the-way places as Ethiopia, Central Africa, Liberia, and British, Belgian, and French territories. Following four recitals in Ethiopia, he received a gold medal from Emperor Haile Selassie. This tour was concluded with a highly acclaimed concert at the Musikverein in Vienna and an appearance in Handel's *Messiah* with the Royal Philharmonic in London, both in December.

WARREN, LEONARD, baritone, was born in the Bronx, New York City, on April 21, 1911. His father, a fur merchant, had been a Russian immigrant who upon coming to this country and becoming a citizen contracted his name from Warrenoff to Warren.

Leonard attended P.S. 11 in the Bronx. After graduation from Evander Childs High School he studied commerce and merchandising during the evening at Columbia University while devoting himself during the day to learning the fur brokerage business from his father. He also studied music at the Greenwich House Music School in New York.

During the depression in the early 1930's, he left his father's firm and held various menial jobs, including one in a service station, while continuing his study of music. In 1935, he auditioned sucessfully for the Radio City Music Hall and was engaged for its Glee Club, which at the time also included Jan Peerce and Robert Weede. During this three-year period at the Music Hall he studied voice with Sidney Dietch.

In 1938 he was dismissed because he wanted two weeks' leave to prepare for the Metropolitan Auditions of the Air. At the final auditions he sang the "Largo al factotum" from *The Barber of Seville* and emerged with first honors from among seven hundred contestants. Though he was now the proud possessor of a contract for the Metropolitan Opera, he was unable to take advantage of it because he did not as yet know a single complete role. A business executive, George A. Martin, presented him with $5,000, a sum which enabled him to go to Milan for eight months of work with Riccardo Picozzi in mastering seven baritone roles.

He returned to the United States towards the end of 1938, and on November 27 made his debut at the Metropolitan Opera during a Sunday evening concert in which he sang excerpts from *Pagliacci* and *La Traviata*. He appeared in several more Sunday evening concerts before making his opera debut, which took place on January 13, 1939, in the role of Paolo in *Simon Boccanegra*. For a few years he appeared only in lesser roles, including those in Gluck's *Alceste* and in the world première of Menotti's *The Island God*. His first leading role, and his first major success, came on December 17, 1943, when he was seen as Renato in *The Masked Ball*. At this time, the New York *Times* said his was a "robust and sonorously sung Renato," and lauded him for his "marked intelligence." Fifteen hours later he was hurriedly called to substitute for Lawrence Tibbett in the part of Rigoletto, since then one of Warren's most celebrated roles. These two appearances, and his subsequent performances in *Falstaff*, *The Barber of Seville*, *Il Trovatore*, *Pagliacci*, *La Traviata*, and *La Forza del Destino*, made critics and opera lovers sit up and take notice of him. By 1948 *Newsweek* magazine was referring to him as the "world's foremost baritone."

Besides singing at the Metropolitan Opera, where he has been a leading baritone, he has appeared in major opera houses in the United States, Canada, Mexico, Puerto Rico, and South America. In 1945 he received a citation plaque from the Municipal Department of Culture of São Paulo, Brazil, for his performances there. In 1953 he made his debut at La Scala, in the role of Rigoletto, which he was then singing for the hundredth time. His appearances on radio and television and on the concert stage have also been extensive.

Warren married Agatha Leifflen on December 27, 1941. She was a graduate of the Juilliard School, and they first met in Milan. They occupy a five-room apartment in New York City and a cottage in Greenwich, Connecticut. Warren finds diversion in fishing, sailing, gardening, and tinkering with machinery. Both of the Warrens are devoted collectors of fine paintings.

LEONARD WARREN

In 1952 Warren established the Warren Scholarship Fund for young singers, to enable a worthy candidate to study for a year with Warren's former teacher, Sidney Dietch.

WEBSTER, BEVERIDGE, pianist. See *Living Musicians*, 1940.

WEEDE, ROBERT, baritone. For his earlier career, see *Living Musicians*, 1940.

* * *

Weede returned to the Metropolitan Opera for the 1944-1945 season. In 1956 he scored a personal triumph in the starring role in Frank Loesser's Broadway musical play *The Most Happy Fella*.

WEINGARTNER, FELIX, conductor. For his earlier career, see *Living Musicians*, 1940.

* * *

Weingartner died in Winterthur, Switzerland, on May 7, 1942.

WEINRICH, CARL, organist. For his earlier career, see *Living Musicians*, 1940.

* * *

From 1942 to 1952 Weinrich taught organ at Columbia University, and in 1943 he became director of music at the Princeton University Chapel. In 1950 he served as visiting lecturer at Harvard University.

WELITCH (WELITSCH), LJUBA, soprano, was born Ljuba Welitschkova in Borissowo, Bulgaria, on July 10, 1913. Her background is rural. As a girl she helped her sisters till the soil on her father's land. Music study began when she was eight, with violin lessons, which continued for several years. Her academic education was not neglected. After the completion of her preliminary schooling in her native city she went in her thirteenth year to the nearby town of Schuman to attend its high school. It was there that one of her teachers first discovered she had a voice worth cultivating. Nevertheless, Welitch continued her academic studies at the University of Sofia, majoring in philosophy and religion, and working all the while at various jobs to support herself. During this period she studied voice with Professor Zlateff and became a member of a choral group with which she sometimes sang solo parts.

After two years at the University of Sofia she went to Vienna to work on an operatic repertory at the State Academy of Music. Her opera debut took place in 1936 at the Graz Opera in the role of Nedda in *Pagliacci.* She soon assumed other lyric soprano roles in the French and Italian repertories. After that she was seen in over forty roles with several provincial companies. After a period with the Hamburg opera and the Berlin Opera, she was engaged by the Vienna State Opera, and in 1943 made her debut there as the Composer in Richard Strauss' *Ariadne auf Naxos.* One year later, during a celebration honoring

Bruno of Hollywood

LJUBA WELITCH

Welitch: vä´lich

Strauss' eightieth birthday, she appeared for the first time in a role which has since become one of her most famous, the title part in Strauss' *Salome.* Besides appearing in the regular repertory in Vienna, she was also seen in such less familiar roles as the Goosegirl in *Königskinder* and Lisa in *Pique Dame.* While appearing in Vienna—and until 1946 when she was made permanent member of the Vienna State Opera—she also appeared regularly with the Bavarian State Opera in Munich.

She made a sensational debut in London as Salome, and once again was seen in that role when she made her American debut at the Metropolitan Opera on February 4, 1949. "Certainly," wrote Irving Kolodin in his history of the Metropolitan Opera, "no Salome since Fremstad had sung the music with the ease and steely thrust of Welitch, and her dance . . . was vastly effective in the sequence of the action." Later appearances at the Metropolitan confirmed the good impression she made in her debut, particularly in *Aida, Don Giovanni, Tosca,* and *Fledermaus.* During the period in which she appeared at the Metropolitan Opera (1949-1952), she also gave performances in other major opera houses, principally in Europe, and at leading European music festivals.

On August 21, 1956, Welitch was married to Karl Schmalvogel, a Viennese traffic policeman.

WERRENRATH, REINALD, baritone. For his earlier career, see *Living Musicians,* 1940.

* * *

Werrenrath died in Plattsburg, New York, on September 12, 1953.

WETTERGREN, GERTRUD, contralto. For her earlier career, see *Living Musicians,* 1940.

* * *

Since World War II Wettergren has appeared with the Stockholm Royal Opera.

WHITE, PAUL, conductor. See *Living Musicians,* 1940.

WHITTEMORE and LOWE, two-piano team, consists of two American pianists, Arthur Whittemore and Jack Lowe.

Whittemore, the son of a famous football coach, was born in Vermillion, South Dakota, on October 23, 1916. He began studying piano when he was five, started composing at six, and at twelve served as organist of the Congregational Church. His musical studies were combined with an intensive academic education, the latter culminating with his graduation from the University of South Dakota in 1934. In that same year he received a teaching fellowship at the Eastman School of Music in Rochester, New York, and in 1935 was made director of music at the University of Rochester College for Men. It was there that he first met and became a friend of Jack Lowe.

Lowe was born in Aurora, near Denver, Colorado, on December 25, 1917. His musical education began in childhood with a toy violin. He subsequently studied on a real instrument, and made a local debut as violinist. When he was sixteen, he joined the violin section of the Denver Symphony Orchestra.

While attending the Colorado State Teachers College he earned his living playing both the violin and the piano in summer resorts. It was during this period that he decided to make the piano his instrument. A scholarship enabled him to continue his study of the piano at the Eastman School of Music. In 1935 he was appointed assistant to Whittemore at the University of Rochester College for Men. He and Whittemore soon joined forces in training the Rochester Glee Club, which in 1935 won a national award in a contest that included 145 entries.

In 1935 Whittemore's aunt invited him to visit her at her home in Puerto Rico. In order to get Jack Lowe to go with him, he informed his aunt that they were a two-piano team and would both like to visit her so that they might be able to continue their piano work in Puerto Rico. When they arrived they discovered that Whittemore's aunt had scheduled a concert for them in San Juan. The next few weeks they spent in a feverish preparation for that performance, practicing together for the first time. Since they had at hand no two-piano music they had to make their own arrangements of classics. This concert was such a huge success that Whittemore and Lowe decided to make their piano partnership permanent. In 1938 they acquired a job playing daily over a Pittsburgh radio station. In 1940 they made their American concert debut with a recital in Town Hall, New York.

The war did not long interrupt their performances. Beginning with 1942 both men served in the Navy, but while filling routine assignments were able to continue their practicing. Finally they were permitted to tour hospitals, Army bases, and combat areas as

WHITTEMORE and LOWE

an entertainment unit, and they gave over seven hundred concerts.

After their discharge from the Navy in 1946, they resumed their concert career. In the first eighteen months they gave over one hundred concerts. They have since then not only made numerous appearances in concerts, but have also been heard as performers with major symphony orchestras and have made numerous recordings for RCA Victor.

Their repertory includes the classical and romantic literature (over two hundred of these works being in their own transcriptions), as well as modern music. They have been responsible for the world premières of many significant two-piano compositions, including works by Quincy Porter (a two-piano concerto which won the Pulitzer Prize in 1953), Vaughan Williams, Francis Poulenc, and Morton Gould. Sometimes at their concerts they also play transcriptions of popular songs.

After their performance of the Poulenc Concerto for Two Pianos in New York, a critic of the New York *Times* wrote: "One could hardly imagine the concerto being better played. It had refinement, wit, spontaneity, and sweetness . . . there was a rare singleness of concept in the . . . partnership. The teamwork was perfect, but there was no sense of mechanical precision."

Whittemore and Lowe live together in Quogue, Long Island, where they can indulge in their mutual interests, swimming and sailing. During its centennial celebration, the University of Rochester honored them with seats in its Hall of Fame as two of the University's most distinguished alumni.

WILLIAMS, CAMILLA, soprano, was born in Danville, Virginia. She was the youngest of four children, the daughter of a chauffeur. When she was eight she sang in the choir of the Calvary Baptist Church. She also attended the public schools, and in 1937 was class valedictorian when she was graduated from the John M. Langston High School. A scholarship brought her to the Virginia State College, from which she was graduated in 1941 with a Bachelor of Arts degree. She was named the "outstanding graduate of the class." After a year of post-graduate work in Italian at the University of Pennsylvania, she was appointed teacher of the third grade and instructor in music in the Danville elementary school system.

One year after her teaching appointment, she was invited to appear as soloist with the University State College Choir. This led to a scholarship for music study in Philadelphia. While studying with Marian Szekeley-Freschi in 1943 she supported herself by working as an usher in a Philadelphia movie house. Her financial situation was somewhat relieved that year, and again in 1944, with the winning of the Marian Anderson Award of $750.

Her career began in 1944 when, on November 14, she appeared as soloist with the Philadelphia Orchestra in arias by Mozart

CAMILLA WILLIAMS

and Bellini. After an additional period of study with Cesare Sodero in 1945 and 1946, she auditioned successfully for the New York City Opera Company, making her debut as Cio-Cio-San in *Madama Butterfly* on May 15, 1946. (This was the first time that a Negro soprano sang a principal role with a major opera company.) She was an instantaneous success. Geraldine Farrar said of her that "she is already one of the greatest Butterflys of our day." Noel Straus wrote in the New York *Times* that she portrayed Puccini's heroine "with a vividness and subtlety unmatched by any other artist who has essayed the part here in recent years. She ran the entire emotional gamut from ecstatic joy to tragic despair with extraordinary conviction and effectiveness, yet always with refinement of feeling and just the needed amount of restraint. . . . There was a warmth and intensity in her singing that lent dramatic force of no mean order to the climactic episodes, and something profoundly human and touching in her delivery of all of the music assigned to her."

This good impression was further strengthened when she later appeared with the same company in the principal soprano roles in *La Bohème, Aida* and *Pagliacci.* Her achievement led the Newspaper Guild of New York to present her in 1946 with its Page One Award as "first lady of opera."

While pursuing her career, she continued her music study with Rose Dirman, Ralph Berkowitz, and Borislava Bazala. On December 19, 1946, she appeared as soloist with the Chicago Symphony Orchestra in Bellini and Mozart arias. "In Paris in the time of the Second Empire," wrote C. J. Bulliet in the Chicago *Daily News,* "the students would have unhitched the horses from her carriage and themselves pulled Camilla Williams triumphantly through the streets." In the spring of 1950 she was a soloist with the New York Philharmonic-Symphony under Stokowski in Mahler's Eighth Symphony. "You infused your part with . . . understanding and intensity of feeling," Stokowski wrote to her after her performance. "It was an outstanding performance." In that same year she also made her first tour of Panama, the Dominican Republic, Venezuela and South America.

In 1954 she became the first foreign-born artist engaged by the Sadler's Wells Opera Company of England, with which she made four appearances in *Madama Butterfly.* On November 14, 1956, she scored a sensation as Madama Butterfly at the Vienna Volksoper, and four days later scored again when she sang the title role in *Aida* at the Vienna State Opera. Other European engagements in 1956 included concerts in Vienna, Stuttgart, Mannheim, and Rome, and radio performances in Vienna, Stuttgart, and Baden-Baden.

WILLIAMSON, JOHN FINLEY, choral conductor. See *Living Musicians,* 1940.

WITTGENSTEIN, PAUL, pianist. See *Living Musicians,* 1940.

WOLFF, ALBERT LOUIS, conductor. See *Living Musicians,* 1940.

WOLFF, ERNST, baritone and pianist. See *Living Musicians,* 1940.

WOOD, SIR HENRY J., conductor. See *Living Musicians,* 1940.

YEEND, FRANCES, lyric soprano, was born in Vancouver, Washington. Her mother was a school teacher and gifted amateur painter, her father a salesman. During her childhood, the family moved to Portland, where, at the age of seven, Frances began taking violin lessons. Three years later, she also started lessons in singing and ballet. While attending Jefferson High School, she appeared in several school productions, winning the *Oregon Journal* award for her performance in *The Taming of the Shrew,* and the Percy Stevens Prize for her part in a musical production.

After graduation from high school, she sang in local performances of Gilbert and Sullivan comic operas and appeared in stage productions with a stock company. Her ambition was to go to New York to complete her music study, but not having the necessary finances she enrolled instead in the Washington State College in Pullman, where she majored in music and languages. During this period she supported herself by holding various jobs, including those of choral director, booking agent for dance bands, and disk jockey playing classical music on a small radio station.

In 1943 she finally arrived in New York, and one day later found a job in the Broadway production of *The Merry Widow,* starring Jan Kiepura and Marta Eggerth. While making her Broadway appearances she was also heard as a singer of hymns on Phil Spitalny's "Hour of Charm" program on the radio. Her vocal study was resumed at the

FRANCES YEEND

same time, first with Peter Herman Adler and subsequently with Otto Lehman and Max Rudolf.

Her ambition for a career in serious music led her to abandon Broadway and radio for an engagement with the Columbia Concerts Opera Company, which toured the country in *Carmen.* This was in 1944. Two years later she auditioned for Serge Koussevitzky who engaged her to make her American concert debut that year as soloist with the Boston Symphony Orchestra in Beethoven's Ninth Symphony. This marked the beginning of a long and eventful career as a soloist with major symphony orchestras, a career in which she has been heard in virtually every celebrated choral masterwork and vocal symphony, as well as in such novelties as Debussy's *Le Martyre de Saint-Sébastien,* Pierné's *Children's Crusade,* Rachmaninoff's *The Bells,* Mahler's Eighth Symphony and Honegger's *Joan of Arc at the Stake.* When, in 1954, she appeared with the Philadelphia Orchestra under Ormandy in Verdi's *Requiem,* it was her 150th appearance with an orchestra (she had, by then, sung with over forty important symphonic organizations). This event was commemorated with the presentation of a specially bound volume of the *Requiem.*

On August 6, 1946, Yeend appeared at the Berkshire Music Festival in the American première of Britten's *Peter Grimes.* Two years after that she made her debut with the New York City Opera Company as Violetta

Yeend: yĕnd

in *La Traviata.* During the next decade she made over one hundred appearances with this company in the leading soprano roles of about ten major operas, including *Faust, La Bohème,* and *The Marriage of Figaro,* in which she scored major successes. After her performance as the Countess in *The Marriage of Figaro,* Irving Kolodin wrote: "The best Mozartian singing of the evening — firm, shapely, and sensitively controlled—was Frances Yeend's rendering of the air universally known as 'Dove sono.' Altogether, her Countess was a superior effort, believable in appearance and forthright in sound." In the spring of 1954 Yeend returned to the New York City Opera Company after a two-year absence. On that occasion the New York *Herald Tribune* critic said: "Singing with glorious tone and greatly matured artistry from first to last, she established her right to consideration as an absolutely first-class Violetta." Besides her performances with the New York Opera Company, Yeend was heard in this country with opera companies in Chicago, San Antonio, and New Orleans.

Her first appearance in Europe took place during the summer of 1951 at the Edinburgh Festival. Her London opera debut followed two and a half years later, when she appeared in Covent Garden as *Micaela* in *Carmen.*

When a group of performers from Covent Garden were flown that year to South Africa for twelve performances in *La Bohème* as part of the Cecil Rhodes Centennial celebration in Rhodesia, Yeend was the only American among them. During that same year of 1953 she also appeared at the Teatro Lirico in Barcelona, the Bavarian State Opera in Munich, the Vienna State Opera, and the Bach Festival in Groningen.

Besides performing in operas and with symphony orchestras, Yeend has made numerous appearances in recitals in America and Europe.

In May 1954 she married her coach and accompanist, James Benner. They maintain a New York apartment which is filled with Oriental furniture and knicknacks, and with Yeend's rare collection of Chinese soup spoons and teacups.

YON, PIETRO, organist. For his earlier career, see *Living Musicians,* 1940.

* * *

Yon died in Huntington, Long Island, on November 22, 1943.

ZIMBALIST, EFREM, violinist. See *Living Musicians,* 1940.

New Biographical Sketches

Albanese, Licia, soprano
Alessandro, Victor, conductor
Alvary, Lorenzo, bass-baritone
Anda, Geza, pianist
Angeles, Victoria de los, soprano

Baccaloni, Salvatore, bass
Bachauer, Gina, pianist
Badura-Skoda, Paul, pianist
Barbieri, Fedora, mezzo-soprano
Baum, Kurt, tenor
Beinum, Eduard van, conductor
Benzell, Mimi, soprano
Berger, Erna, soprano
Bernstein, Leonard, conductor and pianist
Biggs, E. Power, organist
Bloomfield, Theodore, conductor
Boehm, Karl, conductor
Bolet, Jorge, pianist
Borkh, Inge, soprano
Brice, Carol, contralto

Callas, Maria Meneghini, soprano
Campoli, Alfredo, violinist
Cantelli, Guido, conductor
Carvalho, Eleazar de, conductor
Cassel, Walter, baritone
Caston, Saul, conductor
Christoff, Boris, bass
Ciccolini, Aldo, pianist
Cluytens, André, conductor
Conley, Eugene, tenor
Conner, Nadine, soprano
Curzon, Clifford, pianist

Davis, Ellabelle, soprano
Del Monaco, Mario, tenor
Dickson, Donald, tenor
Di Stefano, Giuseppe, tenor
Dixon, Dean, conductor
Dobbs, Mattiwilda, soprano
Doktor, Paul, violist

Dorati, Antal, conductor

Erede, Alberto, conductor

Farrell, Eileen, soprano
Ferrier, Kathleen, contralto
Firkusny, Rudolf, pianist
Fischer-Dieskau, Dietrich, baritone
Fleisher, Leon, pianist
Fournier, Pierre, cellist
Francescatti, Zino, violinist
Fuchs, Joseph, violinist

Gilels, Emil, pianist
Gobbi, Tito, baritone
Goldstein, Ella, pianist
Gould, Glenn, pianist
Graffman, Gary, pianist
Grumiaux, Arthur, violinist
Guarrera, Frank, baritone
Gueden, Hilde, soprano
Gulda, Friedrich, pianist

Hannikainen, Tauno, conductor
Harrell, Mack, baritone
Harshaw, Margaret, soprano
Hawkins, Osie, baritone
Hayward, Thomas, tenor
Hendl, Walter, conductor
Henriot, Nicole, pianist
Hilsberg, Alexander, conductor and violinist
Hines, Jerome, bass

Istomin, Eugene, pianist

Janis, Byron, pianist
Johnson, Thor, conductor
Jonas, Maryla, pianist
Jordá, Enrique, conductor
Jurinac, Sena, soprano

Kapell, William, pianist
Karajan, Herbert von, conductor
Kempe, Rudolf, conductor
Kentner, Louis, pianist
Kirsten, Dorothy, soprano

Krips, Josef, conductor
Kubelik, Rafael, conductor
Kunz, Erich, bass-baritone
Kurtz, Edmund, cellist

Lateiner, Jacob, pianist
Lipkin, Seymour, pianist
Lipton, Martha, mezzo-soprano
London, George, bass-baritone
Lympany, Moura, pianist

Madeira, Jean, mezzo-soprano
Malcuzynski, Witold, pianist
Markevitch, Igor, conductor
Merrill, Robert, baritone
Mitchell, Howard, conductor
Munch, Charles, conductor
Munsel, Patrice, soprano

Nelli, Herva, soprano
Nikolaidi, Elena, contralto

Odnoposoff, Ricardo, violinist
Oistrakh, David, violinist

Paulee, Mona, mezzo-soprano
Pease, James, bass-baritone
Pennario, Leonard, pianist
Perlea, Jonel, conductor
Peters, Roberta, soprano

Rabin, Michael, violinist
Resnik, Regina, mezzo-soprano
Rose, Leonard, cellist
Rosenstock, Joseph, conductor
Rossi-Lemeni, Nicola, bass
Rostropovich, Mstislav, cellist
Rudolf, Max, conductor

Sandor, Gyorgy, pianist
Scherman, Thomas, conductor

Schiøtz, Aksel, tenor
Schippers, Thomas, conductor
Schuricht, Carl, conductor
Schwarzkopf, Elisabeth, soprano
Schwieger, Hans, conductor
Scott, Norman, bass-baritone
Seefried, Irmgard, soprano
Shaw, Robert, conductor
Siepi, Cesare, bass
Singer, Jacques, conductor
Singher, Martial, baritone
Solomon, Izler, conductor
Solti, Georg, conductor

Spivakovsky, Tossy, violinist
Steber, Eleanor, soprano
Stignani, Ebe, mezzo-soprano
Sullivan, Brian, tenor
Svanholm, Set, tenor

Tagliavini, Ferruccio, tenor
Tajo, Italo, bass
Tebaldi, Renata, soprano
Teyte, Maggie, soprano
Thebom, Blanche, mezzo-soprano
Tourel, Jennie, mezzo-soprano

Tucker, Richard, tenor
Turner, Claramae, contralto

Uppman, Theodor, baritone

Varnay, Astrid, soprano
Vinay, Ramón, tenor

Warfield, William, baritone
Warren, Leonard, baritone
Welitch, Ljuba, soprano
Whittemore and Lowe, duo-pianists
Williams, Camilla, soprano

Yeend, Frances, soprano

Classified List of New Biographical Sketches

BARITONES

Cassel, Walter
Fischer-Dieskau, Dietrich
Gobbi, Tito
Guarrera, Frank
Harrell, Mack
Hawkins, Osie
Merrill, Robert
Singher, Martial
Uppman, Theodore
Warfield, William
Warren, Leonard

BASS-BARITONES

Alvary, Lorenzo
Kunz, Erich
London, George
Pease, James
Scott, Norman

BASSES

Baccaloni, Salvatore
Christoff, Boris
Hines, Jerome
Rossi-Lemeni, Nicola
Siepi, Cesare
Tajo, Italo

CELLISTS

Fournier, Pierre
Kurtz, Edmund
Rose, Leonard
Rostropovich, Mstislav

CONDUCTORS

Alessandro, Victor
Beinum, Eduard van
Bernstein, Leonard
Bloomfield, Theodore
Boehm, Karl
Cantelli, Guido
Carvalho, Eleazar de
Caston, Saul
Cluytens, André
Dixon, Dean
Dorati, Antal
Erede, Alberto

Hannikainen, Tauno
Hendl, Walter
Hilsberg, Alexander
Johnson, Thor
Jordá, Enrique
Karajan, Herbert von
Kempe, Rudolf
Krips, Josef
Kubelik, Rafael
Markevitch, Igor
Mitchell, Howard
Munch, Charles
Perlea, Jonel
Rosenstock, Joseph
Rudolf, Max
Scherman, Thomas
Schippers, Thomas
Schuricht, Carl
Schwieger, Hans
Shaw, Robert
Singer, Jacques
Solomon, Izler
Solti, Georg

CONTRALTOS

Brice, Carol
Ferrier, Kathleen
Nikolaidi, Elena
Turner, Claramae

MEZZO-SOPRANOS

Barbieri, Fedora
Lipton, Martha
Madeira, Jean
Paulee, Mona
Resnik, Regina
Stignani, Ebe
Thebom, Blanche
Tourel, Jennie

ORGANIST

Biggs, E. Power

PIANISTS

Anda, Geza
Bachauer, Gina
Badura-Skoda, Paul

Bolet, Jorge
Ciccolini, Aldo
Curzon, Clifford
Firkusny, Rudolf
Fleisher, Leon
Gilels, Emil
Goldstein, Ella
Gould, Glenn
Graffman, Gary
Gulda, Friedrich
Henriot, Nicole
Istomin, Eugene
Janis, Byron
Jonas, Maryla
Kapell, William
Kentner, Louis
Lateiner, Jacob
Lipkin, Seymour
Lympany, Moura
Malcuzynski, Witold
Pennario, Leonard
Sandor, Gyorgy
Whittemore and Lowe (duo pianists)

SOPRANOS

Albanese, Licia
Angeles, Victoria de los
Benzell, Mimi
Berger, Erna
Borkh, Inge
Callas, Maria Meneghini
Conner, Nadine
Davis, Ellabelle
Dobbs, Mattiwilda
Farrell, Eileen
Gueden, Hilde
Harshaw, Margaret
Jurinac, Sena
Kirsten, Dorothy
Munsel, Patrice
Nelli, Herva
Peters, Roberta
Schwarzkopf, Elisabeth
Seefried, Irmgard
Steber, Eleanor
Tebaldi, Renata
Teyte, Maggie
Varnay, Astrid

Welitch, Ljuba
Williams, Camilla
Yeend, Frances

TENORS

Baum, Kurt
Conley, Eugene
Del Monaco, Mario
Dickson, Donald
Di Stefano, Giuseppe

Hayward, Thomas
Schiøtz, Aksel
Sullivan, Brian
Svanholm, Set
Tagliavini, Ferruccio
Tucker, Richard
Vinay, Ramón

VIOLINISTS

Campoli, Alfredo

Francescatti, Zino
Fuchs, Joseph
Grumiaux, Arthur
Odnoposoff, Ricardo
Oistrakh, David
Rabin, Michael
Spivakovsky, Tossy

VIOLIST

Doktor, Paul